EXPERIENCES OF CHINA

Percy Cradock

Experiences of China

JOHN MURRAY

© Percy Cradock 1994

First published in 1994
by John Murray (Publishers) Ltd.,
50 Albemarle Street, London W1X 4BD

Reprinted in 1994 (twice)

A catalogue record for this book is available from the British Library

ISBN 0–7195–5349–0

Typeset in 12/13 pt Baskerville by Colset Pte Ltd, Singapore
Printed and bound in Great Britain by
Biddles Ltd, Guildford and King's Lynn

To Birthe

Forsan et haec olim meminisse iuvabit

Contents

Illustrations

Author's Note

IN TRANSCRIBING CHINESE names I have followed the modern *pinyin* system of transliteration, except in the case of one or two old favourites like Peking, Canton, Chiang Kaishek and, of course, Hong Kong. I hope this inconsistency can be forgiven.

For sources, I have relied mainly on my own memory and that of my wife, supported by notes I made at the time. Since these are memoirs not history I have deliberately not burdened them with footnotes; but I have tried to make them as accurate as possible. I have checked with open records, particularly with the Chinese press. I have also cross-checked by reading, or rereading, some of the excellent books covering each period.

Among the works to which I am indebted, I should mention the following:

On Macartney's Embassy: J. L. Cranmer-Byng, *An Embassy to China* (Longmans, 1962); and Alain Peyrefitte, *The Collision of Two Civilisations* (Harvill, 1993).

For the Cultural Revolution: Edward E. Rice, *Mao's Way* (University of California Press, 1972); Stanley Karnow, *Mao and China* (Macmillan, 1973); and the invaluable little book by my Dutch colleague at the time: D. W. Fokkema, *Report from Peking* (London, C. Hurst and Co., 1972). I must also cite, with my respect and admiration, the works of the Belgian scholar who uses the pen-name of Simon Leys.

For Deng's early years in power: Roger Garside, *Coming Alive* (McGraw Hill, 1981); and Philip Short, *The Dragon and the Bear* (Abacus, 1982).

On Hong Kong, there has been a welter of books, most, I'm afraid, of indifferent quality. Robert Cottrell's work on the negotiations – *The End of Hong Kong* (John Murray, 1993) – is of a more serious kind and, although I do not agree with all his conclusions, I have read it with profit.

More general works I have benefited from include: John Gittings, *China Changes Face* (Oxford University Press, 1989); Harrison Salisbury, *The New Emperors* (Harper Collins, 1992); Evan Luard, *Britain and China* (Chatto and Windus, 1962); John King Fairbank, *The Great Chinese Revolution, 1800–1985* (Chatto and Windus, 1987); and of course the splendid Volume 15 of the *Cambridge History of China*, edited by MacFarquhar and Fairbank (Cambridge University Press, 1991).

The above is inevitably a partial and selective list. In addition, I am indebted to Jim Hoare, formerly of our Embassy in Peking, for allowing me to read his excellent monograph on the history of our mission there. The *South China Morning Post* has kindly allowed me to draw on an article on Sino-British relations I contributed to their edition of 10 April 1993.

My editor, Gail Pirkis, has handled text, and author, with the ideal combination of understanding and professionalism. I have also had much help from the staff of the London Library, the library of the School of Oriental and African Studies and the Reading Room at the British Library.

More generally, I express my debt to my colleagues and staff at various periods.

I am grateful to Faber and Faber Ltd. for permission to quote from *Collected Poems* by W. H. Auden, edited by Edward Mendelson; to His Excellency the Ambassador and the Foreign Ministry of the People's Republic of China for their agreement to the use of a number of photographs taken by official photographers in China; and to Times Newspapers Limited for allowing me to use one of their photographs.

Preface

THIS IS A book about China, one more in the long series recording the impact on Western observers of that remarkable country. It is also a book of reminiscences, an attempt to recover and reorder episodes of a personal past. In it I try to set down, before the images fade completely, my impressions of China at the several times I lived there, some nine years in all. To this I add the period, almost as long, when, though living in London, I was engaged in advising on British policy toward Peking.

There are four phases, with a different China in each. In the first, I was for a short time in 1962 Chinese Secretary in what was then the Office of the British Chargé d'Affaires in Peking. In the second, I spent three years in the same Office, from 1966 to 1969, as Political Counsellor, then Chargé d'Affaires, at the height of the Cultural Revolution. Then a spell of five and a half years as Ambassador from 1978 to 1984 in a reformist China under Deng Xiaoping. Finally, the period 1984 to 1992 when, as the Prime Minister's Foreign Policy Adviser, I included China in my brief and conducted a number of negotiations with Peking, among them those on the Hong Kong Joint Declaration of 1984 and the Hong Kong Airport Agreement of 1991.

Set out in this way it looks a formidable exposure. Certainly it represents a long entanglement, almost an addiction. Whether it has brought enlightenment on China I am less certain.

I can speak with some confidence on relations between Britain and China, particularly as seen from the British side. In the period covered by this book they have swung wildly between hostility and understanding; the extremes are represented, on the one hand, by the burning down of the British Chancery

in Peking in 1967 and, on the other, by the ceremonious welcome for Her Majesty the Queen in China in 1986. Even at
their warmest, they have retained a degree of tension and suspicion. This is only natural: behind them lies a great gulf in
cultures and political systems and a long tragi-comedy, a century
and a half of misconceptions and violence as Britain and China
have tried to adjust to each other. But despite this burden, the
last decades have been the most active and productive in a
chequered history. Certain common interests have been defined
and mutually beneficial agreements have been concluded. Here
the facts are accessible and reasonably firm judgements can be
reached.

When we turn from the interface between the two powers to
China itself, we are on more uncertain ground. The story covers
a generation, from 1962 to 1992. Often tragic, it is at first, in
the days of Mao Zedong, that of a country in the grip of the
revolutionary compulsions of one overwhelming leader. Later,
under Deng Xiaoping, the colours lighten and there is striking
material progress. But a central dilemma remains: how does a
Communist regime reform its economy without losing political
authority? This is a big canvas, much of it still dark. Personal
impressions are sometimes vivid, always incontestable; but they
illuminate only part of the scene, and from one angle only. They
are also outsiders' impressions. We each construct our vision of
China from the limited materials available to us, from our direct
experience and reading, our memories of certain conversations
and scenes; and we cling tenaciously to it. But it remains China
through the foreigner's distorting glass. The real China, whatever that may be, eludes us.

'What does anybody here know of China?' asked Macaulay
in the House of Commons in 1840. 'Even those Europeans who
have been in that Empire are almost as ignorant of it as the rest
of us. Everything is covered by a veil, through which a glimpse
of what is within may occasionally be caught, a glimpse just sufficient to set the imagination to work and more likely to mislead
than to inform.' We know rather more today; but the veil is still
there. Of that vast country and the workings of its government
only a handful of Chinese know more than fragments. In this
field above all, the beginning of wisdom is the confession of
ignorance.

There is a further limitation, that it is mainly official China I am writing about, the world of despatches and telegrams, meetings at the Foreign Ministry and the Great Hall of the People. There are from time to time forays, some involuntary as in the Cultural Revolution, into popular life; but they are not many. The guides and minders of various kinds are usually present. The genre is that of Macartney's Journal (the diary kept by the first British Ambassador), memoirs of puzzled or frustrated Western emissaries under close surveillance. Unofficial travellers have often seen more of the country and talked to a greater range of people. Nor can anything I say compare with accounts by Chinese themselves, writing as only they can about their sufferings and aspirations.

But when all that is said, the book may still serve not only to satisfy myself, which is its main purpose, but also to cast light on our relations with China at certain critical periods in the last thirty years. More tentatively, it may have something worthwhile to say about the recent history of a country which, even today, behind an exclusive culture and Communist secrecy, maintains much of its old reserve, whose wealth and power are rapidly growing and whose evolution, whatever direction it takes, will profoundly affect the rest of the world.

There is another dimension. Increasingly in its later stages the story concerns Hong Kong. Hong Kong is less of an enigma than mainland China, though its problems are sometimes almost as difficult to handle. During the period covered by this book, as the lease of the New Territories has drawn towards its end, the two governments have finally addressed the last great issue between them left over from history, namely the future of the colony. Arduous negotiations have been conducted and critical decisions have been taken. These decisions and the agreements flowing from them have naturally been the subject of intense scrutiny and, in Britain at least, they have been highly controversial. The policy they embody, that of co-operation with China in the interests of Hong Kong, has itself come under increasing question, so much so that in very recent times another course altogether has been attempted.

This book then has among its themes the story of the Hong Kong negotiations from 1979 to 1992 and among its cast of characters the leaders, ministers and governors who took part in those demanding manoeuvres. I hope it will illuminate their decisions and explain a policy of Sino-British co-operation which, in the author's view, was fully justified and indeed remains the only possible course if Britain is to try to meet its responsibilities in respect of Hong Kong.

A Background Sketch:
The Burdens of History

WHEN THIS STORY opens, in the early 1960s, Britain and China had been engaged in diplomatic converse, or, more accurately, struggle, for some one hundred and seventy years, ever since the Anglo-Irish nobleman, Lord Macartney, despatched by the government of Pitt the Younger, arrived at the court of the Emperor Qian Long in 1793. There had been earlier attempts to open official communications: as far back as 1596, when Queen Elizabeth had addressed a letter in Latin to the Chinese Emperor of the day; and as recently as 1787, when the British government had sent a mission to China under Colonel Charles Cathcart, an officer with distinguished Indian experience. Unhappily the Colonel died *en route* and the expedition was abandoned.

There had been private travellers and, since the seventeenth century, commercial contacts, carefully regulated by the Chinese, in Canton. But Macartney's Embassy was the first formal British mission to arrive, to communicate and, of course, to be rebuffed.

No two nations, or governments, could have been more unlike. The Chinese were the inheritors of two thousand years of continuous civilization. Under the rule of a Son of Heaven, assisted by a corps of highly, if narrowly, educated scholar-officials, they felt that they enjoyed a unique system and stood at the centre of the world, on the rim of which obscure barbarian tribes pursued their obscure activities, pausing occasionally to visit China to pay appropriate tribute to the Celestial Throne. Theirs was the Middle Kingdom, coterminous with civilization. They were self-sufficient, ideologically and economically. Under earlier dynasties they had been inventive and technologically advanced, well beyond contemporary European standards. Now, though their population and commerce grew, they were, at official level, static, effete, but still complacent, unconscious of their relative decline. The British were a comparatively new nation, extrovert, dynamic and expansionist, the pre-eminent naval power, with trade and possessions across the globe, leaders of the industrial revolution, technologically advanced and confident in their abilities and strength.

The two parties to the encounter knew little about each other. The Chinese felt no compulsion to study distant barbarians. Their geographers informed them that England was a country that belonged to Holland. 'England consists simply of three islands, merely a handful of stones in the Western Ocean . . . The British are skilled in ocean navigation and can make the voyages as easily as crossing a marshy ground with weeds.' But, the Emperor was assured, they were an insignificant race. As one of his Censors put it, 'True, their guns are destructive, but in the attack on our harbours they will be too elevated, and their aim moreover rendered unsteady by the waves.' As for the British soldiers, they were reliably reported to be so tightly uniformed that once they fell to the ground they could not get up again. There was no cause for concern.

The British for their part were awakening slowly from the eighteenth-century dream of Cathay, in which China had figured as the ideal nation, governed by philosophers, and were moving to a harsher, more realistic appraisal. Macartney in his Journal likened China to a ramshackle man-of-war 'which a succession of able and vigilant officers has contrived to keep afloat for these one hundred and fifty years past . . . but whenever an insufficient man happens to have the command on deck, adieu to the discipline and safety of the ship'.

Macartney's requests, reasonable though they may have seemed to the British, were insufferable to the Chinese. He wanted improved conditions for the British merchants in Canton; the opening of new ports on the China coast; if possible, an island base for British commercial operations; and the establishment of diplomatic relations on an equal footing, with a resident British mission in Peking. In Chinese eyes the request for territory was intolerable enough; but worst of all was the proposal for relations with a foreign sovereign on a basis of equality. This was much more than a matter of protocol: it struck at the root of the Chinese political and philosophical system. How could there be equality in such a case? How could there be two suns in the sky?

So the requests were dismissed as unthinkable, 'absolutely counter to the generous manner in which the Celestial Empire treats foreigners and pacifies the four barbarian tribes'. The carefully assembled gifts from George III, the terrestrial and celestial globes, the planetarium, the clocks, the barometer, were quickly reclassified as tribute. The offers of trade were rejected: 'As your Ambassador has seen for himself, we possess all things. I set no value on objects strange and ingenious and have no use for your manufactures.'

But the Emperor was disposed to be generous and George III was given marks for effort:

> Although your country, O King, lies in the far oceans, yet, inclining your heart towards civilization, you have specially sent an envoy respectfully to present a state message, to kowtow and to present congratulations for the imperial birthday, and also to present local products, thereby showing your sincerity.
>
> We have perused the text of your state message and the wording expresses your earnestness. From it your sincere humility and obedience can be seen.

The Embassy, with its extravagant requests and pretensions, was quietly forced back within the framework of Chinese conventions and the Ambassador, or, as the Chinese preferred to call him, 'the tributary envoy', was sent on his way, empty-handed. China remained a closed world, aloof, superior, self-sufficient.

It is a famous episode, much described. But it is right to dwell upon it at the beginning of any account of Sino-British relations, for it vividly illustrates the gulf between the two sides; and it carries within it the seeds of much of what was to follow.

The rebuff could not hold; Western, in particular British, pressure was sustained. A member of Macartney's entourage had remarked that Chinese prejudices were so deeply rooted as only to be overcome by force. And so, eventually, they were. After one war, an island, that of Hong Kong, was ceded, in 1842. After another, that of 1856–60, a permanent diplomatic mission was established in Peking. The character of the succeeding period was set – incomprehension and compulsion.

Nations, like people, form images of themselves and those they deal with, and are reluctant to change them. Their truth is not the decisive factor. One thinker, Michel Foucault, writes of truth in these situations as a function of power: the stronger impose their vision. Britain and China began with vastly distorted images of each other and with great inequality of power. First contacts in such a situation are likely to be clumsy and painful, a kind of blind man's buff. Or perhaps a better analogy would be the duel chosen by the short-sighted Stuart gentleman in Aubrey's *Brief Lives*, who, asked to decide the weapons for the encounter, specified axes in a dark cellar. Sino-British relations in the nineteenth century contained several such episodes.

Although the British, in the Chinese estimation, were the fiercest and most dangerous of the sea barbarians, they were by no means exclusive in their appetites. They sought trade above all; but, having established the terms for their trade, they were usually content that other powers should enjoy similar, though preferably lesser, advantages. And the other Western powers inevitably followed suit. Nor were British interventions by any means so calculated as simplified histories – or even more simplified sketches such as this – tend to make out: on closer examination policies prove, as usual, to be largely a matter of improvisation and short-term responses. We stumble into history. Nevertheless the general trend, British and Western intrusion and dictation, was clear. By the end of the century China was in the condition Mao Zedong vividly described as half-feudal, half-colonial: foreign missionaries and traders, enjoying special protection, penetrated deeply into the interior; foreign merchants, under special treaty regimes, dominated the ports; significant parts of the territory were under foreign laws or in actual foreign possession. The final partition of China seemed very close. The strange, irrational outburst of the 'Righteous Harmony Fists' (the Boxers) in 1900, mingling magic, violence and xenophobia, reflected the strains and confusion among a suffering but still uncomprehending population. Beginning as a rural insurgency movement against the alien Manchu dynasty, it was hijacked by the Empress Dowager and directed against the European and Japanese interlopers; and when it failed to exterminate these pests was rapidly dropped. The suppression of the rising was inevitably followed by further foreign exactions.

On both sides throughout the nineteenth century there were divided councils on how to handle the new opportunities, or threats, divisions which curiously foreshadow more modern debates. In the treaty ports British merchants, the original 'old China hands', called on the British government for a thorough-going forward policy, nothing less than the foundation of another India, a vast British protectorate over the valley of the Yangtze; while the British Foreign Office, more sceptical of the value of the China market and more alive to the true costs of another Eastern empire, preferred to bolster the tottering Manchu regime, urge moderate reform and pursue a course of limited commitment and limited liability in China.

In the heated internal debates of the time British diplomats were accused of being too sympathetic to China. Sir Rutherford Alcock, the British Minister to Peking in the 1860s, was charged in the British press with being too 'mandarin-minded'; and there was a call for his substitution by 'someone fresh from the political life of Europe'.

On the Chinese side, there was much inherited statecraft on how to handle barbarians, particularly those who were land-based in the north and therefore capable of posing a lasting threat to Chinese security. There were the hallowed precepts 'bridle and restrain' (*ji mi*) and 'use barbarians to control barbarians' (*yi yi zhi yi*). In practice the rule had been: exert pressure on the barbarians when China was strong, come to terms when China was weak. The cautionary tale was that of the Southern Song dynasty, which fell to the Mongols in the thirteenth century, having recklessly pursued a militaristic policy from a weak base. The first Chinese Minister to Britain, Guo Songtao, in a memorial to the Emperor in 1875 feared that his government was emulating the Southern Song, 'considering it disgraceful to make peace treaties but excellent to make war'.

At court in Peking about this time the military-conservative faction was strongly placed and also enjoyed popular backing. A smaller faction, known as the 'foreign affairs group', had no love for the West but were realists and recognized that the only way to salvation was to modernize. But this was usually a minority view; and its adherents tended not to prosper in their careers.

Generally through the nineteenth century, although the

Manchu rulers displayed some dexterity in fending off the more immediate Western threats, and even enrolled Western help in suppressing the great internal revolts afflicting the regime, like the Taiping rebellion in the mid-century, they and their courts remained too frivolous, corrupt and incompetent to take the measure of the challenge facing them. And though individual Chinese statesmen and scholars accurately diagnosed the disease and prescribed the remedy, and there were in fact spasmodic modernization movements, the realists were usually lone voices against a chorus of angry and blinkered conservatism. The imperial tutor Wo Ren reflected the view of the great majority when, in a memorial to the Emperor in 1867, he questioned the need to 'seek trifling arts and respect barbarians as teachers, regardless of the possibility that the cunning barbarians may not teach us their essential techniques'.

So a great opportunity was missed and, for reasons still not entirely explained, China's response to the challenge was slow, partial and inadequate. The old learning was too deeply embedded; Western technology was seen at best as a superficial gadgetry, to be acquired at little cost. In contrast, Japan, confronting a similar crisis, but better at borrowing and adapting, having borrowed a significant portion of its culture from China, reacted with ruthless speed and in the course of a generation transformed itself into a passable imitation of an advanced Western state. So much so that when a clash came with China in 1894 it was China which suffered humiliating defeat. A new predator power had emerged, and one with its base not thousands of miles away, as with the Europeans and Americans, but a next-door neighbour.

As Li Hongzhang, the great realist and international 'fixer' for the Empress Dowager, prophetically observed as early as the 1860s, 'Although the European powers are strong, they are still seventy thousand *li* away from us, whereas Japan is as near as in the courtyard, or on the threshold and is prying into our emptiness and solitude. Undoubtedly she will become China's permanent and great anxiety.'

With the emergence of Japan the balance of power of the area changed fundamentally; and the Anglo-Japanese Treaty of 1902 reflected the fact. For Britain its primary object was to apply a check on Russia, in British eyes the traditional Asiatic menace.

But in China it was naturally seen as an anti-Chinese alliance, imposing a permanent bias on British policy; and such a bias was visible for the next forty years, at first as a result of the treaty and later, when it was not renewed, as a result of respect for Japanese military strength. Britain sympathized with China and proclaimed a policy of safeguarding Chinese independence and territorial integrity; but in practice favoured Japan. Japanese military capabilities at first offered strategic advantage to Britain, decreasingly capable of dealing alone with all comers. In the First World War, when Western energies were concentrated in Europe, Japan had a freer hand in the Far East and Japanese pressure on China became more blatant. The Twenty-One Demands of 1915, if fully pressed, would have reduced China to a virtual protectorate; and the Western powers could do little about it. At the end of the war Britain and her allies supported Japanese claims to inherit German rights in Shandong province. The move provoked one of the great outbursts of Chinese protest, led by the students, in May 1919. From now on the fires of Chinese nationalism burned ever more strongly.

The government of Chiang Kaishek, which came to power in 1928, saw one of its principal functions as being to articulate this deep sense of pride and resentment at foreign intrusions; and Britain, still the leading imperialist power, was a natural target. But the real danger to China now came from Japan, which seized Manchuria in 1931 and began a series of encroachments, culminating in the full-scale invasion of 1937. Britain's sympathy for China and the provision of economic aid were outweighed by continuing British efforts to conciliate Japan. Given the balance of power in the area, Britain may have had little choice; but it was not an elevating course; and it was not until the Japanese attack on the West in December 1941 that Britain was able to follow a more consistent and respectable policy, with China finally in the position of wartime ally.

The Second World War prompted the first collective Western bow to Chinese dignity, the relinquishment by Britain and the United States in 1943 of all special rights in China, the complex of privileges acquired in the 'unequal treaties'. Britain had earlier given up certain concessions and settlements; but this was the first general renunciation. It was made easier by the fact that all the possessions in question were in Japanese hands; and the modern reader is struck by how late in the day the change occurred. Other Western states followed suit. (The new Bolshevik regime had won credit by making a similar gesture as early as the 1920s.) There was a short honeymoon period in relations between China and Britain. But the accumulated resentments of a century and a half were not so easily dissipated. Britain was still felt by the Chinese as an oppressive imperialist presence, visible in its string of consulates and merchant houses, still enjoying a dominant commercial position and still ensconced in its original base, in Hong Kong. Frictions developed over the implementation of the 1943 agreement, and in the councils of the war leaders Britain, unlike the United States, was seen as undervaluing the Chinese contribution to the struggle and the strategic importance of the Far Eastern theatre as a whole.

So civil war succeeded the Anti-Japanese War; and the Chinese agony, which had passed through the stages of the fall of the Qing dynasty, the irresponsibility and corruption of the Republic, the chaos and violence of the warlord era and the horrors of the Japanese invasion, now entered on its final phase. As the Communist armies swept south and consolidated their hold on the country Britain was one of the first to recognize the new regime (on 6 January 1950). But the move seemed to win little credit. Indeed it only prompted Communist demands for further concessions, including the ending of Britain's *de facto* recognition of the Nationalist authorities in Taiwan. Frustratingly, the British discovered that their new Chargé d'Affaires in Peking was simply 'the British negotiating representative', sent 'for the purpose of carrying on negotiations concerning the establishment of diplomatic relations'. It was the first touch of the Kafkaesque style that was to become only too familiar in succeeding years. Though the Nationalist Chinese government had been notoriously difficult and demanding, their successors proved much more so. To the traditional list of nationalist grievances and prejudices they added a new layer, derived from Marxist-Leninist and Maoist dogma. British businessmen in particular suffered under the new, harsh conditions; their properties were expropriated or made worthless; and they themselves were often reduced to the condition of hostages against the continuing remittance of sterling to pay local staff.

Whatever disposition the new regime may have had to come

to terms with the Western world once they had settled into place, any hopes were dashed by the outbreak of the Korean War in June 1950. It was Stalin's war, rather than Mao's; but it brought a fatal rigidity to the Far Eastern scene. Lines were drawn that were not to be easily erased. British and United States troops soon found themselves engaged in ferocious fighting, not only with North Korean but also with Chinese troops, though the British diplomatic mission in Peking somehow managed to survive. Chinese anti-American and anti-Western propaganda reached hysterical levels. On the other side, US hostility to the new China was confirmed. Trade embargoes were imposed which survived until President Nixon's visit in 1972. But, most serious of all, the division of China was perpetuated. The Nationalist rump government on Taiwan was taken under President Truman's wing; arms supplies, which had been cut off, were resumed; the Seventh Fleet 'neutralized' the Taiwan Strait; as Peking saw it, what would probably have been a successful invasion from the mainland was effectively frustrated. The new Chinese regime had demonstrated convincingly that, unlike its predecessors, it could successfully defend Chinese interests against the strongest foreign forces. But China was nonetheless left isolated, excluded from the United Nations, condemned for the next generation to the confines of the Communist and Third Worlds and, for some years, to a galling dependence on the Soviet Union.

In the narrower field of Sino-British relations there was some improvement after the Geneva Conference of 1954, when Britain demonstrated that its position on Indo-China was not automatically that of Mr Dulles. Anthony Eden had some civilized exchanges with Zhou Enlai. China agreed to open a mission in London and to offer better treatment of British subjects in China. High-level British delegations began to visit China.

But this more relaxed tone, which coincided with Zhou Enlai's charm offensive at the Afro-Asian Conference at Bandung in 1955, did not survive policy changes inside China. Mao Zedong, who had seemed to encourage freer political comment with his slogan 'Let a hundred flowers bloom, a hundred schools of thought contend', was, as is usual with Communist leaders in like circumstances, shocked and alarmed at the response he evoked. He reacted with a fierce anti-rightist campaign in 1957.

The Chinese intellectual, again as is usual, was caught by the rapid alternation of warm and cold winds blowing from the centre. Chinese policies at home and abroad grew more militant.

At the same time fissures began to appear in the monolith of Sino-Soviet unity. Mao had come to acquire greater self-confidence with the death of Stalin. He probably felt he had Khrushchev's measure, though he was disturbed by the content, and the implications, of Khrushchev's secret speech, denouncing Stalin, in 1956. He claimed that Soviet achievements in space and rocketry meant, as he put it, that now 'the East wind prevails over the West'. His tone with the Russians grew more assertive and there were Chinese demands for Soviet assistance with the creation of a Chinese fleet and the provision of nuclear weapons. Khrushchev was given no warning of Chinese plans to bombard the offshore island of Quemoy (still garrisoned by Nationalists) in 1958. The strains in the relationship, always latent, began to show, even to the outside world. And at home Mao pushed on, regardless of his colleagues and of Soviet displeasure, into the adventure, and disaster, of the People's Communes and the Great Leap Forward.

So by the early 1960s the wheel had come almost full circle. Britain was no longer a force in China. Power had passed irrevocably to Peking; China had 'stood up', as Mao had put it when he proclaimed 'liberation' from the rostrum of the Forbidden City in October 1949. Britain's military strength had shrunk; her diplomatic presence was greatly reduced; with one exception the old consulates had gone; the old business interests were virtually all erased.

These losses should in theory have freed Britain from the past and allowed a new beginning. But in practice this proved difficult to achieve. Britain was too closely associated with the main enemy, the United States. The slate was not entirely clean: there was still the matter of Hong Kong. There was also the general baggage of history, and not such distant history at that. The Chinese travelled with a full load. There were not only the new Marxist categories of wrong-doing; there were also nationalist memories and aspirations; and always the echo of that sinocentrism, that sense of China as the Middle Kingdom, which Macartney and his company had encountered at the Manchu court in the distant days of 1793. The habits of thought of the two sides were still far apart. And, curiously, under Communism China had again become a closed world, speaking a different diplomatic language, half nationalist, half Marxist, always too ready to reject Western learning and experience and retreat into isolation and self-sufficiency. There was again an ideological gulf.

The new relationship was therefore bound to be thin, harsh, suspicious. Its dynamic would no longer come mainly from the West, but from inside China, as the regime's leaders asserted their sovereignty, reassessed their external relations, planned the recovery of lost national territory and fought among themselves over the gigantic problems of economic development that confronted them. Given such actors, such legacies and the murderous nature of Chinese politics, it would have required no great discernment to predict a rough ride. And so it proved.

But at this point the focus narrows and the story takes a more personal turn.

PART ONE

Mao's China

CHAPTER ONE

First Contact

TOWARDS THE END of 1983, shortly before leaving China, I gave a farewell dinner for one of my staff who was returning to London at the end of his tour. The guests were mainly Chinese-speakers from the Embassy, clever young men who had devoted some years to acquiring and practising an exotic tongue. It occurred to me to ask what had moved them to choose Chinese and what was the main satisfaction it afforded.

I was given some interesting answers. It seemed that there were two main schools, the romantics and the realists. Some had responded to the challenge of far-off places, or had been drawn by the literature or the art. Like the eighteenth-century savants, they had been beguiled by the vision of classical China, the Middle Kingdom governed by scholars and uniquely civilized, the distant country the romantic imagination requires, where things are different and better. Others were drawn by the struggle, the need almost any foreign resident in China experiences, to fight against an all-embracing system intent on imposing its own values. In many cases, I suspect, there was a touch of each school: they had come to admire and stayed to struggle.

If I asked myself, I think the last would be the answer. While still at school I had been fascinated by Arthur Waley's translations from the Chinese, those remarkable pieces of *vers libre*, in form so unlike the bulk of Chinese classical poetry with its rhymes and tonal patterns, which have nevertheless become

synonymous with it for so many Western readers and have
deservedly established themselves as masterpieces of derivative
literature. These sang their siren songs to me. It was the range
as much as the quality that appealed: it seemed that an almost
inexhaustible treasury of poetry and prose lay waiting for the
scholar's attentions. In the seventeenth century Robert Hooke,
the Secretary of the Royal Society, called China 'an Empire of
learning, hitherto only fabulously described'. I think I saw it as
something like that. But Waley, wise in his generation, never
visited China and kept his vision unimpaired. His admirer was
rash enough to live and work there; and so the dream of scholar-
ship faded and was replaced by the coarser satisfactions of the
diplomatic struggle and the clash of political systems.

At Cambridge, where the prizes came easily, the only problem
was one of choice; and that between Chinese and Law was one
of the most agonizing. In the end mundane considerations prevailed, or seemed to prevail. Having taken a degree in English,
I read Law and became a law don. But after a year or so the
prospect of an endless series of undergraduate essays on real property or contract and tort proved too much. I left Cambridge
and the Bar and joined the Foreign Office, as a late entrant.

Here further problems presented themselves. The Foreign
Office ideal of the all-purpose man, equally at home in China
or Peru, seemed to me to offer a prospect of rapid de-education.
I pressed for the opportunity to learn Chinese. But my masters
reminded me that I was a late entrant; hard languages were for
young men with agile brains. This was fair comment: the normal
course is for the two years or so of hard-language training to
follow close on entry. And it was only after a posting to Malaya
and further representations that I was able to prevail and persuade them to let me learn the language.

The promise was reluctantly given and rapidly modified: after
three months of tuition in London and two in Hong Kong I was
told that there was a crisis in our Office in Peking: Edward
Youde, the Oriental Secretary, had to be withdrawn early and
there would be an interregnum of some six months before his
successor could arrive. Would I kindly fill the gap?

And so it was that my wife Birthe and I alighted at Peking
railway station on a January morning in 1962. We were met by
Teddy Youde and taken to our quarters in a block of flats some

way down the main east–west boulevard. As we drove there, we
passed on the eastern city wall the old observatory, with its
strange assemblage of astronomical instruments, constructed in
the seventeenth century by the Jesuit advisers to the Emperor.
The city was grey and flat; few tall buildings; wide avenues with
little or no motor traffic; only bicycles and carts drawn by shaggy
ponies; an air of Mongolia as much as northern China. It was
intensely cold, with a thin almost lunar atmosphere and a
brilliant blue sky. That afternoon we walked the two or three
miles to the great square facing the Gate of Heavenly Peace
(Tiananmen) and the Forbidden City, the small children we
passed gesturing and chanting '*Sulian! Sulian!*' ('Russians! Russians!' All foreigners were automatically Russians in those days.)
We had arrived.

It was an intimidating assignment. My hastily acquired
Chinese was of an altogether lower standard than Teddy's; he
was an old hand, with years in Peking and Chungking behind
him. But the Mission were indulgent. Michael Stewart, the
Chargé (later Minister in Washington and Ambassador in
Athens), had been an Assistant Keeper of Paintings in the Vic-
toria and Albert Museum and he and Damaris, his wife, contrived to turn the stark quarters provided them by the Chinese
into a civilized Residence. Hugh Morgan, the Counsellor, was
the best type of Foreign Office professional, cool, detached,
amused, highly intelligent; and his wife Alexandra provided
enough gaiety and life for several families.

We were well looked after. John Chen, the Chief Interpreter
and head of the small group of locally engaged staff, took me
through the Chinese papers in the mornings for the first weeks
(one of our main jobs was analysing the press). He also gave me
my Chinese name, a task which always afforded the local staff
a certain pleasure: Chinese characters have a variety of secondary and tertiary meanings, and well-chosen ideographs can not
only convey something like the English sound, but also give
opportunities for quiet amusement to the initiated. It was a
milder form of the game which, in the 1830s, had saddled Lord
Napier, our Superintendent of Trade in Canton, with characters
which meant 'Laboriously Vile'.

We were assigned three servants, a cook, a houseboy and an
amah. There was no choice in the matter: they came from the

Diplomatic Services Bureau, a kind of Central Casting set up to provide all our needs, as the authorities saw them, to keep us under supervision, and at the same time to provide a useful income for the state. Of the wages we paid them they saw only a tiny fraction; the government took the rest. But we were lucky, since they had looked after the Youdes and had been trained in the old Legation to old-fashioned standards. They brought with them a small dog, which had been assigned to their care by some long-departed British diplomat. They took their charge seriously, which was remarkable, given the acute shortage of food at the time. But they had been devoted to its owner and regarded the dog as a pledge of his eventual return. When he did not come back and bad times threatened in 1966, the dog, now aged and infirm, was put to sleep by our nursing sister and buried in the Residence garden beside two small stone lions, whose features he resembled.

Our Mission in Peking in those days was called the Office of the British Chargé d'Affaires. Since Britain retained a consulate on Taiwan we could not presume to the condition of an embassy. We also lived in reduced circumstances. The old Legation, the English Palace (*Ying Guo Fu*) as it was known, had been originally the residence of Duke Liang, a descendant of one of the thirty-three sons of the Emperor Kang Xi. Here, on a prime site in the centre of the city, the first resident British diplomats, under Frederick Bruce, Lord Elgin's brother, had established themselves in 1861. But these historic buildings had been lost to us since 1959 and were now occupied by Chinese government offices, allegedly the Public Security Bureau. Our new quarters were two identical concrete villas on the eastern outskirts of the old city, one the Residence, the other the Office. We had in addition staff flats in a large block nearby, shared with other foreign representatives and known locally as the Diplomats' Big Building (*Waijiao Da Lou*), a modern equivalent of the Barbarian Hostel where foreign emissaries were accommodated and insulated under the Emperors. We consoled ourselves with the thought that this was only a temporary arrangement. For appropriate accommodation on a long-term basis the Chinese had been asked to provide a twelve-acre domain, acres that have still to materialize.

Blank, ugly, virtually treeless, the new site was a far cry from the pavilions of the English Palace, but it conveyed more accurately the nature of the new relationship with the Communist authorities. There were no modern luxuries, no air-conditioning, no swimming pool or tennis courts; there was Scottish dancing, the occasional film on loan from home or Hong Kong, and of course excursions to the Ming Tombs or the Western Hills. We had brought with us from the old quarters some household gods, a vine which was successfully transplanted and flourishes still, some statuary and one or two memorials to those who had fallen in the siege of the Legations by the Boxers in 1900. These last I had reassembled years later in a corner of the Residence garden.

Peking at that time was still to some degree a walled city. The demolition of the walls had begun, but the great gateways remained. There was also the occasional ceremonial arch (*pailou*) across a street, built to commemorate loyal statesmen, virtuous widows and like paragons. There was still a Jade Street and an Embroidery Street. There were of course no skyscrapers, no ring-roads. Architecturally the city had three main strata: most recent, some monstrous structures in the Russian monumental style, like the Great Hall of the People; a scattering of English municipal, dating from the turn of the century; and below that the grey dusty mass of the *hutungs* (lanes) and inward-looking courtyard houses, studded with the occasional temple. In the centre the red walls and gold roofs of the Forbidden City.

Our movements were circumscribed. We could not travel far from the city centre; and even within the permitted area a number of the historical sites were out of bounds, though not clearly marked, so that we had regular brushes with the police. Those that were open were often empty: foreign visitors were limited and there was little of the internal tourism common today; ordinary Chinese did not travel and had enough to do to keep alive. Birthe and I could picnic in the grass-grown side courtyards of the Forbidden City: our favourite spot was the Palace of Peaceful Old Age, prepared by the Emperor Qian Long for his retirement, after sixty years on the throne. I also remember a day in February at the Summer Palace with nobody about and a silence broken only by the faint musical sounds of the lake ice cracking in the sun.

We had one other post in China, our great consulate on the

Bund in Shanghai. This was a town in itself, with its lawns, lawcourts, chapel and rows of staff houses, but now a ghost town, inhabited by one diplomatic family, plus an army of Chinese staff, for whom the authorities were constantly seeking higher wages, but whose numbers we were not allowed to reduce.

This trick with local staff was a favourite device of the Chinese government for mulcting British firms who stayed on after 'liberation'. Every pressure was applied to cause the firm voluntarily to surrender its assets. In the end there was no more business to do; but the manager would not be allowed to leave; the Chinese staff were idle but could not be dismissed and their wages had to be remitted to China in foreign exchange. Eventually, when the fruit had been squeezed dry, the unfortunate expatriate might be allowed home.

We had a small British community in Shanghai, centring round the Consulate and going there for film shows or meeting to play bowls at the Hongkong and Shanghai Bank house. They had little to do. Some were businessmen, the last remnants of a great Western commercial centre; some were British nationals married to Chinese or partly of Chinese descent. These last were often tragic cases: a mother might qualify for an exit visa but not her child. Money was usually very short and we administered a small fund for their relief.

There was one other British group in the country, whom we seldom met. These were what Humphrey Trevelyan in his memoir on his stay in Peking calls 'the twilight brigade'. Another name, denoting their extreme loyalty to the cause, was 'the three hundred percenters'. To the Chinese they were 'the foreign friends'. Many of them Communists, they had thrown in their lot with the Chinese and worked with the media or in the Foreign Languages Institute. Their fate was also often sad. Never really assimilated, they were condemned to follow every twist of the Party line; and a number were to suffer in the Cultural Revolution at the hands of their hosts.

The Peking diplomatic corps was highly select. There were East Europeans in strength, led of course by the Russians, who had left their old quarters in the Legation area and built themselves an enormous new Embassy in the north-east of the city, on the site of an old Russian settlement dating from the seventeenth century, when Russian prisoners from an outpost on the

Amur river, including a priest, were first established there. Later an Orthodox church was built on the same spot. The Russians had enjoyed a privileged position in Peking for many years before the first British representatives were allowed to live there. They had had diplomatic dealings with the Chinese going back to the Treaty of Nerchinsk in 1689, the first between China and a European state, and not one of the 'unequal treaties': the Chinese came out of it rather well. Then they had had an ecclesiastical mission and a language school in Peking since the early eighteenth century. All this long before the Soviet Union became the 'socialist elder brother'.

In addition to East Europeans, there were Africans, with strong student contingents at Peking University, acquiring Chinese diplomas few other learned institutions were prepared to recognize. There were also of course Asians: Zhou Enlai had had a triumph at the Bandung Afro-Asian Conference in 1955.

Finally, there was a small Western presence: the Scandinavians, who had the privilege of still inhabiting charming courtyard houses in the centre of town, the Dutch, the Swiss and the British. The Dutch, miraculously, clung on to their old Legation. They held a dance there one evening, enabling me to form a picture of life as it used to be. There were no Americans, Germans, French or Japanese. It was all rather cosy and professionally undemanding. The West Europeans did not have a lot of business with the Chinese; nor, I fancy, did we have a deep insight into what was going on in the government or the Party. The Chargé met Chen Yi, the Foreign Minister, very occasionally. Usually we got no higher than a vice foreign minister; the real leaders were out of reach.

For the Western diplomats then, a quiet time. For the Chinese, hardship and recuperation from a catastrophe, the Great Leap Forward. In 1958 Mao had made one of his periodic attempts 'to get to heaven in a single step'. He tried to project China forward into prosperity and Communism by way of the People's Communes and a mass drive for productivity. Numbers and enthusiasm were seen as the key; with them everything could be accomplished.

The venture began with millions of men deployed on massive irrigation and land improvement projects; it rapidly developed into a rush for production at all costs and in all sectors. Not just in agriculture. Peasants, workers and students were exhorted to produce iron and steel in backyard furnaces in villages, factories and schools, wherever there was a vacant site. Lacking ore and pig-iron to feed the furnaces, they melted down their agricultural tools and cooking utensils. But the metal so produced proved useless. Much of the breakneck irrigation and planting went badly wrong and ruined the soil. The normal economy was disrupted, routine agricultural tasks were neglected, often including the harvest, and famines inevitably followed. There was great loss of life and a sharp fall in the national morale.

China in 1962 suffered in the wake of these events. Mao was in retreat, licking his wounds and, as we now know, conceding that even he was capable of mistakes. The country was in the hands of Liu Shaoqi and Deng Xiaoping on a doctor's mandate. The emphasis was again on agriculture and material incentives. The disasters of the last three years were officially attributed to natural forces; but the meeting of the National People's Congress in March was, unusually, held behind closed doors, and only abbreviated accounts released.

As Birthe and I travelled north from Canton on the two-day train journey to Peking across a wintry landscape we passed the bleak evidence of failure, smokeless factories and walls covered with exploded slogans. 'More, faster, better and more economically'; they had a sad ring to them. There had been a promise that China would overtake Britain's industrial production in fifteen years. But the most striking feature was the shortage of food. We were served meals in our compartment and not allowed to enter the dining car, clearly so that we should not see the desperate nature of Chinese rations, and so that they should not see how privileged we were. The year 1962 was in fact much better than the two preceding years; things were slowly beginning to pick up; but conditions were still extreme. For ordinary Chinese food was cabbage and a little rice; there was virtually no meat. And even cabbage was sometimes replaced by what were euphemistically called 'wild vegetables' – herbs and grasses. I remember puzzling over an obscure recipe I found advertised in Canton, the chief ingredients of which were just such rarities. In Peking Chinese students ate the buds and bark of trees; and our local staff were often near collapse.

China's external relations were for a time less tense. The Sino-

Soviet split had emerged some three years earlier at the time of the first serious Sino-Indian border clashes. It had passed through its first period of open confrontation (Soviet experts were withdrawn in 1960) and was now enjoying something of a lull: there was an agreement to avoid open polemics for a while. But the fires, though banked, still burned. The Chinese still applauded Albania (opposed to the Soviet Union) and condemned Yugoslavia (with whom there was a Soviet *rapprochement*). They also embarked on a series of esoteric essays in their ideological journal, *Red Flag*, about the sins of Bernstein, Kautsky and the Economists (pre-1917 opponents of Lenin). Bernstein and Kautsky, for the initiated, stood for Tito or Khrushchev; Lenin was a surrogate for Mao. I remember being rather proud at discovering these obscure theses and managing to read them, though with some pains. They conveyed a sense of the depth and unmanageable nature of the dispute, not at that time so generally recognized as being irreparable.

Rather less obscurely, we could follow the politics of the Third World as seen from Peking. The Sino-Indian dispute simmered. China's boundaries with Burma and Nepal were being hastily settled in order to emphasize the isolation and intransigence of the Indians. The Algerian cease-fire was celebrated as another victory in the liberation struggle.

There were, however, problems with other Africans, the students from black Africa housed in the Foreign Languages Institute and Peking University. They responded badly to the humourless discipline of their instructors and the over-politicization of their lives. They felt, rightly or wrongly, that they were the object of racial discrimination; and there was the perennial problem of the shortage of girls. A brawl occurred at the Peace Hotel and as a result a large proportion of the African students demanded their passports and left. It did not look well for Sino-African friendship. Echoes of these fraternal scuffles reached even the Western Embassies. They were the early signs of a chronic misunderstanding.

As for Hong Kong, it intruded very rarely. It was there and the Chinese tolerated it, regarding it as a problem left over from history, which would be solved at an appropriate time. It served us as our base camp, a source of supplies and medicines. Only towards the end of my stay did it figure prominently in our telegrams. In May there was a sudden relaxation in the border control exercised by the Guangdong authorities and Hong Kong was threatened by floods of immigrants. It was almost certainly an attempt by the local authorities in the south to relieve their own problems regardless of the wider impact. For a time the situation was tense; and then, in response to our appeals in Peking, control was reimposed. The incident remained only as a reminder of the vulnerability of the territory to events on the mainland.

By June my apprenticeship was coming to an end. I stayed for the Queen's Birthday Party, presided over by Hugh and Alexandra. Michael Stewart was away and *agrément* was sought for Terence Garvey, his successor. My own replacement arrived, Richard Evans, who in 1984 was to succeed me as Ambassador, as I had succeeded Teddy Youde in 1978. I returned to my proper condition as a language student, with a few weeks to prepare for the August examination. The great events of 1962, the Cuban missile crisis and the Sino-Indian War, occurred while I was in Hong Kong.

It had been a gentle introduction. We had come to China in one of the pauses in the revolutionary spasms which punctuated Mao's years of leadership, an interval in a fever. But the interval was not to be long. Already in September of 1962 the Central Committee of the Party in its plenary session resolved that 'class struggle continues after the foundation of the socialist state'. In other words, the left (that is, the Maoist wing of the Party) was beginning its come-back; and though the prelude was to last some years, the foundations were being laid for the biggest convulsion of all, the Cultural Revolution.

CHAPTER TWO

The Cultural Revolution

THE CULTURAL REVOLUTION, once in every headline, has now faded into history. Other excitements have supervened and more topical names, like Tiananmen, have succeeded it in the press shorthand on China. We recall it denoted some violent upheaval, but precisely what and why tends now to escape us. It may therefore help if, before going on with the story, I set down in very generalized terms what lay behind it.

Ever since the Communist victory in 1949 there had been a steady tension between Mao's wish to transform the country and society as rapidly as possible and the more cautious plans of the economists and administrators. As early as 1956 there had been a 'little leap', an attempt, as the *People's Daily* later put it, 'to do everything overnight'. It had to be abandoned when reckless advances brought chaos to agriculture and an unacceptable lowering of quality in industrial production. Mao retreated, but returned to the charge in 1958 with the Great Leap Forward, which again ended in disaster, the 'three bitter years' of 1959 to 1961. Again a retreat, again a regrouping.

By the early 1960s Mao was brooding, not simply on the issue of how to govern China, but also on the example offered by that more advanced socialist state, the Soviet Union. Khrushchev's denunciation of Stalin in 1956 and his apparent penchant for accommodation with the United States raised doubts in Mao's mind about the direction of Soviet society. Far from being an exemplar, it was becoming a warning. How to avoid a similar fate for China?

The Cultural Revolution was his answer. It was called 'cultural' because it began with a rectification campaign against rightist intellectuals; but this was incidental: the struggle had a much wider focus. It was in part an attempt to save China from Soviet-style revisionism, the process of ossification and embourgeoisement Mao saw at work in Eastern Europe, the emergence of a new mandarinate, what Djilas called 'the new class'. It was an attempt to put the clock back and recover the revolutionary simplicities and enthusiasms of the Yenan days, when he and his followers had just emerged from the Long March. The Party organization, and the organization-men at its head, were inevitably seen as the enemy.

The second objective was more visionary. It was nothing less than to change the nature of Chinese man, to 'dig out the roots of self' and produce an entirely public-spirited citizen. To achieve this, the most intensive education was required in order to attain unity of thought based on complete subordination to Mao's teaching. 'Father is dear, mother is dear, but Chairman Mao is dearer.' The new man would not need material incentives: he would have Chairman Mao's teaching. He would not be a blinkered expert, but a man of the all-purpose variety, capable of being at one and the same time worker, soldier, student and revolutionary. It was all outlined in a famous letter Mao wrote in May 1966 to Lin Biao, the Defence Minister and the Chairman's principal acolyte, laying down the blueprint for the good society in China.

As it turned out, the roots of self proved to be not so easy to eradicate and the new all-purpose man bore disturbing resemblances to his predecessor; but the objective was serious and huge efforts in indoctrination, beginning in the army, were devoted to it.

By these vast changes Mao hoped, as he put it, 'to build China into a powerful, modern socialist state in not too long a historical period'. His opponents had similar long-term objectives and in this sense the quarrel was about means rather than ends. Mao's approach was characteristically radical, an extreme example of political voluntarism. He sought to rely on men rather than technology, political fervour and self-help rather than state aid and material inducements. He wanted to bleed the cities of all non-productive manpower, to decentralize industry, to build an educational and medical system concentrating on the country-side and concerned with simple practical needs. The contra-diction between this de-education process and the complex requirements of an advanced socialist state seems not to have deeply troubled the great leader.

These were the ostensible and abstract goals. But how to attain them? And here we come to some much more basic and less idealistic aims. They were first, to recover power; and second, to use it to destroy those who, in his view, stood in his way, a long and ever-growing category, headed by Liu Shaoqi, the heir apparent.

The recovery of power was far from a formality. Though Mao was still Chairman, the Party machine had taken over and was tending to sidetrack his initiatives with increasing ease. He was, he later complained, being treated by Liu Shaoqi and Deng Xiaoping like a dead parent at a funeral. Deng never consulted him and Peng Zhen's power-base in Peking (where Peng Zhen was Party First Secretary as well as Mayor) was a watertight kingdom you could not penetrate with a needle. There seem to have been several attempts by him before 1966 to launch the comeback and purge he wanted, but they were all beaten off.

He succeeded eventually with the help of the People's Libera-tion Army, the PLA. When in 1959 the Defence Minister, Peng Dehuai, was removed for venturing to criticize the Great Leap, Mao had replaced him with Lin Biao. Lin was a brilliant military commander, whose armies had rolled up Manchuria, but an unlikely political leader, sickly, reclusive, uncharismatic to a degree. But he was intensely ambitious and totally committed to Mao. In the early 1960s he set in motion in the PLA a process of revolutionary education and worship of the Chairman, which was the forerunner of the wider ideological revolution attempted in 1966. Moreover, as part of the 'Learn from the PLA' move-ment, there were PLA contingents strategically placed in the government and administrative sectors and in the schools and other places of learning.

The final step to assure military backing was probably the secret purge in March 1966 of Luo Ruiqing, the Chief of the General Staff. Luo differed from Lin Biao on the issue of men against machines, the classic schism in the Chinese defence establishment, and on the imminence of a US attack on China. But, more relevant to the matter in hand, he had wide influence in the PLA; and he was a former Minister of Public Security. With him out of the way the situation in Peking was much more manageable.

Even so, formal authority for the movement was hard to obtain. The meeting of the Central Committee of August 1966 which officially launched it was irregular: about half of the list of full and alternate members were absent and the final session was packed with revolutionary teachers and students and PLA officers.

Once back in full control, Mao employed another instrument against the Party and his opponents, namely the Red Guards, drawn initially at least from middle school and university students. They were the shock troops sent in to criticize and overthrow the established order.

They emerged on the public stage at the first of the great rallies in Tiananmen Square on 18 August, but their origins remain obscure. Mao is reported to have talked to Kang Sheng, his security chief, in March and to have alluded to the old Chinese story of the Monkey King, who stormed the gates of Hell and had the magical power to turn the hairs of his fur into legions of little monkeys to help him. According to the report, which has a plausible ring, Mao remarked, 'We must overthrow the King of Hell and liberate the little devils.'

There are reports of Red Guard groups being set up in the early summer. Their formation and operations were probably assisted by the police and security apparatus and they drew heavily on the army for transport and logistic support. They answered, not to the Party, but to an alternative centre of authority, the Cultural Revolution Group, which was set up to guide the struggle and was headed by Mao's political secretary, Chen Boda. It was revolution of the most artificial kind, dictated from above; but it rapidly acquired a life of its own.

The revolution had a further objective, to provide for the succession. In 1969 at its conclusion it seemed that at the top this work was accomplished: Liu Shaoqi had been brutally removed and sent to a dreadful death; Lin Biao was formally proclaimed the heir. But the heir proved unworthy of his trust. In a manner still not fully explained, he disappeared in 1971. Possibly his plane crashed as he tried to flee to the Soviet Union after a failed coup attempt, as in the official accounts; possibly he was liquidated by Mao before he could flee; certainly the closest comrade-in-arms had come to be seen as a lethal threat.

At a lower level, it was hoped that a new generation of leaders would emerge, tempered in revolution if not in war. But here again there was disappointment. Mao himself conceded, well before the close of the turmoil, that tempering successors had proved a hopeless undertaking. The revolution certainly purged the old leadership, but it left a desert: in 1969, apart from the army and the great survivor, Zhou Enlai, there was only a motley collection of hacks and hatchet-men.

The movement was of course an immense disaster. As it wound to its close after three years of chaos, it left a country in ruins, its economy damaged, its international credit destroyed, its education disrupted, its intellectuals humiliated and brutalized, dead between half a million and a million (no one knows exactly), and a legacy of lasting bitterness and disillusion. Even the Party eventually assessed it as a national catastrophe on an unparalleled scale.

But these truths, now so plain to us with hindsight, were happily concealed in the summer of 1966. Valéry said that we enter the future backwards; it is usually just as well. Mao was preparing quietly for his last ride; few knew what was afoot. He could draw on limitless enthusiasm in China, and, in the West, on a powerful mixture of reverence and incomprehension.

CHAPTER THREE

A Peking Summer

I RETURNED TO Peking in June 1966, as Political Counsellor
and Head of Chancery. Before I arrived the first act of the great
drama had been performed. We were some days out of Hong
Kong (in those more leisurely days sea travel was still permitted)
when we heard the news that Peng Zhen, the Mayor of Peking,
First Secretary of the Peking Party Committee and member of
the Politburo, had fallen from power. This was clearly a major
upheaval: Peng was a very big fish.

But the full scale of what was in store was still not apparent
and it was possible to regard his removal as an isolated episode.
When I first met our Chargé, Donald Hopson, in the waiting-
room at Lowu, the border railway station, I on my way north,
he travelling to Hong Kong and Singapore for a Heads of
Mission conference, this was precisely the view he took. To my
anxious enquiries he replied confidently that it was all over and
things would now settle down. He was off to Singapore to tell
them so. I recall clearly the sight of his erect figure in immaculate
white ducks striding down the platform after having delivered
this definitive statement.

Donald had been our Ambassador in Laos. He was crisp and
military, a commando officer in the Second World War, by all
accounts a good man to have with you in a tight corner. He
bore the trials of the Cultural Revolution with a certain style,
served later with distinction as Ambassador in Venezuela and

Argentina, only to die tragically and unnecessarily in Buenos
Aires of blood poisoning from a small, unattended wound.

We were now a rather larger mission than in the early 1960s.
We were still only an office, not an embassy, but, following
Douglas Jay's visit to China in 1964, we had acquired a Com-
mercial Counsellor, Theo Peters. We also had the usual galaxy
of Chinese-speaking talent in Chancery: Alan Donald, a future
Ambassador in Peking, John Boyd, later Ambassador in Tokyo,
Len Appleyard, now Political Director of the Foreign Office, and
later John Weston, a future Ambassador at NATO.

Ray Whitney joined us in the autumn, succeeding Alan
Donald as Chinese Secretary. He was later to have a distinguished political career. Like me, he was a late entrant to the
Diplomatic Service: he came from the army, where he had
learned his Chinese. He brought us the military virtues of courage, gaiety and resilience, and was to be a tower of strength in
our coming tribulations.

Our foreign colleagues had also grown in number. In particular we had the French, who had been set up in style by
General de Gaulle in 1964, the first full embassy from a major
Western power. We saw much of them, for Donald Hopson's
wife, Denise, was French and had been a heroine of the Resistance. We also felt their influence in the antique shops, which
were now combed in a systematic way unheard of in the old
days.

There was a small Western press corps. In addition to
Reuters' correspondent, Virgil Berger (and later Anthony
Grey), I recall Jean Vincent of Agence France Presse, David
Oancia of the *Toronto Globe and Mail* and Harold Munthe-Kaas.
And of course Hans Bargmann of DPA, a good friend and
always immensely well informed.

Life was still comfortable. Whatever moves were being made
behind the scenes, the prelude to the Cultural Revolution had
been an undemanding time for foreigners. Just before my arrival
a farewell party was given for my predecessor, Michael Wilford,
at the Summer Palace. It was an elegant entertainment. Boat-
men rowed the revellers over the lake as the sun went down.
There were paper lanterns and a dance held near the Dowager
Empress's apartments. Perhaps it was a little like dances at the
Orangery at Versailles on the eve of the French Revolution.

Certainly this was one of the last touches of diplomatic *douceur de vivre* before the storm.

Real life lay elsewhere – at the Peking Party headquarters just opposite the International Club, where demonstrators gathered with lorries and drums. There was turmoil at Peking University, where a radical lecturer, clearly with support from on high, had put up a poster attacking Lu Ping, the University President.

A little later in June a Chinese who had stabbed two foreigners was subjected to trial before the masses as a counter-revolutionary and led away to summary execution. It was an ugly episode, not least for its evidence of the xenophobia underlying the still orderly surface of Peking life, and was made worse by the blatantly political nature of the proceedings, with the crowd chanting slogans about never forgetting the class struggle.

I learned something about the background to Peng Zhen's fall. As with so much else, the threads led back to the traumatic incident at the Party's Lushan Plenum in 1959, when a revolutionary hero, Peng Dehuai, had dared reveal the folly of Mao's policies, and had been dismissed and disgraced for his pains. The story illustrated the esoteric nature of public political debate in China, the habit, necessary under a tyranny, of using historical fables and parables to convey the message. The Chinese proverb is: 'Point at the mulberry and curse the ash.'

Not long after Peng Dehuai's fall, the Deputy Mayor of Peking, Wu Han, a distinguished historian, writing under a pseudonym, had published in the *People's Daily* an article entitled 'Hai Rui reprimands the Emperor'. Hai Rui was an upright official of the Ming dynasty who had been brave enough to rebuke the Emperor on behalf of the oppressed peasants; the author held him up as a model. Obscure and harmless to the Western reader, the piece was painfully clear to the Chinese. Hai Rui stood for Peng Dehuai, the Ming Emperor for Chairman Mao. It was a bold article and a measure of Mao's relative impotence that Wu Han got away with it at the time. Indeed Wu went further and published a libretto for a Peking opera on the same subject in 1960; and there were other articles in the Peking press which, under various guises, belittled Mao. Behind Wu Han and his fellow writers stood the Peking Party chief, Peng Zhen, one of the very few Party leaders not in total awe of the Chairman and one of the few entitled to the designation of his 'close comrade-in-arms'.

Mao picked up this old challenge and launched his revolution by inspiring an article in the Shanghai press on 10 November 1965. It was written by an obscure hack writer, Yao Wenyuan, and entitled 'A criticism of the recent historical libretto, The Dismissal of Hai Rui'. The article had to emerge from Shanghai since Mao lacked control of the Peking propaganda machine. It was long and clumsy, but it concluded with the ominous statement that, 'far from being a fragrant flower', the play was 'a poisonous weed'. 'Poisonous weed' was to become a very familiar phrase in the coming years. When Yao Wenyuan's patron was known, the seriousness of the situation became clear to the Peking circle.

I also learned that, following this exchange, there had been a decision to set up a small group to run a cultural rectification campaign. Curiously, Peng Zhen had been put at its head. He had clearly failed to come up with the right answer. Later information suggested that there was no correct answer: the appointment was probably a trap. If Peng abandoned his protégés to criticism he would in effect be admitting his own responsibility; if he resisted he would find himself in a possibly fatal confrontation with the Chairman. Relying on the strength of the Party machine, Peng had apparently resisted, defending Wu Han and attempting to confine the controversy to the academic world, the field of historical studies.

We saw these events only darkly and fragmentarily at the time; it was an obscure period, when, as we gathered later, the Party organization was making its last effort to keep control of events by sending in 'work teams' to the universities.

But political pressure was building up. Late in July the *People's Daily* announced that Mao had been swimming in the Yangtze at Wuhan. He had apparently swum for sixty-five minutes and covered fifteen kilometres. This was about four times as fast as the world record for ten miles. Even allowing for the swift Yangtze currents, it was a remarkable feat. There was irreverent doubt in the Western embassies whether he had actually performed it, indeed whether he had been there at all. The official photograph was subjected to particularly intense scrutiny in the US Consulate in Hong Kong.

But, whatever the athletic detail, the event was treated in the Chinese media as of immense political importance, a demonstration of the Chairman's continuing political as well as physical vigour. Thousands emulated their leader and took to the water, many swimming in columns or platoons, carrying slogans or Mao portraits, or even weapons, on floats.

By early August Mao was back in Peking and the *People's Daily* published a big-character poster he had composed. It was entitled 'Bombard the Headquarters!' and was a direct invitation to the radical students to assail the leaders of Party and State.

At the same time the Central Committee was meeting and on 8 August issued a directive to guide the Cultural Revolution. This stated that 'the great proletarian cultural revolution now unfolding is a great revolution that touches people to their very souls and constitutes a new stage in the development of the socialist revolution'. The object was 'to struggle against and crush those persons in authority who are taking the capitalist road', and to 'expose every kind of ghost and monster'. The masses must liberate themselves. 'Trust the masses. Cast out fear. Don't be afraid of disorder.' Though there were, mingled with these wild cries, some injunctions not to impede industrial and agricultural production, the general drift was clear, and alarming.

But the event that marked the new epoch most clearly was the great rally of 18 August when around a million people gathered in Tiananmen Square and for the first time the armbands marked '*Hong Wei Bing*' (Red Guard) appeared in public. It was a scene of intense mass enthusiasm. Two figures on the corner of the rostrum, standing apart from the other leaders and surveying the assembled multitude, symbolized the new power structure – Mao and 'his closest comrade-in-arms', Lin Biao. The list of leaders published in the press confirmed a changed hierarchy: Liu Shaoqi had fallen from second to eighth place. Mao's political secretary, Chen Boda, had become a senior leader; and Mao's wife, Jiang Qing, found her place in the official lists for the first time, as the first Vice-Chairman of the Cultural Revolution Group.

The Cultural Revolution Group, now revealed, became the effective power directing the Red Guards and various revolutionary organizations. It was composed of people close to Mao, on whom he now chose to rely in preference to the regular Party organs. In addition to Jiang Qing and Chen Boda, it included one personality who played a dark and influential role throughout the unfolding tragedy, Kang Sheng. Kang, a senior leader for many years, had been trained in Stalin's Russia in the security and intelligence field and seems to have acted for long as the head of the secret intelligence apparatus in China. He was known as 'Venerable Kang' to his associates, 'China's Beria' to others. He was intimate with Mao and had close ties with Jiang Qing, for whom he had found a post in Yenan, making possible her first meeting with the Chairman. At an earlier stage she may even have been on his books. A gaunt and bespectacled figure, with a thin moustache and a thin smile, he had the air of a sinister schoolmaster.

On the Sunday after the 18 August rally, as Birthe and I were driving to the Temple of Heaven, the altar and temple to the south of the city, where once the Emperors performed the ritual sacrifices at the summer and winter solstice, we were struck by the unusual activity, knots of people busy at certain shops and street corners; signs were being changed and decorations removed. At the temple itself the shrine that normally contained the tablets of the Manchu imperial ancestors was empty. Similar changes, we discovered, were taking place all over the city: the Red Guards were beginning their assault on 'the four old things' (old ideas, old culture, old customs and habits).

In his speech at the rally of 18 August Lin Biao had called on revolutionaries to 'launch fierce attacks on bourgeois ideology, old customs and the force of old habits'. A little later Mao remarked that a few months of destruction would be 'mostly to the good'. The response was a wave of iconoclasm, turning to extravagant persecution and finally plain violence.

At the lighter end of the spectrum were the changes in street names. Our road, which also housed the North Vietnamese Embassy, was rechristened 'Support Vietnam Street'. The road to the Soviet Embassy inevitably became 'Anti-Revisionist Street'. Chinese with Western hairstyles came under attack and were invited to have revolutionary haircuts. Jeans, tight-fitting skirts and blouses and what the press called 'obnoxious photographs and journals' came under heavy fire.

But this was only the beginning. John Boyd and Len Appleyard came back from one of their fact-finding tours to report,
'They are breaking into people's houses.' As indeed they were.
Bourgeois furniture, that is anything traditional or Western, was
seized and carted off to be sold in second-hand shops. Books were
burned. Anything giving a touch of individuality, paintings,
porcelain and, of course, any items of foreign origin were
smashed. Private houses themselves were seized and the owner
assigned one or two rooms. Savings over a thousand yuan were
confiscated. The inevitable next stage was reached when John
and Len saw a Chinese being savagely beaten in the grounds of
the Temple of the Sun adjoining our Mission. Beatings and killings soon became common.

China's historical relics and artistic treasures were under
serious threat. Some monuments were too large to be destroyed;
but they could be defaced. The Forbidden City itself was pru-
dently closed. The press proudly reported inexcusable acts of
vandalism. The students of the Central Institute of Arts removed
the Institute's collection of dynastic sculptures as well as *objets
d'art* from abroad and, according to the New China News
Agency in an approving article, 'completely destroyed these by
burning and crushing'. Similar acts of destruction or defacement
took place throughout the country. As Lin Biao put it in his
speech at a rally at the end of August, 'the revolutionary torrents
of the masses are washing away all the sludge and filth left over
from the old society'.

Personally disturbing were the visits by our Chinese office
staff, begging us to take back small mementoes we had given
them, photographs of some office party and the like. They were
obviously very frightened.

I recall a party at an Indian colleague's house. We sat out
under the trees in the garden. From next door, a Chinese residence, came the noise of destruction, blows, cries, the sound of
breaking glass and furniture. I recall too a diplomatic dinner
with the Danish Chargé, Arne Belling, whose flat overlooked the
main east–west boulevard. As we sat with our candles and silver
we could see below in the darkened street groups darting out
from the pavement to intercept the buses plying along the main
road, stopping them and dragging out individuals. There were
no police, or none visible. For a moment we had a sense of the

thin partition between our polite world and the growing disorder outside.

I recall the same evening learning from a student at Peking University that posters were up in the campus pointing at Liu Shaoqi.

The incident that touched us most at the time was the Red Guard occupation of the international school run by the Franciscan nuns of the Sacred Heart, the only establishment for foreign children in Peking. The nuns were handcuffed and beaten. The foreign nuns were allowed to leave the country after a day or two. One of them died a few hours after crossing into Hong Kong. Out of some twenty Chinese nuns, four died; the rest were reportedly dispersed to their places of origin and an unknown fate.

There was naturally much feeling in the Mission over this brutality, affecting the school British children attended. We held a meeting for staff and families to establish there was nothing more we could do to intervene and to convey some sense of reassurance. Theo Peters and I argued that the revolution was an internal matter, affecting only Chinese. This was true for a while, but not for so very long.

CHAPTER FOUR

The Revolution Gets under Way

THE RALLY OF 18 August was succeeded by a series of others on similar lines throughout the autumn and early winter, each involving around a million demonstrators. There was something of a pause before National Day on 1 October and an effort to tidy up. Then the rallies resumed. The official figure was that some nine million Red Guards visited Peking between 18 August and 21 November.

The National Day parade itself was on strange lines. Instead of the usual orderly march past, there was first a gigantic statue of Mao in military uniform, his hand pointing forward, then a horde or flood of revolutionary youth streaming across the great square in a kind of deliberate disorder, as if to convey a sense of the turbulence and power of the movement sweeping the country.

The effect, particularly in Tiananmen Square, of the vast numbers present at the rallies, the enthusiasm and the rhythmic chanting was overpowering. On the basis of my own limited observation, there was individual frenzy and hysteria, but the scene remained disciplined and the atmosphere generally good-humoured and joyful. The PLA were always present in strength, but more as ushers or participants than as armed guards. The faces were remarkably like those in the propaganda posters, young, round, smiling, uncomplicated, the faces of converts at any revivalist gathering, washed clean of doubts.

To the strains of 'The East is Red', Mao would appear on the rostrum overlooking the square. There would be thunderous cries of '*Mao Zhu Xi, Wan Sui! Wan Sui! Wan Wan Sui!*' ('Ten thousand years to Chairman Mao!'), the old greeting for the Emperor transposed in a new devotional setting. Everyone brandished the Little Red Book, the collection of the sayings of Mao, originally designed by Lin Biao for political education in the armed forces, but by now the indispensable equipment of any revolutionary.

Sometimes on these occasions Mao would come down from the rostrum and be driven through the square among the adoring ranks. He did not speak. Usually Lin Biao and Zhou Enlai would deliver speeches, the first calling for all-out attacks on revisionists and capitalist-roaders, the second indicating that, while revolution was vital, there were other tasks not to be neglected, such as the harvest or industrial production. Perhaps we imagined it, but Zhou did not appear entirely at ease, despite his Red Guard armband and vigorous performance with the Little Red Book. His task throughout was that of riding and restraining a runaway horse.

The press revealed that at the rallies there were student representatives from other parts of China. The Red Guards, encouraged to exchange revolutionary experiences, or simply determined to cast eyes on their Chairman, were fanning out across the country. Some marched great distances in order to emulate the Long March of 1934, in which the Chinese Communist Party had been steeled. Many more took to the trains, and Peking station and the square outside it were packed with pilgrims. We threaded our way round mounds of sleeping figures. Trains were diverted or taken over and before long the whole railway system was in confusion.

To many Red Guards this must have been the blissful dawn of revolution. For the first time they were able to leave their own districts and travel, free of charge, across the country. They were the élite of the movement, charged to criticize and drive out revisionists and capitalist-roaders from all positions of authority. They carried the word of Mao. In the Little Red Book he had said, 'The world is yours as well as ours, but in the last analysis it is yours.'

I recall one who was given a lift by my Norwegian colleague.

Was he not afraid of being seen driving round with a foreigner?
No, he was a Red Guard and the police would not touch him.
What was it like in Peking? Fine. The girls there were much
prettier than in his home town. Initially at least, there were
simple pleasures for some in the Cultural Revolution.

But of course it was more complicated than that. Transport
was being diverted from essential purposes. Peasants and workers
were being harassed and were reacting angrily. Orders had to
be issued emphasizing that they could not leave their posts in the
same way as the students: they could make revolution only in
their spare time. Party authorities outside Peking found themselves under attack from visiting Red Guards and defended
themselves with the help of local youths. There were signs of
division among the students themselves: they were forming
factions and competing in extremism; violent clashes between
them were growing more frequent. The colours were darkening
rapidly.

For the foreign diplomat in Peking at the time life still maintained its normal outward forms: the embassies were well
guarded; there were still the telegrams, the National Days; there
was even some business with the Chinese. But it was getting
more uncomfortable and distinctly more odd. Movement by rail
was disrupted; even movement inside Peking was difficult. The
streets were packed with the visiting masses; they were not just
students; there were workers and peasants, availing themselves
of the general disorder to petition about their grievances, but also
to gaze at the shops and the foreigners. The shops were plastered
over with posters and hard to identify. There was in any case
little inside them.

For the Embassy political officers it was a time of great interest
and excitement. We knew now that we were in the presence of
a great historical convulsion; we understood its general direction;
we still did not know how far it might go. But there were now
gaps appearing in the screen normally interposed between the
Chinese authorities and their foreign guests. We were increasingly being supplied with information by the revolutionaries
themselves. The wall posters carried reports of trouble in distant
cities or provinces as delegations came to the capital to complain,
stories of oppression of revolutionaries by local cadres, or of
fights between rival revolutionary groups.

More important, reports were appearing critical of government or Party leaders and apparently drawing on privileged or secret material. Though the immediate authors were Red Guards, the leaks clearly came from much higher, presumably from the Cultural Revolution Group itself, and were deliberate. Allowing for some distortion, the reports were probably accurate. In a tightly closed society, where any information, however harmless, was secret, such revelations were pure gold.

The Chinese-speakers from the embassies and press corps gathered eagerly with their notebooks round the hoardings, mingling with the equally eager Chinese audience. At that stage there was no hostility to our presence, rather a kindly interest and some admiration that we could cope with the language. There was competition among the embassies for the best poster service; the Japanese journalists were usually thought to have won. Many of them, brought up in Manchuria, were bilingual and they worked in teams, the reader at the poster-face shouting his translation to the scribe, hunched over his typewriter on the pavement.

Later this activity became more hazardous. Indian diplomats, who were good at the poster game, were accused of spying and we were all warned off. Diplomatic cars were then often seen making strange deviations in the main streets as the occupants tried to catch at least the headlines of the posters as they drove past.

Posters were also later supplemented by Red Guard newspapers, conveying much the same information, though in more permanent form. Small boys touted them and could sometimes be induced to sell to the foreigner for a few coins. They were much sought after; but they too were contraband, inviting a charge of espionage. Birthe, going about quietly on her bicycle, became one of our chief suppliers and came back usually well padded, with several layers of newsprint beneath her coat.

The cult of Mao was by now assuming extraordinary proportions: from a revered political leader he was rapidly becoming a god. He was no longer just Chairman Mao: the full title was the Great Helmsman, Great Leader, Great Supreme Commander, Great Teacher, Chairman Mao. He was shown in posters and pictures with rays of light emanating from his head, a kind of halo. We were told that he was the red sun at the hearts of his people, that his presence, even his writings, had an inspirational effect. His words were judged of greater potency even than those of Marx and Lenin; indeed, according to Lin Biao, every word of his equalled ten thousand words by others. It was therefore not surprising that sick men revived looking at his portrait; and athletes were inspired to supreme feats after studying his sayings. There was unfortunately one recorded instance of a Chinese table tennis player who broke off his match for this spiritual refreshment, but then lost. But these were rare lapses.

When a fire broke out in the flat above my own, the firemen, late at the scene, insisted on an inspirational session before getting down to work and chanted the text, 'Be resolute, fear no sacrifice and surmount every difficulty to win victory', an exercise listened to with some impatience by my neighbours and myself. And when we flew from Peking on Chinese airlines, the air hostesses entertained us with a charming dance in the aisles, using the Little Red Book and inviting us to join the reading of such texts as 'All reactionaries are paper tigers.'

The revolution produced other art-forms. There was a crop of powerful cartoons and caricatures. In them young revolutionaries of Brobdingnagian proportions, their features set in righteous anger, crushed beneath their feet or skewered with their bayonets or pens small, ugly, wriggling creatures representing revisionists or capitalist-roaders, or simply charged forward to some unspecified heroic confrontation, while behind or above, radiating light like the sun, floated the benign figure of the Chairman. In later variants Liu Shaoqi would be personally identified, often wearing a sinister trilby, always associated in Communist demonology with Chiang Kaishek's followers. He would be shown abasing himself before top-hatted capitalists or learning ignominiously from Khrushchev, or simply fleeing, like some noxious insect, from the light of Mao's thought.

There was much misplaced skill in these productions. I admired one in particular, which came out some time later and showed the gang of Cultural Revolution villains winding across the page in the guise of the entourage for some travelling mandarin of the imperial era. Here was the whole rogues gallery, each engaged in some typical activity or making some characteristic utterance. Liu, as the principal figure, was borne in a sedan chair under a banner inscribed 'bourgeois reactionary line'. Deng, by his side in another litter, held a pack of cards, appropriate to a bridge enthusiast. Wang Guangmei, Liu's wife, rode on a bicycle in a 'bourgeois' dress, such as she had worn on her visit to Indonesia when she danced with President Sukarno, and adorned with a large string of pearls. Yang Shangkun, then a senior official in the Central Secretariat, alleged to have bugged Mao's office, carried earphones and a notebook. Led by Lu Dingyi, the disgraced chief of propaganda, the cavalcade headed for a precipice marked 'To capitalism'. Drawn with skill and obvious enjoyment, the work was entitled 'The Rogues Gallery' (see Plate 5).

More intrusive than the cartoons were the revolutionary songs. For these, quotations from the Chairman's writings had been selected and set to catchy tunes. Some of the material was refractory, to say the least. For example, the words of one well-known song consisted of the passage: 'The force at the core leading our cause forward is the Chinese Communist Party. The theoretical basis guiding our thinking is Marxist-Leninism.' But the tune did wonders for the lyric.

Some of the songs were less forbidding and were simple devotional pieces.

> Beloved Chairman Mao,
> The red sun shining in our hearts,
> Beloved Chairman Mao,
> The red sun shining in our hearts,
> How many words so deep in our hearts we
>   long to say to you,
> How many warm and fervent songs we
>   wish to sing for you,
> Ay!
> Millions of red hearts excitedly beating,
> Millions of smiling faces turn to
>   the red sun.
> From our hearts we wish you,
>   beloved Chairman Mao,
> A long life, a long life, a long
>   long life to you!

The favourite was 'Sailing the Seas depends on the Helmsman', the helmsman naturally being Mao. This was sung at

every rally. Even now, after the passage of more than a quarter
of a century, I cannot listen to a recording without being carried
back to the hot, dusty days of that Peking autumn and those
scenes of mindless enthusiasm and mindless noise.

Noise in fact was the hallmark of the revolution and before
long earplugs became standard Embassy issue. The songs were
the enforced accompaniment of our waking hours. We had them
in grand chorus at rallies, less formally from radio and television,
and *passim* from the innumerable loudspeakers rigged up at road
junctions or outside blocks of flats. From these latter also came,
at high volume, interminable political harangues. The con-
tinuum was punctuated by the sound of drums and gongs as
demonstrators rode by in lorries, sometimes with banners, but
sometimes, and increasingly, with victims, wearing dunce's caps
and carrying placards reciting their sins. The drums had an
unmistakable rhythm.

The victims were now growing in numbers and seniority. The
first swathe, Peng Zhen and his associates, were 'dragged out'
by Red Guards to face 'struggle meetings' in December, and
again in January 1967. 'Struggle meeting' was a term of art,
denoting violent confrontation and denunciation with the object
of destroying the victim's 'face' and self-respect. It did not mean
immediate physical destruction; that might come later, but only
when the discrediting and humiliation were complete. Nor, in
practice, did it preclude lesser violence or torture. In the case
of Lu Dingyi, the disgraced head of propaganda, the Red
Guards had been over-enthusiastic. He had been suspended by
ropes attached to his arms and legs, and swung about so violently
that he was seriously injured. Kang Sheng is reported to have
reproved the young men for going too far; this was presumably
not out of any humanitarian impulse, but because it meant that
Lu could not be used for further struggle sessions.

In photographs in Red Guard newspapers Peng and his fellow
prisoners were shown in the 'jet position', that is held with their
arms bent backwards and upwards, forcing them to bow their
heads. They had clearly been subjected to various kinds of
physical violence. Luo Ruiqing, the former Chief of the General
Staff, whose removal had been kept dark for months, was part
of the group and had one of his legs in plaster. He had reportedly
tried to escape his tormentors by jumping out of a window to

commit suicide, but had only succeeded in breaking a leg. He was hauled about from struggle meeting to struggle meeting in a kind of basket.

At the same time the revolution was aiming higher. Liu Shaoqi was by now clearly targeted, as was Deng Xiaoping, the State President and the General Secretary of the Party. They were still not named in official publications. Liu was 'the top person in authority taking the capitalist road', or 'China's Khrushchev'. In January Liu and his wife, Wang Guangmei, were forced to attend a struggle meeting, the first of many.

There was also poster criticism of a number of senior ministers, including Chen Yi, the Foreign Minister, and Li Xiannian, the Finance Minister, plus a list of provincial leaders. Zhou Enlai managed to give some protection to his closest colleagues in the State Council, but had to abandon others: the Coal Minister, for example, died under persecution.

Zhou's own position was an almost impossible one. We constantly read that he had received this or that delegation, from Red Guard groups, or visiting workers or peasants who had come to the capital with their problems; he endeavoured to look after his ministers and keep the administration going; he was required also to perform at the rallies. He worked regularly through the night to three or four in the morning. Some of the criticisms of his lieutenants amounted to covert attacks on himself from the left and there was one occasion at least where he was directly assailed. But, by a consummate display of tact and adroitness, he survived and was able to do something to limit the excesses. It was common ground among the foreign community that if he fell it was time to leave.

These were the dramas at the top, but at lower levels too the casualty lists were lengthening fast. There were frequent stories of suicides, particularly among the intellectuals. We heard of many cases in Shanghai. In Peking, Wu Han, the author of the libretto on Hai Rui, ended his life in this way. Lao She, the famous author of *Rickshaw Boy* and *Teahouse*, was reported to have drowned himself in a lake near his home. We were also beginning to get increasing reports of torture and beatings and killings by Red Guards. At the time we hesitated to believe them all. Later knowledge suggests that they were only too true.

CHAPTER FIVE

The Foreigners Join the Proceedings

BY THE END of 1966 the Cultural Revolution was well on its way to its objective at the centre, namely the removal of a group of senior Party leaders whom Mao saw as opposed to his plans. But immense questions remained unanswered. How far was the revolution to go outside Peking, where Mao's writ was less certain and regional military commanders and Party leaders still wielded great influence? And how far was it to go in other sections of society, in industry, in agriculture, in the army itself? What were the limits of revolution? And what were to be the new institutions once the revolutionaries had successfully seized power?

These were the issues addressed in the first nine months of 1967, the most critical and violent period of the movement. As we guessed at the time and now know all too well, they were not addressed in any systematic way by Mao and his coterie; they lived hand to mouth. And to Western observers in Peking the battlefield was even more obscure.

I recall writing to London about articles in the Chinese press praising the Paris Commune of 1871. There were also references in the Sixteen Points of August, the founding document of the revolution. The Commune was commended as a system of extensive democracy, naturally under the dictatorship of the proletariat. There was a constitutional assembly, whose leaders were directly responsible to the masses and could be elected or recalled by them at any time. It seemed that this might be envisaged as the model for post-Cultural Revolution China.

In fact, on 5 February, Maoists in Shanghai, after a protracted struggle to seize power in the city, proclaimed just such a Commune and it was praised on the local radio as Mao's latest contribution to international Communism. But at this point it seems Mao drew back: the new system was too fluid, too visionary, the change too sweeping; what would happen to the Party? His vote went to the Revolutionary Committee that had just been set up in Heilongjiang province, based on a triple alliance of rehabilitated cadres, revolutionary rebels and the army.

This was of course a very different creature from the Commune; and, as soon became apparent, in any such grouping the dice were loaded, not in favour of the revolutionary masses, but rather the old *apparatchiks*, whether within the Party organization of the military, or the battered but still surviving civilian Party organization. The men in charge of the new Revolutionary Committees tended to be the old army commanders. In expressing his preference, Mao had acknowledged the requirements of order. Perhaps he had been compelled to make a deal with the army in return for its intervention. But he had in effect said enough was enough; and though there were to be many backslidings, and the struggle was to sway back and forth between the left and the right in the coming months, February may be seen in retrospect as a watershed.

As regards the scope of his revolution, Mao seemed to have answered the question in his New Year's Day proclamation, which called for a general attack on monsters and demons, not only in offices, schools and cultural circles, but also in mines, factories and rural areas. The effect was to deepen a confusion which was already profound. Workers and peasants, particularly workers, since the Cultural Revolution was a predominantly urban phenomenon, seized the opportunity to ventilate a variety of grievances and to demonstrate for better conditions. There were strikes of a kind the socialist system was supposed to have eliminated long ago, crippling Chinese ports and railway communications; there was unauthorized movement to the cities of workers, peasants and many who had been exiled to the countryside years before; and worker units became powerful forces in the sanguinary struggles already in progress between contending revolutionary factions in cities throughout the country.

But the crucial element in the equation was the army. It was sacrosanct. Though Maoist extremists, the so-called Group of 16 May, advocated extension of the revolution to the army and wanted to 'drag out the handful of capitalist-roaders' there, such attempts were always defeated in the end. Individual military leaders suffered, some very eminent, like Marshal Zhu De, or colourful, like Marshal Ho Long, but military discipline was usually preserved.

The critical question, however, was how far the army should intervene in the struggle and on whose side? To some extent it was already intervening on the side of the rebels by servicing the Red Guards. But at the same time it was filling in the great administrative gaps opened up by the collapse of the Party machine.

In late January Mao called on the PLA to 'support the left'. This highlighted the army's predicament as at one and the same time the ultimate preserver of order and now its challenger. It also faced army commanders with a painful choice: how to identify the left in disputes where each contending group claimed to represent the essence of leftism? And even when the purest faction had been identified, what degree of force was permissible?

Over this issue there were painful and visible heart-searchings throughout the first part of the year and it was not until September that the military received the clear authority they wanted. During this period the army resembled an ineffectual referee at a particularly ugly football match, holding the ring, darting from group to group, reproving and cajoling, but never applying the ultimate sanction.

After investigations in February had revealed too much zeal for order and stability on the part of army commanders, Mao removed from them the power to judge a faction 'counterrevolutionary': in future such decisions could only be made by Peking. Activists jailed for raiding army installations were to be released. The army was forbidden to shoot at unruly elements, even when the troops themselves were under fire. The result, not surprisingly, was an intensification of fighting between Red Guard groups and of attacks on army installations. Throughout the summer violent turmoil, amounting, on official admission, to civil wars, reigned in most of the provinces of China, concentrating on urban centres and provincial capitals.

It reached its peak in the Wuhan incident of July, which came near to splitting the army. In Wuhan an armed struggle was in progress between radical students and workers on the one hand and a federation of more conservative groups, the 'Million Heroes', on the other. The local military commander favoured the Million Heroes. Peking despatched two leftist emissaries from the Cultural Revolution Group to pronounce on which faction was the more truly revolutionary. But the emissaries were seized and humiliated, one of them beaten up, by the Million Heroes, helped by local troops. They were only released after Zhou Enlai's personal intervention.

At least in outline these dramas were known to us in Peking. But diplomats there were having to concentrate on events closer to hand. The revolution was beginning to spill over into foreign affairs; involuntarily the foreign guests were being drawn into the proceedings.

There had been a warning in the summer of 1966, in an incident involving the Netherlands. In July one of a delegation of Chinese welders attending a conference in Holland died in highly suspicious circumstances, probably after jumping or falling from a window. The other members of the delegation refused to submit to questioning by the Dutch authorities and stayed in their quarters under police watch. The Chinese Chargé was declared *persona non grata* and left for home.

The Chinese response was a fascinating mixture of European diplomatic forms and Eastern hostage-taking. The Dutch Chargé in Peking was declared *persona non grata*, but prevented from leaving his residence. He was kept there under effective house-arrest for several months until eventually, at the end of December, the Chinese welders were allowed to leave the Netherlands, uninterrogated. I went to a party at his house during this period of incarceration; some of the guests appeared in convict costume in honour of his special status. The incident was a reminder that diplomatic immunities carried little weight with the Chinese government in their mood at that time.

Trouble deepened in January 1967, when Chinese students in Moscow sought to pay their respects at Lenin's tomb by reciting choice extracts from Mao, one eulogizing Stalin. Soviet police

intervened; there were incidents involving both students and
Chinese Embassy property and in the end Chinese students were
expelled *en bloc* from the Soviet Union. This led to massive
demonstrations at the Soviet Embassy in Peking, lasting for three
weeks, and a high threat of violence. The atmosphere can be
gathered from the *People's Daily* headline at the time: 'Hit back
hard at the rabid provocations of the filthy Soviet revisionist
swine!' My own favourite among the anti-Soviet slogans then
current was rather more succinct: 'Fry Kosygin!'

Eventually the Russians decided to withdraw their women
and children, an enterprise beset with delays and humiliations
inflicted by the Chinese administrative machine. At the airport the departing travellers were spat upon and struck and
made to stoop under a Sabine yoke, a low arch adorned with
portraits of Mao and Stalin. Various missions, including our
own, sent contingents to help their Russian colleagues and a
kind of camaraderie developed between Communists and non-
Communists, particularly among the China specialists.

The Russians naturally had pride of place; but there were also
about this time lesser frictions involving East European embassies. The Yugoslavs, or, more accurately, 'the renegade Tito
clique', were a regular target; I recall dinners there held to a
background chant of slogans such as 'Bash Tito's head in!'

There was also an ugly incident at the French Embassy. The
Chinese government claimed that Chinese students in Paris, on
their way to the Soviet Embassy to protest against Soviet persecution of their compatriots, had been attacked by the French
police. Demonstrations ouside the French Embassy in Peking
followed, together with a two-day strike of Chinese staff. The
Red Guard demonstrators carried slogans such as: 'Your days
are numbered', 'Sooner or later the revolutionary people will
smash your swine's heads', 'No reactionaries will come to a good
end'. And so on.

The French Commercial Counsellor and his wife, driving to
work, had the misfortune to encounter the demonstrators and,
trying to back out, hit a Red Guard truck. The Counsellor's wife
spoke vigorously to the crowd, unhappily in good Chinese.
She and her husband were thereupon forced out of the car and
made to stand outside the Embassy surrounded by the masses
for over six hours in freezing weather. Efforts by colleagues to

give the pair refreshment were permitted, but regularly frustrated: at the last moment the extended cup was always dashed aside. Eventually, as night fell, the two were released, but faced prolonged police questioning and had to be withdrawn from China.

Throughout this period the Chinese Foreign Minister, Chen Yi, was himself under steady Red Guard attack and could be only partially protected by Zhou Enlai. A man of taste and spirit, a *bon vivant* as well as a brilliant general, he, almost alone among Chinese ministers, replied to the Red Guards as they deserved. He told them to put cold towels round their heads and cool down. If they wanted to fight so badly, why didn't they go to Vietnam and fight the Americans? It did not avail, but it preserved his dignity. The attacks continued. Chinese rhetoric against the two great enemies, the United States and the Soviet Union, grew even more strident; policy towards South-east Asian neighbours, an area where China had hitherto shown some flexibility, lost any traces of sophistication; and the general xenophobia, never far below the surface, became ever more apparent.

Chinese ambassadors abroad, accused of succumbing to the bourgeois life, were all withdrawn for re-education, with the exception of Huang Hua in Cairo. Embassies were left in the hands of juniors and zealots and transformed into stations for disseminating Mao's thought, in the form of literature and Mao badges and portraits, regardless of the susceptibilities of host governments. Before the summer was out China had antagonized a range of well-disposed neighbours, including Nepal, Burma, Cambodia and Ceylon, on this score.

In all, according to the *China Quarterly*, there were at this time diplomatic incidents of varying magnitude with thirty-two countries. One or two, like Pakistan and Romania, continued to enjoy courteous treatment, and North Vietnam and Albania were always in a special category. Relations with North Korea, which currently favoured the Soviet Union, were not at all easy: the Red Guards called Kim Il Sung 'the fat revisionist'. But it is safe to assume that North Korea still enjoyed special consideration. Otherwise the impression was that China could dispense with governments and rely on the support of the revolutionary masses across the world. A series of articles in the local press, entitled 'The people of the world love Chairman Mao', supported this impression.

Among the serious cases were Burma, where Peking switched support from the Burmese government to the local hard-line Communists; India; and Indonesia. With India, of course, the dispute went back many years, but it was exacerbated by the violent expulsion from Peking of two Chinese-speaking Indian diplomats in June on the charge of spying. They had been too assiduous in reading the wall-posters. Following the expulsion, the Indian Embassy came under siege for four days.

In the case of Indonesia, relations had plummeted in September 1965 with the failure of the Indonesian Communist coup, in which Mao had probably had a hand; and there had been a series of incidents involving the Chinese Embassy in Jakarta. Eventually, at the end of April, the Chinese Chargé d'Affaires, Yao Dengshan, was withdrawn and given a triumphant reception in Peking as a 'red diplomat fighter'. As a result, Yao developed large ambitions and had an important role to play in the later disturbances of the summer.

It would have been surprising if Britain had not been drawn into this turmoil. In early May a labour dispute at the Sanpokong artificial flower factory in Hong Kong rapidly developed into violent demonstrations across the colony. After some initial hesitation, the Hong Kong government responded firmly. Arrests were made for breaches of the peace and among those arrested were Communist and pro-Communist Chinese journalists. These very necessary actions were inevitably presented in the mainland press as sanguinary suppression of the masses, and on 15 May Donald Hopson was summoned by Luo Guibo, the Chinese Vice Foreign Minister dealing with Western Europe, to receive the first of many protests. In peremptory language we were required to stop the atrocities, set free those arrested and guarantee against any recurrence. The stage was now set for confrontation.

In the week beginning 15 May over a million demonstrators marched past our Office in Peking. There was also a big rally in the Workers' Stadium. On 22 May the Chinese protested again, this time about intemperate language used by the Foreign Secretary, George Brown, to the Chinese Chargé, Shen Ping, and told us that our Consulate in Shanghai would have to be closed within forty-eight hours. Peter Hewitt, the Consul, and his wife and two children had to be got out and Ray Whitney was sent down to assist. The help was necessary. A mob had broken into the Consulate, frog-marched Hewitt round and smashed his belongings. The two men were spat on, struck and smeared with glue as they left Shanghai.

In June there was an escalation as the Six Day War broke out in the Middle East. Because Britain was accused of collusion with the United States and Israel, there were further large-scale demonstrations, and effigies of President Johnson, Harold Wilson and Moshe Dayan, the latter as a dog, the 'running dog' of Chinese polemics, adorned the pavement in front of the Mission. Pro-Arab demonstrators broke into the Office, wrestled with staff and smashed a picture of the Queen. They included British fellow-travellers from the 'twilight brigade', no doubt summoned at short notice to prove their loyalties.

The Queen's Birthday Party on 9 June was barred to all guests by Red Guard cordons and our staff drank the champagne alone, while our Chinese employees marched round the garden shouting their slogans. The sole guest was the Danish Chargé, Arne Belling, who had managed to climb over the wall.

During July the rioting in Hong Kong grew more violent; there were incidents on the border and a number of policemen were killed. But the colonial authorities were firm and the population supportive. There was also a certain ambivalence in mainland Chinese statements: the rhetoric was extreme, with references to 'blood debts' and calls for a fierce struggle against British persecution; but it was unspecific and Peking's actions, as opposed to its words, remained cautious: the necessary supplies of food to Hong Kong were maintained. There was no response to an appeal from the Hong Kong government in July for an extra two billion gallons of water to meet shortages caused by the drought; but the water agreement, which ensured supplies between the beginning of October and the end of June each year, was not breached. Some at least of the Chinese leaders presumably remained aware of the benefits Hong Kong brought to the Chinese economy.

Perhaps what they sought, in so far as they planned anything, was a public humiliation like that the revolutionaries had been able to inflict on the Portuguese in Macao in the winter of 1966, and a consequent permanent weakening of British administration in the territory. In Macao in December, after two months of rioting, the Governor had been compelled to sign a confession of guilt, release arrested rioters, pay compensation, ban pro-Nationalist activities and hand over Nationalist agents. Macao never recovered.

There was therefore some restraint. But the involvement of Chinese journalists from the mainland, often as ringleaders in the riots, and their consequent arrest suggested a pleasingly symmetrical form of reprisals, and Peking's eye fell on Reuters' correspondent, Anthony Grey. Grey had arrived only in April, pitchforked into a revolution, and had barely had time to find his feet. As he recounts in his book, *Hostage in Peking*, he began to realize in late June that the Hong Kong crisis could have personal implications for him. But, on 11 July Xue Ping, a reporter of the official New China News Agency, was arrested in Hong Kong for unlawful assembly and Grey found that there were no seats on planes or trains out of China. On 19 July, after Xue Ping had been sentenced to two years' imprisonment, Grey was called to the Foreign Ministry and not seen again for two years. Public Security men drove him back to his house and shut him up there. The official statement was that his freedom was restricted because of illegal persecution and fascist atrocities against Chinese correspondents in Hong Kong. For a short time we were able to keep up telephone contact with him; then the line was cut. Another personal ordeal was added to the millions already imposed by the Cultural Revolution and another intractable problem presented to those who were trying to retain some sense in the relations between the British and Chinese governments.

CHAPTER SIX

Strong Action against the British Office

SINCE I WAS away from Peking on leave for some weeks in the first part of the summer of 1967 I missed some of the excitements described in the last chapter. But in August I returned, via Moscow – because of the chaos in the south of China, the only reliable route – in time for what was to be the denouement.

It was plain as soon as Birthe and I landed at Peking airport that the situation had grown a great deal worse. There was much more hostility and harassment. It was claimed that our medical documents had been stamped by an inappropriate authority and we had to endure a session of readings by health officials from the Little Red Book. We were invited to translate into English, but did not oblige. Eventually a compromise was reached by having the translation laid in front of us. There were angry outbursts when we were thought to be paying insufficient attention to the passage about reactionaries and paper tigers.

At our flat the servants explained that they could serve us, but not any guests. And so on. The problems of administration, of getting simple things done, always exhausting in China, had grown to nightmare proportions. And in a country where all was of a piece and virtually nothing happened by chance, this could only indicate that Sino-British relations were under the most serious strain.

In the evening we walked from the diplomatic compound where we lived to the Office, past the Mongolian Embassy.

Everything was clothed in the lush green of the Peking summer. The Mongolian Embassy was under siege. A few days earlier the Mongolian Ambassador's driver had 'callously treated' a portrait of Chairman Mao and the Ambassador's car had been set on fire in consequence.

The outer walls were surrounded by PLA men, most sitting in groups on the pavement, studying the Little Red Book. It was hot and humid. The actual demonstrators straggled past in small detachments, carrying triangular paper flags and chanting the approved slogans, carefully written out on small slips of paper. They looked slight and tired in their summer cotton. It seemed that this was a slack period in the action by the masses.

Our own Office was battered, most of its windows broken and the walls plastered with ageing posters. But the grounds were in good order, the trees we had planted in the spring were doing well and the swimming pool was functioning. The staff were also in good heart and the security guard on duty regaled us with stories of the summer's happenings.

I wrote to the Foreign Office, setting out my impressions on getting back. The main worry was not the administrative difficulty of our position, though that was great, but its precariousness. It was plain that diplomatic immunity was virtually at an end. The Hong Kong crisis would continue. We therefore had to expect further and worse attacks. The only question was the form they would take.

My guess at the time was that there were probably two more moves in the game: a siege such as the Indians had had, and then a final sacking. The Indonesians had reached this ultimate stage. Some of our people had visited them and reported that their Embassy was almost completely destroyed. Literally nothing in the way of movable property was left intact. After some effort the Indonesians had reconstructed a telephone out of surviving pieces and the remnants of a teapot. It did not sound encouraging.

The first week back was occupied with drawing up emergency plans, catching up on the news of the chaotic situation inside China and following the round of diplomatic outrages. The Russians had moved back into the headlines with a Chinese attack on their Consulate. The Kenyans were in trouble over a traffic accident involving Red Guards. And there were demonstrations against the Ceylonese for alleged interference with a shipment of Mao badges.

Our turn came on the evening of Sunday, 20 August. Donald Hopson was summoned to the Foreign Ministry, but since there was apparently disorder there, the meeting had to be transferred to the International Club. In that curious setting, with its tennis courts and cane chairs, redolent of the privileges of the old order, Mr Xue, the Head of the West European Department, carried out his instructions. A quiet, bespectacled, scholarly man, he was not at his best on such fraught occasions. He looked flustered and incongruously produced his papers from a string bag. But the message was stark enough. Within forty-eight hours the British must cancel the ban on three patriotic newspapers in Hong Kong, declare innocent and set free nineteen patriotic Chinese journalists there, and call off the lawsuits pending against two Hong Kong newspapers and two printing firms. Otherwise they would be answerable for the consequences.

There was nothing we could do about this. It was a demand for total surrender, and compliance or even partial compliance was out of the question, given the due legal processes in Hong Kong. We could only prepare for the worst. We telegraphed recommending that the Foreign Office summon Shen Ping, the Chinese Chargé d'Affaires, and warn him that the Chinese were answerable for our security. If nothing else, it would place the responsibility firmly where it belonged.

The next day we prepared riot shutters and collected in the Chancery and the adjoining Chargé's residence food, mattresses and other requirements for emergency accommodation. We began burning papers. There were small-scale demonstrations from press and broadcasting circles, and we went through the routine of standing at the gate to receive written representations and generally be shouted at.

That evening I had dinner with Ray Whitney to celebrate his departure the next day on mid-tour leave; his wife had already left. The next day, however, he was to learn that his seat on the plane was cancelled.

On the morning of Tuesday, 22 August, our Chinese staff held a meeting on the terrace of the Office and asked for the Chargé to come down to talk to them. Rather unwisely, Donald, accompanied by several of us, went down. It was a violent meeting, with much brandishing of fists, and before long the staff had manoeuvred behind us, cutting off the exit and forcing us out into the direct August sun. We spent about three hours in that uncomfortable position before the demonstrators disbanded; they seemed to be keeping union hours. But we found the gates closed when we tried to leave; twenty-three people, eighteen men, five women (four secretaries and one wife), were now besieged.

A siege was a situation we had prepared for and our arrangements went reasonably well. I spent the afternoon checking the precautionary destruction we were undertaking and drafting telegrams home reporting what we had done. In the evening most of the staff entertained themselves watching for the second time the Peter Sellers film, *The Wrong Arm of the Law*. At about ten o'clock I had finished my work and stepped out to take a quick swim in the Office pool and to see what was going on in the street outside.

It was a fine warm night. The compound wall and trees made it hard to see what was happening at the gates, but there was an impression of great numbers of people and powerful lights. The crowds were orderly and still. Someone was haranguing them on Hong Kong; it was not a particularly rabble-rousing speech and ended in a round of polite applause. I stood listening behind a pillar for a few minutes before going back into the Office, then went upstairs and thought of trying to lie down. A few moments later Donald Hopson, who had been playing bridge in his room giving on to the gates, put his head in to say the crowds were looking more boisterous. As I started to go downstairs I heard him shouting 'They're coming in!'

We had a rough plan of action in case of an all-out attack on the Office. I had drafted it two days before and called it 'Armageddon'. I remember at the time it was something of a joke. It consisted of retreats behind a series of defence points, first the door behind the security guard's desk, then the sliding metal grille leading to the secure zone and finally the registry grille protecting the registry itself, where all classified papers were held in the strong room. We would retreat behind each as need arose, with the door at the back of the registry, opening on the grounds, as our escape route. This plan was followed, but it was rather as if the tape had been moved to

Fast Forward. Each line was barely manned before it fell.

Outside there was a sound of rushing feet, the noise of break-ing glass, heavy blows against the door, then flames as cars were set alight. We moved to Position Two, behind the sliding metal grille. Filing cabinets were dragged up to strengthen it and we stood in the narrow corridor leading to the registry, occasionally looking out at the burning cars at the back of the Office. But the line would not hold and we were soon on the move again, into the registry.

We stood there in the dark, a dim group of figures, and waited and listened. There were heavy blows at the registry door, our escape route. The outer wooden door soon gave, but the inner steel door remained. Blows began on it. Outside the registry windows we could hear shouts of '*Sha! Sha!*' ('Kill! Kill!'); the Chinese speakers wisely did not offer any translation. There were blows on the wooden riot shutters protecting the registry win-dows and some unidentified liquid began to pour through. We wondered if it was petrol. One of the girls tasted it and reassured us it was water.

Then the water stopped. Flames appeared outside. Someone peered through the shutters and said they were burning effigies. If so, they were burning them very close and the flames were spreading to the riot shutters. We doused the shutters. But there was a lot of smoke, probably from upstairs, where the mob were in full cry.

There was a pause in the attack and some blowing of whistles. We thought perhaps it was being called off, but very soon the blows began again; they were specially heavy on the steel escape door. I checked that we had someone reliable there, but there was the unpleasant thought that the door might jam.

There were more flames outside and it was becoming clear that the building was on fire; smoke was getting very thick. I spoke to Donald Hopson and said we had better get the door open and get out. By this time there were cries that they were coming through the wall at the side of the escape door. We gathered the girls together and moved them up to the door. Just before it was opened I remember Donald saying that we must have an agreed rendezvous. We settled on the tennis court, although even then it seemed an unlikely target.

The door was opened. Donald went first and I followed just

behind. Our immediate worry was that if the mob rushed in as we tried to get out we would all be trampled. So we raised our hands in a generally reassuring way and said 'We're coming out.' They stood back for a moment, then seized us. I was dragged down the steps and had a glimpse of Donald grappling with the crowd and half-strangled by his tie.

Surrender to the crowd was a strange sensation. Mixed with fear there was even a sense of relief. No more decisions. I had spent most of the day locking up, destroying, making anxious provision. Now it was straightforward and out of our hands. Perhaps it was like going over the side of a sinking ship.

I was swept along by the mob and beaten mainly about the shoulders and back. Someone had hold of each arm. Occasionally someone would hit me in the ribs. The man who had hold of me on the left kept saying '*Bu da! Bu da!*' ('Don't hit him!'). It seemed to have little effect, but there were perhaps some restraints operating: the blows were painful but not crippling and I remember thinking that it required only one good blow to the head to finish me off.

There was a circle formed in the crowd and I was carried to a soap-box, where I was put up in order to be knocked down again, by the simple expedient of two men holding my arms and another hitting me in the stomach. Someone came up and brandished his fist in my face, asking whether I thought the Chinese people were to be trifled with. I did not reply: it seemed the sort of question that did not call for an answer. Someone then demanded that I say 'Long Live Chairman Mao!' I remained silent and fortunately the demand was not pressed.

A photographer appeared and for his benefit – I remember he seemed rather fussy and wanted lots of preparation – my head was pulled up by the hair or forced down, while the usual two men held my arms. It was difficult to decide where I was, since as soon as I tried to lift my head to look about, it was knocked down, or pulled down, to cries of '*Di tou! Di tou!*' ('Lower your head!').

I was then carried off the soap-box and the man on the left, who turned out to be a soldier, began dragging me through the crowd. Someone disputed me with him but, after a struggle, I was flung into a gate-house belonging to the Albanian Embassy, which stood directly opposite our own. Here I found four members of the staff already collected. Ray Whitney and Frank Holroyd, the Administration Officer, were flung in. An army man, told off to guard us, gave us water and spoke reassuringly about our security, saying that several PLA men had been hurt trying to protect us. He made rather anxious enquiries about the number of people in the building. Were there any in the cellars?

We kept our heads down and talked a little. Despite the danger, there was an immense sense of relief that we had come through so far. I remember quoting 'Perhaps even these things it will one day be a joy to recall.' '*Forsan et haec olim . . .*': Virgil's lines on his shipwrecked mariners floating back over years in the way the Classics masters assure us they do. I also talked with Ray Whitney about the future of the Office and the need to keep our hands on the Chinese diplomats in London.

After a while we were led off by the PLA to the side-road between the Office and the Residence, where we found most of the rest of the staff, sitting or crouching against the wall, guarded by military. Donald Hopson, his head in a bloodstained bandage, was brought to join us. We were led off to a lorry, where we were concealed by standing soldiers and then driven to the diplomatic flats.

Here there had naturally been great anxiety as the flames rose from the Office. There had also been physical danger. Two small blocks of flats, wholly occupied by British families, were thought to be vulnerable to attack and hasty arrangements were made with friendly missions to evacuate the occupants. This operation was still in progress when a body of Red Guards burst into the compound. Birthe recalls snatching the Appleyards' youngest daughter from their path and carrying her up to a top flat. There in the dark she watched from a balcony while down below the Dutch Chargé, Dr Fokkema, intervened with the Red Guards, arguing with them and the PLA until the intruders finally withdrew.

There were many similar experiences that night. But eventually order was restored. We checked that all our people were back and said goodnight to the diplomatic colleagues who had turned out to help us. I took Donald Hopson with me to sleep in my flat; he was to stay there for the next four months (Denise was in London). I remember thinking what a beautiful, still

night it was as we walked across the compound at about three
in the morning.

The Residence had been sacked; the Office itself had been
burned down. There had been no fatalities, though there were
cases of concussion and all had been badly bruised and beaten.
It seems likely that the army had had orders to save lives; beyond
that, given their equivocal position, they probably could not go.

For their part the official Chinese media acknowledged that
something unusual had happened, but their account was brief.
The New China News Agency recorded that 'over ten thousand
Red Guards and revolutionary masses surged to the Office of
the British Chargé d'Affaires in a mighty demonstration against
the British imperialists' frantic fascist persecution of patriotic
Chinese in Hong Kong'. It went on to say that 'the enraged
demonstrators took strong action against the British Chargé
d'Affaires' Office'.

The next morning we held a council of war in my study. We
needed to get messages to London reporting our position and
reassuring them of our safety. We advised against a rupture of
relations, but proposed an evacuation of women and children (a
forlorn hope as it turned out). A break in relations would not
only be against our long-term interests, but might also have the
effect of leaving us in Chinese hands, deprived of the remaining shreds of diplomatic protection. We were also anxious that
Chinese diplomats and officials in London should not be allowed
to slip out of the country, leaving us as hostages for events in
Hong Kong, while lacking any Chinese counterparts.

There were also urgent practical issues. We had to establish
a new Office. We chose Ray Whitney's flat: it was big and he
was on his own. We had to reconnoitre the ruins to see what
remained and what could be saved. For safety's sake this would
have to be done in non-British transport. We also had to seek
exit visas for the women and children. Finally, for the record,
I dictated a short note to the Foreign Ministry, condemning the
outrage of the preceding night and reserving all our rights. Since
we had no means of delivery, it went by post.

The reconnaissance party, carried in a French car, came back
with good news: the strong room was intact. But this in turn
posed considerable new problems: the strong room was packed
with classified papers, which had to be destroyed urgently. We

began by bringing back small quantities to our flats, where fortunately we still had coal-burning stoves in which they could be disposed of. But the main bulk called for more dramatic action and, as we thought, scientific methods.

A bizarre episode followed. The Foreign Office in its foresight had provided us with a remarkable chemical compound in the form of a powder, possibly sodium nitrate. We were told that this only needed to be scattered on the files, left for a period with the doors closed and we would find a tidy pile of ashes, all secrets consumed. We followed the instructions, scattered the magic powder in the strong room and retired. Unfortunately, when we returned we found the files neatly charred round the edges, rather like funeral stationery, but still perfectly legible. And there was a side-effect of which we had not been warned: powerful and tenacious fumes had been generated, turning the strong room into an effective gas-chamber. The only way to retrieve the documents was for each of us to wrap a towel round his face, plunge in to the gas-chamber, seize the nearest file and get out before succumbing.

So we did, fearing interruption by the Chinese at any moment. In the darkness and confusion of the strong room Ray Whitney crushed his foot under a filing cabinet. It bore too great a resemblance to the situation the Chinese slogans were constantly reminding us of – the reactionary lifting a rock to drop it on his own foot – and there was much heartless merriment.

In these desperate and unusual activities we spent a good proportion of the next few days. In the end the offending papers were burned in the open in perforated petrol-drums, an old-fashioned but effective technology. Some time later we drew the lesson from all this and arranged to carry no more paper than could be destroyed in our old-style shredder in half an hour. That we judged to be the longest we could hold out. The diplomatic bags were therefore delivered, conscientiously read and as conscientiously destroyed. We experienced a great sense of relief and functioned quite as efficiently as before.

Meantime the office in the Whitney flat was beginning to take shape, to the considerable inconvenience of its owner. In the main room Donald Hopson, very trim in a suit provided by the French, received a string of calls from colleagues, offering condolences and help of all kinds. The international response was warm and heartening. Wives and children were looked after. Messages were sent, commissions carried out. Since we had no cook and it was dangerous for Birthe to venture out, the Swedish Embassy stepped in and sent their Cultural Attaché to the market, to return loaded with meat for the whole Office.

At night Ray gathered the more vulnerable office effects into his bedroom for greater safety. I recall that then or shortly after he slept with a strange device, an incendiary deed-box, close to him. It was supposed to consume its contents in a crisis, at the same time emitting a high-pitched whistle. I had the same faith in it as in the incendiary powder.

Quietly, two days after the burning, our house servants returned. Service as before. I also found our Chinese office staff reporting for duty, or more precisely, hanging about in a guilty fashion. This enabled us to set up an administration office again. Money problems were mounting and we needed the help of our Chinese accountants.

But the atmosphere remained very tense. Reports of further Red Guard incursions into the compound, real or threatened, and there were many, were sufficient to provoke serious alarms. We drew up a hair-trigger plan for evacuating families at a moment's notice to friendly foreign flats in the same building. Coming across it some eighteen months later, just before leaving Peking, I was reminded vividly of the kind of pressure under which we had had to operate.

The great question, however, was the attitude of the Chinese government. We had had no word from them since the ultimatum of 20 August and for a week we existed in a kind of diplomatic limbo. The reason for this pause was presumably that the Chinese were preparing the strange episode of 29 August, what came to be known as the Battle of Portland Place. On the morning of that day the British police posted outside the Chinese Mission in London were startled to find themselves facing an eruption of angry Chinese officials, armed with baseball bats, axes and broom-handles. There were naturally injuries on both sides.

This curious piece of theatre was undoubtedly engineered by the Chinese so that they could claim to match us in terms of outrage and work themselves into the position of moral superiority from which they loved to operate. Late on Tuesday, 29 August, we were telephoned with orders to present ourselves at the Foreign Ministry at two the following morning. The timing of the interview indicated extreme displeasure. By a refinement of cruelty it was later shifted to three o'clock.

I accompanied Donald Hopson on this as on most succeeding interviews and, since my car was one of the few that had survived the burning, I drove him to the Foreign Ministry. The question that hung in our minds was whether we would be received as diplomats, or held as prisoners. We recalled how Grey had not been seen again after his call at the Ministry on 21 July.

It was worrying. We had no faith in our host government and our anxieties were not lightened by the sight of two large black cars from Public Security parked outside the flat. I remember John Weston, who came with us as note-taker, being rather puzzled when I explained to him how my car, which had automatic gears, operated.

As it turned out, the Chinese had decided to preserve some shreds of propriety. Luo Guibo, the Vice Foreign Minister, delivered a 'most serious and strong protest'. He noted that the British government had on 22 August taken illegal measures against the Office of the Chinese Chargé d'Affaires and other Chinese establishments in London. (This was a reference to the movement restrictions we had placed on the Chinese following the burning.) These must be immediately cancelled. Moreover, on the morning of 29 August the British government had instigated ruffians to beat up Chinese personnel in London. On the afternoon of the same day police and ruffians had gone further. British policemen, clubs in hand, had flagrantly and brutally beaten up personnel of the Chinese Office. Three were severely wounded and more than ten others injured.

As a result, the Chinese government had decided that no personnel of the British Office were to leave China without permission. All exit visas were cancelled. British activities were to be confined to their Office and residences and the road between. An application forty-eight hours in advance would be required for any attempt to move outside that area.

This was severe but not entirely surprising. Our principal reaction was one of relief that we were recognized as diplomats and that the Office could continue to function. We had early breakfast in a relaxed mood. But we noticed that the compound was filling up with soldiers, the usual prelude to trouble. Later that morning a group of Red Guards appeared at our temporary Office, the Whitney flat, and posted a notice calling on us to come down and face the masses. A large crowd was gathering just in front of the building. We telephoned the Protocol Department at the Foreign Ministry and reminded them of our status and the Chinese duty as host country. They told us we must face the masses.

I found this the most trying moment of the saga. It was partly the fatigue from the night before, but more the bleak realization that the flats were not immune and that our families could face repeated incursions by violent men. As planned, we dispersed families to foreign flats. The Office valuables were taken down to a French apartment just below: I recall leaving Birthe sitting there on a laundry basket containing the Mission's remaining stock of money. A group of us then went out to meet the demonstrators. This was necessary; without it the violence could have become general.

It was an ugly demonstration, based of course on the alleged brutalities of Portland Place. I remember some very large and very wild men, literally hopping with rage in the front ranks. The army were there in strength but did not interfere. There were calls to bow our heads. When that did not happen one of the dervishes rushed forward and seized Donald Hopson's hair, forcing his head down. The shouting and threats continued. At one point the officer in charge of the military detachment asked me quietly whether we could not perform a simple obeisance – a gesture would do. I explained it could not be done. Eventually, to our intense relief, the demonstrators marched away. We returned wearily to our Office under the eyes of some of our diplomatic colleagues, who had watched the episode from the flats without being able to intervene.

Yet, after that low point, the situation gradually eased. We were of course marooned, but the sense of physical danger lessened. There was a curious incident the next day, when our servants demonstrated, together with Chinese office staff, outside my flat. They told me they had to leave to attend a meeting, but that lunch was ready on the stove. A few minutes later there were loud knocks on the door and I was confronted with raised fists and familiar faces contorted in ritual rage. I had a glimpse of the complexities of existence for the ordinary Chinese and the adjustments they constantly had to make between the demands of human reality and those of Maoist ideology.

That evening we had a small celebration for Donald Hopson's birthday and a showing of *Les Belles de Nuit*, borrowed from the French. Perhaps the worst of the crisis was over?

CHAPTER SEVEN

Hostage Games

THE BURNING OF the British Office proved to be the turning-point of the Cultural Revolution, at least in its foreign policy manifestations. The extremists had overplayed their hand and given an opportunity for brakes to be applied. As we learned later, for a period of some weeks in August the Foreign Ministry had been in the hands of Yao Dengshan, the returned Chargé from Jakarta, and Wang Li, who was a member of the ultra-left 'Group of 16 May' and had been one of the emissaries to Wuhan.

On the domestic front, at about the same time, Mao conceded, as he did from time to time, that a restoration of order was essential. He had been on a tour of inspection of a number of provinces, which had brought home to him the prevailing state of chaos. According to Zhou Enlai, he had remarked that it was 'like a country divided into eight hundred princely states'. He was also reported as saying, 'I think this is civil war.'

Early in September decisions were taken to restrain action against foreigners. There was a later Central Committee directive in explicit terms. It was also decided to purge Wang Li and another member of the group of extremists, Guan Feng. Very rapidly, under the iron rules of Communist denunciation, these two, and later other colleagues of the 16 May group, were transformed from heroes of the revolution to comrades of Liu

Shaoqi and 'schemers of the Khrushchev type', and duly passed into darkness.

On 5 September, Jiang Qing herself in a remarkable U-turn addressed the Red Guards and denounced armed struggle. Most important of all, on the same date Mao finally gave the army the authority it needed to fire as a last resort on violent elements who defied its orders.

The pendulum had swung again; and, though there were the inevitable twists and turns, and the coming year was to see appalling violence and bloodshed throughout the country, the fever had passed its crisis.

In our very temporary quarters we had some sense of this amelioration. But the Hong Kong crisis, to which we were closely tied, continued. Two Hong Kong policemen had been seized after accidentally crossing the border and there were incidents in which students at Communist schools in the territory tried to make bombs, sometimes blowing themselves up in the process.

Our minds were also inevitably occupied with the predicament in which we found ourselves. We did our work on the reporting and consular side and did it well, given the unusual circumstances; but much energy was diverted into a long struggle with the Chinese over hostages, ourselves and others, to which was added, unhappily, a long argument with the Foreign Office over tactics.

Diplomats and hostages have close family ties. The 'honest man sent abroad to lie for his country' readily becomes personally answerable for his country's conduct; and the corpus of diplomatic rules and immunities is a necessary invention to prevent the link being taken too literally. In China hostages had a long tradition. In the Warring States period, before the country was unified, scions of princely houses were regularly left at other courts as pledges of their rulers' good faith; the father of the first Emperor languished many years in exile in this way. The Chinese were also well aware of the connection with diplomacy; and in the nineteenth century, when China was setting up permanent missions abroad, at a time when self-respecting Chinese gentlemen recoiled from the idea of foreign service, a critic reminded the authorities that 'the envoy of today is the hostage of yesterday'. In our position after the burning we needed no reminding of the point. We found we enjoyed a dual status, diplomats in name, hostages in fact. The trick was how to get rid of our more ancient function and be treated again according to the Vienna Convention.

It is in some ways an inward-looking story. But it has relevance, not only for the historian of Sino-British relations, but also for those who wish to study the Chinese negotiating style.

The position at the end of August 1967 was that the Chinese held the staff and families of the Mission in a tight grip. We were allowed to go from our flats some four hundred yards by a designated road to the remains of the Chancery building and the Residence. In effect we were held under house arrest. In return, the British government limited Chinese diplomats and officials in London to five miles from the centre of London rather than the normal thirty-five miles; this seemed to us in Peking at the time an extremely comfortable form of confinement. Both sides withheld exit and entry visas. The Chinese claimed that they were only reacting to illegal restraints imposed by us after the burning; in fact they had begun preventing exit from China by our diplomatic staff a day earlier, on 21 August. But the precise sequence was not so important; what mattered was the resulting impasse.

In Hong Kong, we had arrested or sentenced for breaches of the peace a number of New China News Agency correspondents and reporters from pro-Peking newspapers, the so-called 'patriotic press'. In return Anthony Grey was held by the Chinese. His detention had been provoked by the sentence on Xue Ping of the NCNA; but it later became clear that he would not be released until all the journalists held in Hong Kong were free. We were not sure of his condition but feared the worst. As we learned later, on 18 August his house had been invaded and vandalized by Red Guards and he himself attacked and confined in a tiny room.

Our original plan had been to evacuate women and children. When that proved impracticable, we tried for permission to leave for the more vulnerable categories, schoolchildren who had come out for the holidays and wives needing medical attention. We registered some success in this and throughout I found it possible to argue for exit visas on urgent medical grounds and occasionally to succeed. But for the great bulk of the staff there was no release.

We therefore began turning our minds to ways of de-escalating the situation. The first move would have to be some relaxation of the movement restrictions on Chinese diplomats in London. It had been right to impose them: otherwise we could have been left without bargaining counters and could have seemed inexcusably weak in the face of a major outrage. But the thought, in my mind at least, was that after a suitable interval, if the situation was peaceful enough to warrant it, we should quietly wind down.

But here we ran into trouble, not so much on the Chinese side as on our own. There was a reluctance to make the first move; the Foreign Office seemed at times to believe that we could outplay the Chinese at the game of being tough. Besides, the Foreign Secretary, George Brown, appeared to want a man-to-man meeting with his Chinese opposite number, at which these and other problems, including Hong Kong, could be settled. Given the chaotic state of China and that of its Foreign Ministry in particular, with Chen Yi under sustained criticism and moving into the shadows, a less realistic idea would have been hard to conceive. But, for one reason or another, our persuasions were not very effective in London.

The Chinese Foreign Ministry, with whom we still had some contact, almost entirely in the context of Hong Kong, pointed us in the same direction. They were abusive, dogmatic and rigid. They lectured and threatened and made demands. But they also let fall hints that any progress depended on easing restrictions in London.

October came and with it National Day. Naturally we were not invited, but it was a holiday. Birthe and I sat in the garden at the Residence in the mellow sunshine which only Peking autumns can provide. For a few weeks, between a sub-tropical summer and an arctic winter, there is a pause; the asperities of a savage climate are softened. Dragonflies drift in the still air; the persimmons hang like yellow lanterns; a golden calm descends. In that light even the empty reception room of the house, despoiled and with telephone wires draped from the chandeliers, took on a surreal beauty. We sat and watched the sunlight slowly move. It was wonderfully still. Far off, for there could never be total silence in those days, rose a confused, high-pitched baying from the loudspeakers. It was the voice of Lin Biao, proclaiming from the rostrum the decisive victory in the Great Proletarian Cultural Revolution: 'an epoch-making new development of Marxism-Leninism, which Chairman Mao has effected with genius and in a creative way'. It was remote and irrelevant. For a moment the natural order had reasserted itself and the absurd violence in which we lived was relegated to its proper place.

A few days later we heard of fighting at Tilbury between British dockers and seamen from a Chinese ship, the *Hangzhou*. A docker had refused a Mao badge offered by a Chinese sailor. The Foreign Office refused access to the ship by Chinese officials, saying they would permit visits only if the same facilities were given British diplomats in China.

These incidents did not encourage flexibility on the British side. By the end of October all that London was prepared to contemplate was the lifting of surveillance on Bank of China officials there; and this was apparently only prompted by the wish to save money.

We returned to the charge. By this time life was getting back to a tolerable level. Our servants went out to market for us and proved generally helpful. The lift-boys in the flats were now ready to operate the lifts for us, instead of leaving us to walk up three or four flights, though sometimes they would compromise by spitting as they did so. I was even allowed out to buy a fountain-pen, after an elaborate application and accompanied by a large posse of police.

Another and parallel hostage drama was by now drawing to an end. The Indonesians were in fact more advanced players than we in what I called at the time 'the Marat-Sade school of diplomacy'. But they had the immense natural asset of a mob in Jakarta which proved a match for the Red Guards. We watched in wonder as counter-sack followed sack. In the end it was Jakarta who brought the curtain down. On 25 October, the Indonesian government announced the closure of its Embassy in Peking and China had little option but to follow with an announcement of a reciprocal closure in Indonesia. On 31 October, a Chinese plane carried the remaining eight Indonesian diplomats home and brought back twenty Chinese diplomatic staff. A delighted Mr Darwoto, the Indonesian Acting-Chargé, paid a farewell call on us. We envied him. We had to follow a different route.

By mid-November there were at last signs that the Foreign Office was coming round and on 14 November we were able to to inform the Chinese Foreign Ministry that the movement limits on Chinese in London would revert to the old thirty-five miles. Mr Xue, who received us, was supported by no less than four colleagues, no doubt including minders to keep him up to the mark. Our police escort kept the door open and pushed inside the room, determined to miss nothing.

Donald conveyed his message. He added the hope that this would make possible the restoration of normal working conditions for the two missions and the return of Sino-British relations to a better footing. This modest comment provoked a long outburst from Xue about the impossibility of normal relations while the British continued their persecution of Chinese compatriots in Hong Kong. The exchange became heated. A simple announcement about restrictions would probably have been better. But Xue undertook to report.

A week later we were told that our freedom of movement within the old limits in Peking was restored. Also, that applications for exit and entry visas would be dealt with in the normal way. This last statement aroused great hopes, which were rapidly disappointed. The unspoken message was that we had only taken the first step; strict equivalence was to be observed.

There then followed the most difficult passage in our long wrangle with the Foreign Office. To us the message was now clear: de-escalations by us would be likely to prompt similar relaxations by the Chinese; but we would have to move first. Moreover, the problem would have to be solved step by step and not in one package. The London and Hong Kong threads would have to be disentangled: the Mission staff were held against their counterparts in London; Tony Grey was held against Communist news-workers in Hong Kong. If we unpicked the easier parts of the knot we would be better able to concentrate, and concentrate the attention of others, on the hard part, Hong Kong and Grey. Also on other British detainees: Grey was not alone.

But alas, these arguments, drafted, as I thought, with unanswerable logic, received dull, evasive and, as it seemed, uncomprehending replies from London. The Department's approach was different. There was this question of making the first move. In reliance on what? Never more than hints on the Chinese side. Where was the clear understanding we needed: if you do this we shall do that? What about Hong Kong and Grey? There was also the delicate question of appearing to look after diplomats while a journalist continued to suffer in harsh detention. This last consideration, I suspect, weighed heavily.

There was an answer, or, more accurately, several. To refuse to do anything until we could do everything merely intensified the agony and disabled the Mission. There was also the constant fear that the internal situation would worsen, making any negotiation impossible. Time was not necessarily on our side. But these arguments did not prevail.

At the turn of the year we had reports that two Chinese diplomats might be planning to leave Britain. I urged the Foreign Office to let them go. All that was called for was inaction on our part. The move could be made without publicity, but the Chinese would take the point and a de-escalation process could be set in motion. The recommendation was not accepted and the travellers were turned back.

It was about this time that I evolved a rule to which I gave the title of Cradock's First Law of Diplomacy, namely that it is not the other side you need to worry about, but your own. Born out of the trials of the Cultural Revolution, it stood up well to the tests of later experience.

This inability to influence London on a matter on which we had both special knowledge and interest naturally had its effect on the morale of the staff, who were in any case coming to feel the strain of the strange life they led. Resilient during the demonstrations of the preceding summer and, without exception, brave during the burning, they were beginning to wear in the long haul. A number were separated from wives or families. There were many nervous complaints and some wild schemes. One couple planned to send their baby home on his own by plane via Irkutsk. I spent a lot of time on the telephone to doctors at home. (We only had a nursing sister with us in Peking, though she performed wonders, and we carried only limited medical supplies.) The connections were laborious; there was no direct London-to-Peking line and I recall we had to have a link with Paris.

Occasionally there would be incoming calls on bad lines from the British press, seeking a story. We weren't able to say much. One of the more serious papers did an authoritative article on the Mission's situation, accompanied by a street map. Unfortunately, it showed us still in the old Legation quarter, which we had left eight years before.

One project we were able to busy ourselves with, to good effect, was the creation of a more permanent Office in the Residence, which was still structurally sound, though bare. The communications staff moved first and the rest of us followed. By December we were installed.

In late January 1968, prompted by an unusually broad hint from the Consular Department of the Foreign Ministry, we addressed a grand remonstrance to London. We repeated that the only way out of the impasse was to grant outstanding Chinese entry visa applications and abolish our UK exit visa requirement. The door would thereby be opened, as far as the Mission was concerned. We could then concentrate on Grey. We drafted what seemed a powerful telegram and waited anxiously for the answer. It came after some delay. The Foreign Office were almost persuaded, but not quite. They were prepared to abolish exit visas and all outstanding entry applications to London, only excepting applications for entry visas for NCNA officials. These they were not willing to grant while Grey remained in custody. They were sure we would understand.

We could not. By jibbing over the NCNA visas, London had missed the point and, instead of untying the knot stage by stage, had entangled it further with the separate problem of Hong Kong. We were back where we had begun and the Chinese told us so.

So we continued in deadlock until April. I would go down to the Foreign Ministry to argue about visas and would be treated to long harangues about Hong Kong and Sino-British relations, delivered in a very loud voice. There was, I fancy, an instruction about volume circulating in the Ministry, or perhaps the Chinese officials felt they could prove their revolutionary bona fides in this way. At the end, as I got up to go, the official might add, 'My personal opinion, Mr Cradock, is . . .' That was the message; the rest was verbiage. But how to convey that convincingly to London?

Then in April there came an intervention from on high. George Brown resigned and was replaced as Foreign Secretary by Michael Stewart. Very shortly afterwards our recommendations on tactics were approved. We dismantled our exit visa regime in London and granted outstanding entry visas. Looking back, it is tempting to place the whole responsibility on a gifted but temperamental man. But I fear that officials were also to blame: he was wrong-headed, but also wrongly advised.

The Chinese response to our move was encouraging. We received exit permits for a number of junior staff and entry visas for new staff. But it was not complete: applications for senior staff were still refused. Ray Whitney left in June, but on medical grounds. Donald Hopson was still held. I think the reason for this was a rise in tension over Hong Kong. The Chinese protested over the visit there of US warships engaged in the Vietnam War, particularly the arrival of the nuclear-powered carrier, *Enterprise*. Such visits, they said, could only result in a further worsening of the situation in Hong Kong and of Sino-British relations generally. The visa flow was checked. But the Chinese position was now unsustainable and the last restrictions were removed when we let it become known that we were planning a full-scale diplomatic campaign, with much publicity about our imprisonment while Chinese diplomats were free to come and go. Late in July normal travel was finally restored and on 14 August Donald Hopson left China.

The problem had been solved by a series of de-escalations between London and Peking. There was no explicit causal connection. We had to move first. We also had to move on the strength of hints only. Unfortunately, the equation had not been perfect: from time to time the Chinese muddied the waters by bringing in the general issue of Hong Kong, and tension there always fed back to Peking. Nevertheless it was a useful lesson.

During this time we had been doing all we could to find out more about Anthony Grey and to improve his conditions by getting messages or parcels to him, or by making concessions over comforts for Chinese prisoners in Hong Kong. We had not made much progress, though a parcel and some letters got through.

In March we explored the possibility of deporting to China Communist prisoners in Hong Kong and solving the issue in that way. Two left-wing film stars were brought to the border but, after hours on Lowu bridge, had to be taken back into custody. The Chinese authorities refused to accept them and demanded release in Hong Kong.

But on 24 April Grey was allowed his first consular visit and Donald Hopson, now Sir Donald, and John Weston were able to see him. The move no doubt reflected calmer conditions in Hong Kong and lower tension in the diplomatic confrontation.

There were, however, other British detainees, their number rapidly mounting. George Watt, a British engineer working for Vickers Zimmer, had been held since September and in March was sentenced by a rally in Lanzhou to three years' imprisonment on charges of spying. Our repeated requests for details and for consular access were refused. A free-lance writer was lifted from a ship in Shanghai. British ships' officers were seized as their ships docked at Chinese ports. Again we had no information. The general charge was spying; it seemed there was a spy mania, particularly threatening British citizens. It affected even the small British community of 'foreign friends' who worked with the Chinese, teaching or translating. Their loyalty was being severely tested.

Strangest and saddest of all was the case of Frans van Roesbroeck, a Belgian citizen arrested in Shanghai in June on a vague charge referring to his personal activities. Frank, as we knew him, was a long-time member of the foreign residents' community in Shanghai. We met him on every visit. He had been put in charge of the liquidation of the Shanghai branch of the Belgian Banque pour L'Etranger in 1952. His task was completed in 1953, but he had been refused an exit visa ever since. He was apparently hostage for Chinese funds held by his bank in blocked American dollars. His wife was free to travel, but he stayed. Measured against his case, our problems seemed slight indeed.

CHAPTER EIGHT

The End of a Revolution

I TOOK OVER as Chargé from Donald Hopson in August 1968. It was a time of rapid turnabout in our staff. London was anxious to recall those who had been through the burning and replacements for most were available, ready to come in via Hong Kong. John Weston and Alistair Hunter, the First Secretary Commercial, stayed on for a while and were an enormous help; but before long I was the only one who could recall the first Red Guard rallies and the excitements of the summer of 1966, now seemingly ages ago.

Among the newcomers were Roger Garside, later author of an excellent book on Deng's first years in power, and George Walden, a future education minister and already wise beyond his years, speaking fluent Chinese and Russian.

We were now installed in reasonable comfort on the first floor of the Residence and accepted again as respectable members of the diplomatic corps. I was asked to the government banquet on the eve of National Day, the first invitation to an official function we had had since May 1967.

Our concerns were still heavily consular, dealing with a long list of British detainees, headed by Grey. To this list on 25 August was added David Johnston, the manager of the Shanghai branch of the Standard Chartered Bank, who, for some obscure reason, was suddenly declared 'an enemy of the Chinese people'. This came as a shock and a setback, since there had been signs that the tension might be easing: one or two of the merchant navy officers seized earlier in the year had been deported. But the omens were mixed: Johnston's colleague, the manager of the same branch of the Hongkong and Shanghai Bank, who, with his wife, had been unable to obtain an exit visa, despite the arrival of his replacement, was able to leave in September.

In Hong Kong tension was still high, the trouble centring round Communist schools and home-made bombs, and the consequent deregistration of those establishments. With the detainees in mind, particularly Grey, I was anxious that we should tread as lightly as possible and entered into an exchange of correspondence with the Governor, Sir David Trench, which became rather sharp. The Foreign Office did not fault the reasoning but were upset by the tone of the telegrams and gently said so, not the last of such admonitions I was to receive. The Governor, who was not accustomed to having his policies dissected, was even more upset.

An issue much in my mind at the time was whether we were right to shun publicity over Grey and the other prisoners. Our policy hitherto had been to do so. There were good arguments in support: it is usually easier to make concessions quietly and there was a particular danger with the Chinese that, having taken up a public position, their national prestige would seem involved and they would dig in. Reuters and the press generally had accepted this advice.

But in Grey's case the Chinese were now already on record. There were also vast resources of publicity world-wide that had not been tapped. Nor were the Chinese impervious to pressure. Their foreign policy was no longer one of total isolation and defiance; they were cultivating friends again and even considering establishing relations with new countries.

I was able to pay a visit to Hong Kong at the end of October and used the occasion to speak to the press – on the record – to express our concern for the ten British subjects detained in China and to condemn the Chinese refusal to grant consular access. This was thought rather daring, coming from one who had only just ceased to be a detainee himself. But it was a deliberate move, using an instrument that was available to us.

I also pointed out that Grey, who was in solitary confinement, had not been treated in accordance with normal standards, had not been charged with any crime or sentenced in any court. He had been held without explanation. The Chinese incantation, 'You are well aware why Mr Grey has been treated in the way he has,' was not good enough. Again a risky line: the Chinese could have cooked up a charge and a trial if need be without difficulty. But the calculation was that the time for such antics had passed.

Again, publicity was very much an issue in late November when we were allowed a second visit to Grey and I went to see him, accompanied by Roger Garside. It was not an easy interview. His mind was naturally on the Hong Kong prisoners. When would the last be released? I could give him little comfort. But later, in a press conference and in a telegram home, I was able to describe the conditions in which he was held. The telegram was published in full and the final sentence, 'He lives in a void,' got home. A storm of publicity followed. I think it helped.

The background to these debates was a revolution which was still violent and confused, but arguably moving into its terminal phases. The army's writ ran with growing effectiveness. The list of redeemed provinces, those that had succeeded in establishing their Revolutionary Committees, was lengthening. In many the new organizations were headed by familiar names, those of the old army commanders.

This persistence of old forces in the new order, plus second thoughts on the part of Mao, provoked a further lurch to the left in the spring of 1968 and coincided with the removal of Yang Chengwu, the PLA Chief of Staff. There were further outbursts of violence in the provinces, with particularly heavy fighting in Guangdong and Guangxi. The Vietnamese Consulate in Nanning was stormed by Red Guards in June and trains carrying military supplies to Vietnam were raided.

Again the growing chaos prompted directives from the centre demanding moderation. There had to be more than one: the first were ignored.

These final convulsions revealed themselves to us in Peking in the form of fighting between student factions in the universities. Two great Red Guard coalitions had been formed, the Earth faction and the Heaven faction, each embracing a collection of smaller organizations, whose leaders had made their names in two years of zealotry, agitation and violence. They included Nie Yuanzi, who had put up the first big-character poster at Peking University, and Kuai Dafu of Qinghua University, the epitome of radical virtue, fierce, extreme and intransigent, who as early as June 1966 had opposed the work teams sent out by the old Party centre to smother the revolution. He enjoyed great fame, a kind of revolutionary pop-idol. I recall his appearance in the audience during a performance of *The White-haired Girl*, one of Jiang Qing's model operas, almost stopped the show. But his virtue was not of the lonely variety: it was supported by powerful and sinister connections. Liu Shaoqi thought that Kang Sheng stood behind him and he was probably right.

These groups, each claiming to represent the pure milk of Mao's doctrine and the true wishes of the Cultural Revolution Group, now turned their energies to an internecine warfare which curiously mingled the modern and the medieval. They occupied and fortified campus buildings and conducted siege operations, tunnelling under enemy posts and constructing siege machinery, huge sling-shots made of bicycle inner-tubes attached to window frames and firing nuts and bolts and rocks. Some had more up-to-date equipment, including sub-machine-guns. Occasionally a body, laid out on blocks of ice, would be carried through the hot Peking streets to Peking Party head-quarters, where the mourners demanded redress.

It was a grotesque interlude even by contemporary standards and one not appreciated by leaders increasingly driven into moderate courses. Official references to the Red Guards became critical, even scathing. They were reminded of the sins of petty-bougeois factionalism, egoism and small-group mentality. Mao began to rediscover the virtues of the workers, a much less divisive and more orthodox component of socialist society. It was decided that they should be sent to straighten the students out. On 29 July a body of such workers, forcing their way into Qinghua's fortifications, were fired on by Kuai Dafu's cohorts; five were killed and many hundreds injured.

The next day Mao summoned the five most prominent Red Guard leaders and spoke of his deep disappointment. They had let him down. He urged them to unite. The alternative was martial law. Kuai Dafu, arriving late from his battles, claimed

that a 'black hand' was behind the incident of the day before.
'I am the black hand,' said Mao.

Massive propaganda teams, composed of workers and peasants, liberally supported by the military, then descended on the
Peking campuses and imposed peace. This intervention was
accompanied by one of those gestures from Mao which, like his
swim in the Yangtze two years before, acquired vast symbolic
significance. He made a gift to the workers on the teams of some
mangoes he had been presented by the visiting Pakistan Foreign
Minister. The news was greeted with fervid demonstrations and
the mangoes were preserved with formalin and kept in a glass
case. It was the official blessing for the worker-peasant teams and
the cause of order. Similar teams were soon being despatched
to other educational centres throughout the country.

In this way the Red Guards, conjured up to suit a tactical need
two years before, were cast aside. Briefly they had been the uni-
versal exemplars, the 'little generals'. They were now told that
they had performed meritorious service, but that they must not
assume airs, a failing to which intellectuals were prone. They
must learn modestly from the workers and peasants, earnestly
accept the leadership of the working class and gradually mature.
Very soon they were to be sent off to the great school of the
countryside, some fifteen million of them, despatched to remote
border lands or inhospitable rural wastes. They were to become
the 'lost generation', a further category in the endless list of
victims of Mao's final venture.

The revolution was winding down, growing stale. The audience too. In a despatch describing another long hot summer, I
quoted some lines of Auden.

> The Emperor's favourite concubine
> Was in the Eunuch's pay,
> The Wardens of the Marches turned
> Their spears the other way;
> The vases crack, the ladies die,
> The Oracles are wrong:
> We suck our thumbs or sleep; the show
> Is gamey and too long.

But the show had one preordained end. In late October the
Twelfth Plenary Session of the Eighth Party Central Committee

issued a communiqué decreeing the formal expulsion of Liu Shaoqi from the Party. For the first time in an official document he was named. He was declared 'a renegade, traitor and scab, hiding in the Party and a lackey of imperialism, modern revisionism and the Guomindang reactionaries, who has committed innumerable crimes'. We were told that he had wormed his way into the Party in 1921 and for forty years had 'consistently employed counter-revolutionary and double-dealing tactics to recruit renegades and defectors, to make contact with foreign countries and to oppose wildly the proletarian revolutionary line represented by Chairman Mao'.

The question how with such a record he could have remained undetected so long was not addressed. Unrelieved and consistent villainy, or virtue, was demanded by the rules of the game.

From his first self-criticism in late 1966 Liu and his family had suffered increasingly savage persecution. His self-criticisms were rejected: no compromise was possible; for the purposes of the revolution it was necessary that he be shown guilty of the most heinous crimes. It was also necessary that he be kept alive until he could be formally condemned and expelled. But short of death, there was room for every variety of cruelty and many were practised on him. After the Plenum of October 1968 and the more formal proceedings at the Party Congress of April 1969, he was expendable. In October 1969, barely alive, he was moved from Peking, wrapped only in a blanket, to Kaifeng, the former Song dynasty capital, and was left to die in the bitter cold on the floor of an old prison, naked and deprived of the medication on which he was wholly dependent for survival.

Liu was of course the show case, but only the tip of a mountain of senior Party and government victims who were persecuted, tortured, cast into prison or killed. In this sense at least, Mao had achieved his aim.

One other event marked the end of the era, the Soviet invasion of Czechoslovakia in August 1968. We had seen something of our Czech colleagues as the Prague Spring developed: they were anxious to borrow our copies of English newspapers so that they might read reliable accounts of what was happening at home. When the news of the invasion came I called on the Czech Ambassador to express my condolences; it was a poignant interview.

I recall there was palpable tension when Zhou Enlai spoke at the Romanian National Day party on 23 August. The Chinese had been equivocal about Dubček: he was approved as a rebel against Soviet authority, but unwelcome as a super-revisionist. The invasion, however, made things simpler. Though still swinging at both superpowers and portraying the invasion as the result of US-Soviet collusion, Zhou drew a direct parallel between Brezhnev and Hitler. He declared Chinese support for Romania, now also facing the threat of foreign aggression. The Chinese were getting alarmed.

By the autumn they were noting a Soviet military build-up on their northern borders and were beginning to speak of the need for vigilance. They were also beginning to show a greater regard for the health of Western Europe and my Norwegian colleague reported favourable references to NATO. The sense of relative security the Chinese had enjoyed over the last few years, an environment making less hazardous the madness of the Cultural Revolution, was fading and the Soviet Union was beginning to be seen as an expansionist power and the main threat. On 26 November, the Chinese called for the resumption of the Sino-American ambassadorial talks in Warsaw. The first steps were being taken on the road to Kissinger's visit.

CHAPTER NINE

Reflections on a Disaster

THOUGH HISTORIANS DIFFER on the point, it is, I think, reasonable to say that the Cultural Revolution proper ended with the Party Congress of April 1969, which confirmed Lin Biao's position as Mao's designated heir. It was, of course, by no means the end of the time of troubles. (The Chinese speak of a ten-year span from 1966 to 1976.) Mao was in undisputed control, presiding over a ruined country and talking of further cultural revolutions, a regular cleansing to be carried out every decade or so. Lin Biao's death and disgrace lay in the future. Jiang Qing and her cronies were still about and Mao, as usual, jockeyed between the factions, playing off the leftists against Zhou Enlai and the moderates. The heyday of the Gang of Four, the period of 'Criticize Lin, criticize Confucius', which meant in effect 'Criticize Zhou', was still to come. As long as Mao survived, the fever was there. But the Red Guards' quietus at the meeting with him on 30 July 1968 and the verdict on Liu Shaoqi in October that year round off a distinct and unique period.

I left Peking in February 1969 and briefed my successor, John Denson, in Hong Kong on the way home. Despite our travails, the Mission had been kept open and was now in good working order. Most of the detained British subjects would trickle out over the next year. Tony Grey was set free in September 1969, when his equivalents in Hong Kong were granted early release.

I had been in China for rather less than three years. Not a

very long spell; but time counted twice in the Cultural Revolution. Birthe and I were tired, marked by the demands of running a post under siege conditions and the wider pressures of living in a demented environment, an Alice-in-Wonderland world, governed only by its own mad logic.

From a purely professional point of view the Cultural Revolution, for all its horrors, had been a source of intense interest, a fascination. I had been a spectator at an immense and historic convulsion, a movement whose course I understood and which I could analyse and report and even, to some very small degree, predict. It was like having the French Revolution performed in the road outside and occasionally being required to join in. It had its dangers, but, for the historian, the student of Communism, or the sinologist, there were great compensations. They were increased by the access, via Red Guard posters and publications, to information normally closed to all foreigners and to virtually all Chinese. The workings of a Communist state and the manoeuvres within the Chinese body politic were briefly visible. If much of what one saw only served to confirm the darkest views of human nature, or to evoke cynical laughter, it was nevertheless a unique insight.

But outside this narrow professional context there was little to comfort or encourage. The country was in the grip of a nightmare, a regime under which the normal vices of a Communist system were swollen to monstrous proportions. The standard lies and persecutions were now on an Orwellian scale; the tyranny both complete and capricious; the link with reality almost non-existent. As the Han dynasty historian wrote of the reign of terror under the first Emperor, Qin Shi Huang Di: 'The condemned were an innumerable multitude . . . From the Princes and Ministers down to the humblest people everyone was terrified and in fear of their lives. No man felt secure in his office; all were easily degraded.'

Moreover, it was a regime whose energies were largely directed to destroying its own resources, political, intellectual and economic. Under the strains it imposed, the downward potential of human nature was brutally exposed: one noted how rapidly respect had been turned into mindless adulation, criticism into torture and killing. There was only a short step from absurdity to atrocity.

It was impossible to avoid a deep sense of waste at the spectacle of the talents and devotion of a gifted people rejected or misused. Even in our confined world we had seen examples enough of personal shame and suffering: the doctors condemned to scrub the ward floors, the old amah with her long hair forcibly cropped, the Chinese office staff terrified of interrogation by students, or indeed of their own children, and one by one removed to be punished and re-educated, some to return, some not. We had seen ourselves a little of the beatings and vandalism. And outside this small circle there was the immense national suffering one could divine from the official statements, the posters and the various reports available to us.

These self-inflicted wounds were too large to assess accurately. Though certain sectors seem to have been protected, notably those concerned with nuclear weapons, and agriculture came off lightly, the economy had slipped back several years, at a time when population growth made rapid progress critical. The Great Leap Forward was indisputably a major disaster; Chinese writers put the deaths resulting from it at twenty million. But the official Chinese judgement in 1981 placed the Cultural Revolution in a league of its own, as the greatest national catastrophe the Communist regime had had to endure: 'the most severe setback and the heaviest losses suffered by the Party, the state, and the people since the founding of the People's Republic'. The fatalities were much less than in the Great Leap and the associated famines; but the political and spiritual damage and scars were greater and longer-lasting.

What had the revolution achieved? It had brought Mao back to full power and had eliminated those he feared or suspected. As an engine of destruction it was effective. But it could construct nothing and it changed much less than it claimed. The emerging Revolutionary Committees were dominated by the army and later by old Party *apparatchiks*; the new revolutionary elements did not last long. The nature of Chinese man, which was to have been fundamentally improved, remained unregenerate. And in classic style the revolution devoured its children. The Red Guards were sent off lamenting into the countryside. The *enragés* of the 16 May Group were rapidly discarded and condemned. Chen Boda, Mao's secretary and shadow, who had helped organize the whole show, fell in 1971 and was linked with, of all people, Liu Shaoqi. Finally Lin Biao, the closest comrade-in-arms and acknowledged heir, was found to have been a plotter and a traitor all along. What had it all been for?

Mao's own conduct could scarcely be matter for surprise: his character had been sufficiently revealed in the Great Leap Forward and the punishment of Peng Dehuai for venturing a dissenting opinion on that earlier adventure. Even so, one could only wonder at the vanity and egoism that could inflict so great a calamity on his country.

But there was also puzzlement. How could it be allowed to happen? How was it that leader after leader acquiesced in the madness, often actively assisted as long as he himself was not the target, and, when he was, meekly accepted his fate?

The answer was in part the extraordinary ascendancy attained by one man on the basis of earlier undoubted achievements and a long reign. The support of the military, in particular the troops round the capital, helped. It was also in part the effect of Communist discipline, the loyalty to a Party which had liberated and unified the country, given it dignity and begun to tackle some of its basic problems.

But this carried one only part of the way. At a deeper level the answer had to be the weight of Chinese history, of successive despotisms, the absence of any experience of tolerated dissent or open debate. One was driven back to the tyranny of the first Emperor and beyond that to the chilling Legalist philosophers who, two thousand years before modern dictatorships, provided the intellectual underpinning of the totalitarian state. It was they who required total conformity and a ban on private knowledge. As Han Feizi, the greatest of the Legalists, put it: 'In the state of the enlightened ruler there are no books written on bamboo slips; law supplies the only instruction. There are no sermons on former kings; the officials serve as the only teachers.' It was they who advised that people should be organized into groups, who would be responsible for each other and obliged to denounce each other's crimes, thereby foreshadowing the Communist street committees. And, of course, it was the first Emperor who burned the books and buried the scholars, though Mao, who liked to draw parallels with the Qin ruler, used to boast that he had outclassed his mentor in that department.

Chinese tradition therefore required an Emperor and inculcated total obedience. If, as was bound to happen from time to time, the Emperor proved to be a monster, the only course for his followers was to obey and endure. In a way, he was their creation.

Whatever explanations could be offered for the phenomenon of the Cultural Revolution, there was little danger that any dispassionate observer of it would retain an idealized view of China. Yet it was remarkable how many in the West, including the well-informed, were anxious to put the best possible construction on Mao's fiasco. It was presented as a way to democratize Marxism-Leninism, to achieve a new democratic consensus by giving ordinary folk a hand in government. The idea that Mao, or his opponents, ever contemplated democracy in the Western sense was of course grotesque, but the line was a fashionable one. The Cultural Revolution was praised as the wave of the future, pointing the way forward for the world as a whole. Mao was invoked in the student riots of 1968, in Paris and in the United States; and it was seriously claimed that the great helmsman had a cure for Western society's ills.

Even when that claim was not pressed, it was possible to argue that his policies were justified and successful in the special Chinese context. A significant number of Western writers and experts, some still prominent today, eager to defer to their hosts and anxious to retain access in Peking, were only too ready to draw a veil over the less appetizing features of those policies and did not recover their analytical vigour until Mao had gone. Remarkable intellectual contortions were performed. Much was written about struggle through reasoning, not force, as a Chinese characteristic (*wen dou*, not *wu dou*). The Chinese, it was claimed, did not physically liquidate opponents in the way the Russians did. Indeed, some went so far as to suggest that analysis from the point of view of the power struggle was peculiarly inappropriate in China: the Chinese were concerned with principles, not personalities. One group of scholarly visitors, looking at the country in the early 1970s, one of the grimmer periods in the decade of troubles, praised the enrichment of people's lives by the new art and culture and found vitality and humour, relaxation and euphoria.

In retrospect, these willing delusions are laughable enough; but they constituted a small, discreditable episode in intellectual history, worthy of mention beside the better-known examples of whitewash for Stalin's enormities. They were a reminder of the sad fact that tyrannies have rarely lacked their apologists among the intelligentsia; and of the further fact that even in its ugliest moods China retained the power to confuse and beguile its Western audience.

PART TWO

Deng's China

CHAPTER TEN

Deng's China

I CAME BACK, as Ambassador, in June 1978. There had been a happy interlude at home, as Head of the Policy Planning Staff, then Head of the Assessments Staff in the Cabinet Office. This was followed by a taste of Soviet-style Communism as Ambassador to East Germany and some negotiating with Russians and Americans over nuclear matters in the Comprehensive Test Ban talks in Geneva.

In Peking we were now an Embassy, having finally closed our Consulate in Taiwan in 1972; but the Chancery building, rebuilt by the Chinese at their own cost, was unchanged. The patched-up room in the Residence, where I had worked as Chargé in 1968 and 1969, had reverted to type and was once again the Head of Mission's bedroom. There were identifiable faces all round, though wearing different expressions. The Chinese recognized the returned wanderer and courteously put him in the category of 'old friends'. We were all survivors, and having been there before showed at least interest and persistence.

Nothing was said about the burning. Zhou Enlai had summoned my successor as Chargé, John Denson, late one night and formally apologized to him for the incident, which he attributed to 'extreme elements'. He had added that the Chinese government would pay for the rebuilding. On social occasions over the next few years I was occasionally asked by leaders and officials 'Were you there? Were you actually inside?' When I said I was, there would usually be a laugh. This was partly the laugh of embarrassment; but I suspect there was also an element of pure glee, that for once the foreigner, particularly the British, had been dealt with firmly.

These were small continuities. But of course in other, much more important ways the scene was very different. The old leaders had gone, dead or disgraced, or both: Jiang Qing and her Shanghai cronies, who rode the revolutionary wave, now imprisoned and anathematized as the Gang of Four; Lin Biao, with his Little Red Book, possibly the victim of an aircraft crash as he fled to the Soviet Union, but undoubtedly dead and condemned as a traitor; Zhu De, the army commander, once equal in rank with Mao; Zhou Enlai, who held the country together while Mao enacted an old man's fantasy and tried to recover the revolutionary vigour of his youth; Mao himself, the great primal force, appropriately preceded to his grave by a disastrous earthquake. All, all were gone, the old familiar faces.

But not quite all. Deng Xiaoping, purged in the Cultural Revolution and reinstated in 1973, purged again in 1976 and again reinstated, was now the driving force in the government. He shared power with Hua Guofeng, Mao's acknowledged successor.

The regime was gradually distancing itself from what had gone before. The crimes and excesses of the decade of troubles were now conveniently ascribed to Lin Biao and the Gang of Four, and any Chinese presentation on the internal scene began with a litany on this subject. Mao himself was not criticized; indeed there were still ritual obeisances to him and a great mausoleum disfiguring Tiananmen Square; but he was rapidly being cut down to size. On the Party's anniversary in July, just after I arrived, I was intrigued to find on the front page of the *People's Daily* the text of a hitherto unpublished speech by Mao in 1962, shortly after the Great Leap, in which he admitted responsibility for shortcomings and mistakes in the Party's work over the preceding ten years. It was the first official recognition that the great man was capable of error and had erred. From that a host of earth-shaking questions flowed.

But the principal characteristic of the new regime, as it struck me in those first few weeks, was its commitment to the modernization of China and to the opening to the West which was a precondition of any such process.

Modernization as a general aim was something the Chinese had been intermittently engaged in since the nineteenth century. The question was how to come to terms with a more advanced outside world and how to recover for China a place and power appropriate to her size and traditions. China's modern history was largely the story of abortive attempts to answer that question.

The old China, the Middle Kingdom, was a world in itself. China had no need of barbarian skills or wares. The Emperor Qian Long's dismissive response to George III in 1793 is the *locus classicus*: 'As your Ambassador can see for himself, I possess all things . . .' But, as the nineteenth century wore on, this bland self-sufficiency showed increasing signs of wear. The repeated humiliations of that time in the Opium Wars and at the hands of Europeans and Japanese served to discredit the philosophical basis of Chinese society, but put nothing in its place.

The Self-Strengthening movement, launched in 1861, was perhaps the first serious attempt to face the issue. Western techniques were studied, Western-style factories were erected. But it was a superficial reform: the groundwork of Confucianism remained untouched. 'Chinese learning for substance; Western learning for practical use.' The formula reflected only a half-hearted conversion. And the inadequacy was brutally demonstrated in the Sino-Japanese War of 1894–5.

Following that experience, in 1898 the young Emperor, Guang Xu, inspired by a group of modernizing scholars, instituted his 'hundred days of reform', but then lost power to the reactionaries, headed by the Empress Dowager. The Chinese government remained too conservative, too arrogant and too corrupt to recognize reality and make the wholesale adjustment that the situation demanded and that their Japanese neighbours accomplished.

In the succeeding years, under Sun Yatsen, the warlords and Chiang Kaishek, the aspiration persisted but China remained weak and divided. After 1949, the Communists had a better chance and, in their earlier years at least, a better record. They sought to learn from the Russians but, in true Chinese fashion, found themselves uncomfortable *in statu pupillari*. Mao soon

manoeuvred himself into a position in which he was no longer
the pupil Marxist, but the teacher and in which in terms of
political philosophy China could once again claim to be the
centre of the world. Moreover, under his rule economic development was too often subordinated to political fervour and China
too often retreated into itself.

Modernization therefore was a word with a long and chequered
history. In its latest phase it had been proclaimed by an ailing
Zhou Enlai at the National People's Congress in 1975. The
object was the modernization of agriculture, industry, science
and technology, and defence, so as to turn China into an advanced
industrial state by the year 2000. The cause had been espoused
by Hua Guofeng, who in February 1978 announced an ambitious ten-year programme (much too ambitious as it turned out).

On modernization, Hua and Deng apparently saw eye to eye,
though only Deng had the pragmatism necessary for its accom-
plishment. His celebrated remark, 'It doesn't matter whether the
cat is black or white; what matters is whether it is good at catching mice', had given him a lot of trouble during the Cultural
Revolution; but it fairly conveyed the atmosphere of 1978. And
with modernization went a readiness to seek the help of more
advanced nations, in particular Western Europe, Japan and the
United States. At a state banquet for the King of Spain in June,
Deng said, 'We are prepared to learn modestly from others.' An
interesting statement from a Chinese leader.

And, it was clear, a sincere statement. In pursuit of the
necessary knowledge high-level delegations were scouring Europe
and Japan. Scientists of all kinds were welcomed and cross-
questioned. A kind of open-ended seminar was in progress. The
Chinese were particularly interested in the German and Japanese examples.

They were also ready to import advanced equipment and
technology, and as a means to this were apparently prepared
to think the previously unthinkable and consider government
loans. They were interested in everything from machinery for
making high-class toys to nuclear submarines. There were
enquiries about Harrier jump-jets, to Mr Brezhnev's alarm. It
was far from clear how it was all to be financed, but the commercial opportunities were obvious and the business delegations
multiplied.

As part of the same process, education was being revived and intellectuals again accorded some respect. Education had naturally been a major casualty of the Cultural Revolution and even when classes were resumed, the students remained disaffected and the teachers were often afraid to teach. Not long before, a young man who handed in a blank examination paper had been praised as a hero.

At a national conference on education in April 1978, Deng laid down that the main task of students was to study and that schools should enforce strict standards and rigid discipline. The élitist, and therefore anti-Maoist, concept of key schools was restored. A large-scale movement to teach the basics of the English language was mounted on radio and television and in the schools and aroused great enthusiasm. Most interesting of all, it was decided to send ten thousand students, eighty per cent of them scientists, abroad in 1979. There was a story that Deng had written in the margin of the policy paper, 'If a few run away, it doesn't matter' ('*Pao le jige bu yaojin*').

China's foreign policy reflected the same priorities. Fear of the Soviet Union and hostility to it remained central; but to this was added the positive element of the need to develop relations with advanced countries. A host of delegations travelled between the relevant capitals and Peking. Deng himself visited Japan in October for the ratification of the Sino-Japanese Treaty of Peace and Friendship, which ended Japan's equidistance between the Soviet Union and China and assured the supply of Japanese machinery and technology to fuel the modernization programme. At the end of the year there was an even greater prize, normalization of relations with the United States. In January 1979 Deng was to visit America.

There was also a blossoming in unofficial contacts. China was much more accessible; new provinces and cities were open to travel. The visitors from home whom I briefed and dined departed for ever more exotic destinations, Xinjiang, Sichuan, even Tibet. China was realizing what an immense reservoir of interest and sympathy it could tap if it were only to smile. Foreign tourists had multiplied tenfold from the previous year and, in addition, hundreds of thousands of overseas Chinese were now admitted for short visits to relatives. Urban life was visibly easier. There was more food in the shops than a few years before;

people were better dressed; and they were also more relaxed. The new policy was popular.

One measure of better times was the return of some of the old pleasures for Peking people. They had not been wholly exterminated in the time of troubles, but they had gone underground. Now we saw again the old men airing their caged birds in the parks and heard the strange, aeolian music of pigeons wheeling overhead with small bamboo flutes attached to their tails. Life was seeping back. Even traditional opera, banned by Jiang Qing, was restored in 1978.

Altogether then, for the returned Cultural Revolution veteran, a new and more hopeful China. Allowing for all the exaggerations and disappointments inherent in vast modernization plans, there were opportunities which we and our Western partners could not afford to miss. It was much more than a matter of business contracts, though they were not negligible. The development of a strong, peaceful, well-disposed China would be an enormous gain to Asian and world stability. In return, China apparently favoured a strong, united Europe, a healthy Atlantic Alliance and a Japan equipped to play her full role in the security of East Asia. A China that had abandoned the current enterprise and turned in upon itself would be a much more uncertain and dangerous neighbour.

Nor was there any inconsistency between this and our search at the time for a constructive relationship with the Soviet Union, unless we accepted that this relationship could only be pursued on Soviet terms. There were bound to be Soviet protests about defence sales to China; but that was scarcely ground for avoiding a course we judged to be in our overall interest. There was no foreseeable danger of China attacking the Soviet Union; it faced a long period of overwhelming Soviet military superiority and would need a peaceful environment if modernization was to have a chance.

It also seemed to me that the role of the Embassy was radically changed by the new Chinese policies. In the past our major concern had been reporting and analysis. We had been spectators at an esoteric, sometimes alarming, play, exchanging learned comments with fellow experts in the audience. Now, if we played our cards right, analysis would take second place to growing bilateral activity in education, science and technology, in the commercial field, in political contacts and possibly even in military matters. China had become a country we had to deal with, rather than simply study. We needed the right instructions and we needed more staff. My existing complement, able and hard-working as they were, were run off their feet, facing levels of activity almost double that of the preceding year and going up fast.

It was along these lines that I argued in a series of telegrams, pressing for a rapid and positive response from home. Happily, the telegrams caught Mr Callaghan's eye and things began to move.

CHAPTER ELEVEN

Reversing the Verdicts: The Peking Spring

A CURIOUS FEATURE of the internal situation in the new China was the co-existence and, to some degree, co-operation of Deng Xiaoping and Hua Guofeng. They were men from very different backgrounds, one Mao's heir, one his chief surviving victim. To many of my Western colleagues this did not seem so strange: coalition governments were common; the two men needed each other; both believed in modernization; why should they not continue to work together?

I found this reasonable scenario somehow unconvincing. As Mao, and many leaders before him, had said, there could be only one sun in the sky. And, in China of all places, the logic of Lenin's 'Who, whom?' applied. In fact, the history of the next few years was to turn on the struggle by Deng to dislodge Hua; and on the larger question, how far could Deng dismantle Maoism itself, without undermining the foundations of post-1949 China.

Hua Guofeng was a strange, anonymous figure. Large, shambling, round-faced, soft and slightly sinister in manner, he was the regulation senior cadre, without any distinguishing features. He also looked rather like Mao, a resemblance he strove to cultivate. He had come up through the Hunan provincial machine, where he had been Vice-Governor. At the time of the dispute with Peng Dehuai in 1959 he seems to have done some devilling for Mao. He also had the good fortune to be in charge of the area that included Shaoshan, the Chairman's native village. This brought him into contact with Mao and he was able to devote resources to beautifying Shaoshan and improving its communications.

He had had a good Cultural Revolution and emerged as Party leader of Hunan. He was then brought to Peking as a rising Mao loyalist, where he probably enjoyed Kang Sheng's patronage. He was promoted to the Politburo in 1973 and in January 1975 became Minister of Public Security and a Vice-Premier.

Mao's choice of him as Acting-Premier in February 1976, just after Zhou Enlai's death, may have been prompted as much by who he was not as by who he was. Deng Xiaoping, rehabilitated in 1973, and in day-to-day charge of the government for the last year, had again fallen into Mao's disfavour, allegedly for pushing ahead too fast with modernization. On the other hand, Mao did not want to become a prisoner of the left by appointing their candidate, Zhang Chunqiao, one of Jiang Qing's Shanghai coterie. Hua was a compromise; he also no doubt approximated as closely as possible to the ideal of having no successor at all.

As Acting Premier and Minister of Public Security, Hua became involved, on the wrong side, in one of the watershed incidents of the 1970s, the demonstration in Tiananmen Square from 30 March to 4 April 1976 in honour of Zhou Enlai. There had been recent press attacks on Zhou, alleging that he was a 'capitalist-roader' and threatening a new Cultural Revolution. They had been inspired by Jiang Qing and her following, but probably also had had Mao's countenance. These attacks had provoked an explosion of popular anger and of mourning for Zhou, which for once was unorchestrated and which extended beyond condemnation of the Gang of Four to embrace defiance of Mao himself. The scenes occurred at the time of Qing Ming, the traditional Chinese festival for the dead, and the square was filled with white memorial wreaths and mourning poems, which were political as well as elegiac.

On the instructions of the Politburo and after reference to Mao, the square was cleared overnight of wreaths and elegies. The next day (5 April) the crowds reacted in violent demonstrations, overturning police vehicles and storming a police command post. That evening, when most of the demonstrators had gone home, strong forces of troops, militia and police swept through the square, beating and arresting anyone they encountered. The demonstrations were officially condemned as counterrevolutionary. The Politburo also seized the opportunity to blame Deng for them. He was stripped of all his offices. At the same time Hua was appointed First Vice-Chairman of the Party, in addition to his post as Acting Premier. The same decisions that elevated Hua cast Deng out for the second time.

Later in that same momentous year of 1976, when Mao finally died in the early hours of 9 September, Hua as the heir apparent had faced a showdown with Jiang Qing and her three cronies from Shanghai (Zhang Chunqiao, Yao Wenyuan and Wang Hongwen), who formed the surviving core of radical beneficiaries of the Cultural Revolution. This was the infamous Gang of Four, a name originally given them by Mao himself. With their patron dead they made their bid for supreme power, seeking to assume Mao's ideological mantle and attempting, not very efficiently, to take over the central Party apparatus. Realizing the threat they posed to him as well as more conservative colleagues, Hua flung in his lot with a group of senior Party and military figures led by the old marshal, the Defence Minister, Ye Jianying, who were determined to move first. With the help of the guards regiment that had protected Mao, three of the Gang (Zhang, Yao and Wang) were seized on 6 October as they appeared for a meeting Hua had called in Zhongnanhai, the leadership complex to the west of the Forbidden City. Jiang Qing was arrested in her house and taken away, reviling her captors and reviled by her servants. When it was finally released, on 15 October, the news prompted further spontaneous crowd demonstrations, this time of relief and joy.

The credit for this decisive move, bringing down the curtain on the ten years of troubles, must lie with Ye Jianying, who had planned it for some time. Deng was a fugitive in the south, under military protection, reduced to verbal exhortations of the need for a fight to the finish. Hua was a late convert. Nevertheless he enjoyed some popular acclaim as the man under whose leadership the country had been saved.

His main strength, however, lay in his position as Mao's acknowledged heir. He had arranged to be put in charge of the construction of Mao's mausoleum and the editing of Mao's works, thereby becoming the high priest of the cult. It was also announced, in October 1976, that Mao has said to Hua shortly before his death: 'With you in charge I am at ease'; and pictures of the scene in Mao's study, with Mao conferring these dubious credentials, were, at the time I returned to Peking in 1978, on sale in all the shops. They later became extremely rare.

In formal terms therefore, in the summer of 1978 Hua was very much in charge. He was Chairman of the Party, Prime Minister and Chairman of the Military Affairs Commission, a combination of offices Mao himself had not held. He had developed a minor personality cult as 'the heroic leader' or 'the wise leader'. Decisions were reported as coming from 'the Central Committee under the leadership of Chairman Hua'. But he had a shady record, particularly in relation to the Tiananmen demonstration in 1976. He was also a creature of the Maoist past, from which, at Deng's prompting, the country was only too ready to recoil. The more Maoist dogmas were denounced, the more Maoist verdicts were reversed, the more uneasy his position became.

The publication in July of Mao's 1962 speech admitting the possibility of error was one major blow at the edifice of belief. Another, and in some ways more serious, was Deng's call, again in the summer of 1978, to 'seek truth from facts' and his assertion that this represented the essence of Mao's thought. Deng was picking up a remark of Mao himself in 1937; the sacred writings were sufficiently rich to provide ammunition for most causes. Deng saw Mao's great strength in his application, in his younger years it was stressed, of Marxist-Leninist principles to actual conditions in China. Even Mao's thought had to be tested in practice, with the implication that it might not always be the answer. Holy writ was being turned into the basis for pragmatism.

Deng also condemned those who used Mao's word blindly as dogma. The target here was the group of leftists in the Politburo, who were allies of Hua and had acquired the name of 'the Whatever Faction', from their claim to defend whatever decisions Mao had made and follow whatever instructions he had given. Their leader was Wang Dongxing, who had risen from being Mao's bodyguard to the position of Vice-Minister of Public Security and then that of Director of the Central Committee's General Office and Party Vice-Chairman. They included Wu

De, the Mayor of Peking, and Chen Xilian, the Commander of
the Peking Military District. They were Hua's allies, but they
also represented his vulnerable left flank. He was careful not to
identify himself with them and manoeuvred for a central position
where he could balance Maoists against reformers. But if the
Maoists fell he was exposed.

Throughout this time the pressure on leftists was building up
as the provinces replaced many of those who had done well out
of the Cultural Revolution. In 1977 and early 1978 there were
a number of violent struggle meetings recalling the scenes of
1966–8.

There was also by now a dangerous fragility in the official
ideological position. The Cultural Revolution was still adjudged
a good thing, a revolutionary event. It was explained, however,
that it had been distorted by the Gang of Four and later by Lin
Biao. But the revolution was known, instinctively and univer-
sally, to be an extremely bad thing; and questions naturally arose.
How could Mao be unaware of what the Gang of Four had been
up to? Something had to give.

The material that proved most explosive, however, was that
connected with the Tiananmen demonstrations of 1976. There
was steady popular criticism of Wu De who, as Peking Party
leader, bore special responsibility for the official response to
events in the great square on 5 April that year, and who also
happened to be disliked as a bad manager of the city's affairs.
An article in *China Youth* in September described the riots as a
'demonstration of real and full social democracy on the part of
the people'. Another article in the same issue attacked the cult
of Mao.

The issue was banned on the instructions of Wang Dongxing.
But the decision was reviewed at a Politburo meeting late in the
month and Wu De was removed from his Peking post, though
retaining his place on the Politburo.

There was public rejoicing at the decision, with immediate
calls for a full-scale reappraisal of the events of 5 April 1976. The
lid had been lifted. The press now described the demonstrations of the time as being anti-leftist and in support of Deng.
And on 15 November the Peking Party Committee announced
that they were completely revolutionary. Far from being a
counter-revolutionary incident, as two years before, they were

declared 'a brilliant page in China's revolutionary history'.

Hua adjusted himself deftly to the new situation and ensured that the decision was presented as one taken 'under the leadership of the Central Committee headed by Chairman Hua Guofeng'. He also wrote an inscription for a memorial volume of Tiananmen poems. But his position was nonetheless dangerously weakened. If the demonstrations were entirely revolutionary, why did he, Minister of Public Security at the time, suppress them? More worrying still, if the Politburo decision condemning the demonstrations was a major error, what of the other two decisions of the same day, appointing Hua Premier and dismissing Deng? Hua survived for a long time and retained the outward trappings of authority; but, from November 1978 onward, he was not the same: power slipped more and more into Deng's hands; and the events of the past became fatally incriminating material, which his opponents could use against him at any time.

The shift in power was exemplified in the results of the Third Plenum of the Central Committee, which was held in December 1978 and was one of the turning-points of China's recent history. At the work conference which preceded it Hua made a verbal self-criticism, presumably about his incipient personality cult. Thereafter he was no longer 'the wise leader Hua Guofeng', but simply 'comrade Hua Guofeng'. The Plenum reaffirmed the principle of collective leadership. His leftist allies, the 'Whateverists', Wang Dongxing, Chen Xilian, Wu De and company, made formal self-criticisms and lost effective power; and a number of Deng supporters were brought into the Politburo. They included a prominent associate of Deng, Hu Yaobang, who had been leader of the Youth League in the 1950s.

Certain general principles of great importance were laid down at the same time. It was declared that large-scale class struggle, which above anything had been the distinguishing feature of Maoist ideology, was now over. There would be no more mass political movements. The priority would be modernization.

On Mao himself, the communiqué of the Plenum was cautious: it went no further than affirming that he had made errors and that the Cultural Revolution (still referred to as 'Great') also had shortcomings and mistakes. But it turned out that the work conference preceding the Plenum had been braver and had re-evaluated a number of aspects of the revolution. Moreover, the public caution was balanced by the wave of rehabilitations of senior cadres which began about this time. A memorial meeting was held for Peng Dehuai, who had died under persecution in 1967. Peng Zhen, the former Peking First Secretary, returned in January and was later given high office. Wang Guangmei, Liu Shaoqi's widow, reappeared in the Great Hall of the People during the Spring Festival of 1979. Despite years of suffering, she retained her old brilliance and charm and rapidly became one of Peking's great ladies. We saw much of her at the Embassy.

The December 1978 Plenum also sought to create a less divided society. Elements held vicious and irredeemable in the revolutionary years, such as former landlords and rich peasants, were to be readmitted. Property seized from former capitalists was to be restored. The United Front, a device for bringing into alliance with the Party other segments of society, such as intellectuals, members of 'democratic parties' and professional people, was to be rebuilt. Modernization was seen as requiring more popular participation. The word democracy was used. It was of course qualified and subject always to the Party's centralized leadership. But there was direct official encouragement for a greater freedom in thinking and self-expression.

The Plenum was in fact held against a background of popular debate and agitation which was unprecedented in China and which excited intense interest, not only in cities throughout the country, but also in the West. It was the period of Democracy Wall or, to use two sadder titles, the Second Hundred Flowers or the Peking Spring.

In part this was a continuation of the practice of poster-writing which had been deliberately stimulated and guided during the Cultural Revolution and had survived and re-emerged spasmodically through the Decade of Troubles. It had been given new life by the reopening of the discussion of the Tiananmen incident of 1976 and by the questions prompted by an implausible official line on Mao and the Cultural Revolution. It was also affected, inevitably, by the subterranean struggle between Hua and Deng; and in this instance, Deng, by no means a natural democrat, found himself on the side of the angels: the more that was revealed about the riots and their suppression, the stronger his position; and the faster the temple of Maoism was dismantled, the better the prospects of modernizing and getting China on the move.

The centre of this blossoming was an unprepossessing spot, a scrubby stretch of wall lying to the west of the Square of Heavenly Peace and shielding a municipal bus depot. This became Democracy Wall (Minzhu Qiang). There were posters elsewhere, in the great square, and, at one time, on almost every hoarding in the centre of the city. There were also democracy magazines. But this stretch of wall was the focus. It was enthusiastically attended and worked over, not only by the Chinese crowds, but also by Western observers and reporters.

There were many kinds of posters. Some were confined to specific grievances, for example bad housing or pollution; some were silly, or cranky. But, in addition to, and dominating the inevitable dross, there were more general pieces of great political significance. Some of these raised questions about Mao. Over the weekend of 17–19 November there appeared the first poster criticizing Mao by name. It referred to his mistaken judgement of the class struggle and his erroneous support for the Gang of Four in striking down Deng Xiaoping. Another, conceding that Mao was a great leader, asked how, without Mao, Lin Biao could have climbed to power, or the Gang of Four have flourished, or the Tiananmen riots have been condemned as counter-revolutionary. Very natural questions; but earth-shaking at the time.

Another poster-writer suggested that Hua was to blame for the delay in rehabilitating the Tiananmen demonstrators. There was widespread criticism of Wu De and of fellow leftists in the Politburo and calls for the return of Peng Zhen. Kang Sheng, who had died in 1975 in the odour of sanctity, and had been buried with full honours and praised by Hua and many others, was now denounced as a monster. The truth was coming out. The posters began to refer to Mao as seventy per cent good, thirty per cent bad; and even the press were taking to describing the Cultural Revolution as wrong from the start.

All this was grist to Deng Xiaoping's mill: it hastened the process of revisionism and undermined Hua's standing. Some of it might have been prompted by him; certainly it was welcome;

and in interviews with foreign correspondents he gave the wall-poster movement a cautious blessing.

But quite soon there appeared another strain, much less welcome and more fundamental. Poster-writers had hitherto kept within the framework of the socialist system. Now they began to raise more general issues. They looked at Communism from the outside and with an unsparing eye. They began to claim the classic elements of liberty, constitutional government, governments elected and recalled by the people, freedom of expression, an independent judiciary, the rule of law. The authorities were referred to sceptically: 'Don't expect our leaders to make us a present of democracy. We shall have to fight for it.' America, Britain and Japan were held up as examples, particularly America. Deng visited the United States in January 1979 and for the first time undistorted pictures of life there were seen on Chinese television screens.

The most powerful critique appeared in a poster of 5 December. It was entitled 'Democracy, the Fifth Modernization', and it swept aside the slogans and dogmas of thirty years of Communist rule with an angry eloquence which was both exhilarating and moving.

There is an old Chinese saying which tells of 'feeding the people by painting cakes' and there is another one about 'quenching thirst by contemplating plums' . . . During these last few decades, the Chinese people docilely followed a 'Great Helmsman', who fed them with cakes which he painted by using a brush called 'Communism' and who quenched their thirst by dangling in front of their noses plums which were called the 'Great Leap Forward' or 'the Three Red Flags'. And the people kept on bravely marching onward. Thirty years passed like a day and gave us this lesson: the people are like the monkey grasping at the reflection of the moon in a pond. Don't they realize there is nothing there?

Go on, old yellow oxen, taking the Four Modernizations and 'unity and stability' as the key link, continue the revolution. You will reach your heaven in the end – Communism and the Four Modernizations . . . I advise everyone to disbelieve political swindlers of this kind. We are no longer stupid . . .

Statements about the people being the masters of history are no more than empty talk. The people cannot control their own destiny. Their merits are ascribed to another and their rights are woven into his imperial crown. What sort of masters then are they? I say they are more like slaves.

The people must retain the right to dismiss and replace their representatives at any time . . . In Europe and in the United States the people enjoy precisely this type of democracy . . . Whereas in our country, if in a private conversation you express the slightest doubt concerning the historical sublimity of our Great Helmsman, Mao Zedong (even though he has already passed away), you immediately see in front of you the gaping gates of a jail . . .

Without the Fifth Modernization [Democracy] the other four modernizations are only a new lie. I call on the people to rally round the banner of democracy. Don't believe in the despots' 'stability and unity'. Totalitarian fascism can only bring us disaster . . . Democracy is our only hope.

The author of this philippic was a young man named Wei Jingsheng, who worked as an electrician in the Peking Zoo. Interestingly, he had been an enthusiastic Red Guard, a fervid believer in his time and therefore doubly disillusioned. He belonged to the lost generation. He was by no means an intellectual and was largely self-taught, picking up information on the West from translations of Russian novels and articles in Chinese magazines. But his criticism went to the heart of the matter and he was fearless.

In his background he was not untypical. Many of his fellow activists had been denied university education by the events of the Cultural Revolution. There were posters by railwaymen, electricians, workers in factories. In this they differed from their historical antecedents, the students who rose in protest against the provisions of the Versailles Treaty in May 1919, and the intellectuals who were deceived by Mao into speaking their minds in the Hundred Flowers of 1957. If anything, this made their questions more impressive: they had thought it out for themselves.

But criticism of this order could not be tolerated by a Communist government, whether of the Hua or the Deng variety.

It was only a matter of time. In fact the time given was surprisingly long, from November 1978 to March 1979. There was a check in December, then a further efflorescence. More posters, more democratic magazines, more permitted contact between ordinary Chinese and foreigners, more excited questions put to diplomats and reporters by crowds of young Chinese about life and politics in the West. We kept closely in touch with it all, in my own case with much foreboding.

In February there were signs of official misgiving. The climate of greater freedom had been exploited, not only by activists in the cause of democracy, but also by petitioners of various kinds, hoping to have unjust verdicts reversed, and by rusticated youths, sent off into the countryside years ago and given no hope of returning permanently or retrieving their lost education and lifestyle. The latter swarmed back into Shanghai for the Spring Festival in January 1979, refused to return and paralysed the city for several days.

The government had more general worries. How was it to balance democracy and the more cardinal principle of centralism, that is, political dictatorship. There were concerns too about fraternization between Chinese and foreigners, carrying with it the risk of secrets leaking and, potent for all those who had survived the Cultural Revolution, a fear of a general breakdown of discipline. China was by now fighting another war, against Vietnam, and not doing too well; and over-ambitious plans for modernization were having to be scaled down. The warm breezes of the Peking Spring were turning distinctly cold.

Deng held the position for some time. He had his visit to the United States to complete and no doubt saw advantage in keeping up the pressure on leftists a little longer. But by March the returns from the democratic movement were diminishing. He began stressing the importance of discipline and stability. He drew distinctions between socialist democracy on the one hand and bourgeois democracy and ultra-democracy on the other. When I took Malcolm Macdonald, the former Cabinet minister and Commissioner-General for the UK in South-east Asia, to see him on 21 March he was talking in terms that clearly indicated a clamp-down. It duly came.

Wei Jingsheng with characteristic courage condemned the new repression in a special issue of his magazine, *Exploration*, on

25 March. But, on 29 March, he was arrested on the charge of counter-revolutionary activity. Other activists were seized. The Peking authorities forebade any writings or representations that opposed 'socialism, the dictatorship of the proletariat, the leadership of the Chinese Communist Party, and Marxism-Leninism-Mao Zedong Thought, as well as the disclosure of state secrets and violations of the Constitution and the law'.

On 16 October Wei was tried for passing state secrets to foreigners and for counter-revolutionary agitation and propaganda, and was condemned to fifteen years' imprisonment. He had apparently spoken of Chinese casualty figures in the Vietnam War and of other details of the conflict in a talk with a Western journalist. But his real crime, in the eyes of the authorities, was something else; and the object clearly was to make an example of him. Democracy Wall lingered on into the autumn, with written protests at Wei's treatment, but was finally closed down on 7 December 1979 by the Peking authorities.

The episode had been a sad, unsurprising but at the same time inspiring one. The young activists were in the direct line from the student protesters of the 4 May movement of 1919 and, more recently, the three young men who put up a celebrated poster in Canton in 1973, attacking Lin Biao and, by extension, Mao. They were the forebears of the young people who protested against Hu Yaobang's removal in 1986 and mourned his death in 1989. They reminded the Western observer of the existence of a strong, subterranean river of dissent, free thought and idealism flowing below the grim uniformities of Communist rule; of that and of the universality of human aspirations: Peking man was in the end not so different from his Western counterpart.

For Deng it had been on the whole a helpful period; it had pressured his opponents and cleared away some of the ideological obstacles in his path. On the other hand the conservative reaction, when it came, was so strong that he had to struggle hard to control it; the first months of 1979 were occupied with such manoeuvrings. Though he benefited from the movement and for a time exploited it, I do not believe he engineered it; it had independent springs.

But for Deng and his fellow leaders it must also have been a worrying experience. The fact was that the most indoctrinated population on earth, relentlessly moulded and drilled for thirty years, had shown that it was irrepressible. In a matter of weeks the critics, many of them self-taught, had moved from narrow complaints or grievances to unsparing comment on their leaders and from that to fundamental analysis and condemnation of the whole system. For the Chinese government it was an alarming message, for the outside world a testimony to the resilience of the human spirit.

CHAPTER TWELVE

Reversing the Verdicts: Judgement on Mao

THE REVERSAL OF policy involved in the suppression of the democracy movement and the circumstances in which the move occurred amounted to a setback for Deng. The Maoists, backed in this case by the great mass of middle-ranking cadres, were able to say: 'I told you so.' Hua Guofeng's stock rose and for a time, in the spring and early summer of 1979, the ground won at the Third Plenum in December came under attack.

But it was only a temporary reverse. Deng rapidly recovered and from then on the movement was all one way. The 'Whatever Faction' were accused of trying to turn back the wheel of history, and incriminating information on them was leaked to the public via posters (even in its dying days Democracy Wall had its uses). At the end of the year they were to lose their places on the Politburo.

The demolition work on Mao also resumed. At a speech to mark the thirtieth anniversary of the founding of the People's Republic, Marshal Ye Jianying, speaking on behalf of the leadership, redefined Mao Zedong Thought as the crystallization of China's collective experience in revolutionary struggle, not simply Mao's own wisdom. He also described the Cultural Revolution as 'the most severe reversal to our socialist cause since the founding of the People's Republic . . . an appalling catastrophe suffered by all our people'. He still contrived to play down Mao's personal role in the tragedy, ascribing the errors and crimes to 'Lin Biao, the Gang of Four and other conspirators and careerists'. This was, however, only a preliminary assessment, he said; a considered judgement would be prepared later. The leaders were getting nearer to the nerve; but they were still inclined to shy away.

Hua's base was crumbling; but he still held the posts of Party Chairman and Premier, as well as that of Chairman of the Military Affairs Commission; and it was in these capacities that he carried out a series of visits to West European capitals in the autumn of 1979, to be received with full honours. In particular, he visited Britain, lunched with the Queen and had talks with Mrs Thatcher. Though I accompanied him, I have little recollection of the substance of the discussions; substance, in fact, was elusive: Hua spoke in generalities, sticking closely to a carefully prepared brief. In this he was the antithesis of Deng, whose throw-away remarks, uttered with casual authority, always represented the end of the road on any topic. Agreements on educational and cultural co-operation and on civil aviation were signed in his and the Prime Minister's presence; and there was some unrewarding discussion on Hong Kong; but there was little else of note.

In some ways the visit was more memorable to me for its insights into the style of the host than that of the guest. It was my first meeting with Mrs Thatcher, for whom I was later to work, as her Foreign Policy Adviser, for a spell of some seven years. It was also my first experience of those bruising but searching meetings which were a distinguishing feature of her administration. The ministers and officials gathered for the standard briefing were put through the mill in a way which was to become very familiar. What was the visit for? What would we get out of it? She wanted precise answers. The Chinese were not favourites and the onus of proof lay heavily on those who had saddled her with the engagement.

There was also a revealing incident at the welcoming ceremony. It was a little complicated. There was present a representative of the Queen; there was also the Prime Minister. The first turned out to be rather hazy about his exact movements. The second was not at all hazy and, realizing that her colleague in the receiving line needed briefing, proceeded to give him one, which was impressive in its detail. She knew the arrangements as well as I did, and it was my business to know them thoroughly. But that was not all; she concluded by pointing to the corner of the VIP room and telling the startled gentleman: 'Now go over there and learn it.'

Hua returned from these foreign travels to watch the fall, at a December meeting of the Politburo, of his Maoist allies, led by Wang Dongxing. He was also faced with the emergence of two new leaders, threatening his positions as head of Party and government.

One was Hu Yaobang, an old associate of Deng, who had twice been purged and rehabilitated with him. He was put at the head of a restored Party Secretariat as General Secretary, a post that had been abolished in 1966, when Deng himself held it. He also joined the inner core of the leadership as a member of the Standing Committee of the Politburo. His responsibilities suggested he might eventually take over Hua's place as Party leader.

He was a tiny man, much slighter than Deng, whose barrel-like build made up for his lack of height. He was unlike his fellow leaders, who sought, at least on public occasions, to maintain an impassive dignity. He bubbled with energy, bounced and gesticulated, could not sit still. When he spoke it was in the Western style, with expression, as if the words were his own, rather than those of a committee. Some of his colleagues may have thought he lacked gravitas, but he had courage and reforming zeal and was a new and refreshing phenomenon.

On the state side, the new man was Zhao Ziyang, who became Vice-Premier charged with handling day-to-day government work. Zhao had been the First Party Secretary in Guangdong before the Cultural Revolution, had been purged and persecuted along with other senior cadres there and on return had been moved to the vast, rich province of Sichuan as Party leader. Here he had been responsible for a number of pioneering measures which foreshadowed the immensely successful reforms in agriculture in the next few years. There were two trial provinces, Sichuan under Zhao and Anhui under Wan Li, a future Vice-Premier. The two men were commemorated in a popular rhyme.

Yao chi liang
Zhao Ziyang,

Yao chi mi
Zhao Wan Li.

If you want to eat wheat,
Look for Zhao Ziyang.
If you want to eat rice,
Look for Wan Li.

We had identified Zhao as a rising star while he was still in his Sichuan post and had invited him on a visit to Britain in the summer of 1979. I had him to lunch and heard his account of his reforms. We were not sure who his host should be in Britain; we had no equivalent for a man running a province larger than France. Eventually we hit on Michael Heseltine, in his capacity as Minister of Local Government.

I had no very clear impression of Zhao, except as a smooth, high-powered functionary, from that first meeting. Men of his generation, though they had had their share of trials, lacked the deeply etched characteristics of the old leaders, the men of the Long March. But I saw something of him later in the Hong Kong talks and came to respect him as a quiet, skilful negotiator, able to put over a hard line in unprovocative terms. It also became apparent from his record that, as well as a good administrator, he was a committed reformer, who, left to himself, would have tried to take China into unexplored territory of economic and eventually perhaps even political change. He could have been China's Gorbachev, though that is, I suppose, a two-edged compliment, and to China's leaders today, surveying Russia's torments, a condemnation in itself. His misfortune, and to some degree that of Hu Yaobang, was to hold high office while the older conservatives still survived. Surprisingly and sadly, the urbane high-flier of that first lunch meeting was to become a tragic figure, the reformer too far ahead of his time, who in the end was destroyed by the student idealists whose best practical hope he represented.

By 1980 Mao's sayings were becoming less obtrusive; Mao's statues were disappearing. In February 1980 his principal victim, Liu Shaoqi, was formally rehabilitated. The labels of scab, renegade and traitor were removed and the accusations against him were described as 'the biggest frame-up in Party history'. He was praised as a great Marxist, who had always been loyal and who had made 'indelible contributions'. There had been no plotting, no revisionist headquarters. There was a state funeral. In May there was an exhibition opened in his memory at the Museum of the Chinese Revolution. The old photographs were all there, with many others I had not seen before, covering a lifetime's service. The effect of this total reversal of history was bewildering, even for an outsider. Its impact on Chinese brought up over the last thirteen years to regard him as the arch-villain, the epitome of evil, was hard to imagine. The official statement proclaimed the intention to ensure that 'frame-ups such as befell Liu Shaoqi and many other comrades inside and outside the Party' should never happen again. But the Chinese reader could be forgiven some doubts on this score. The overall effect could only be to induce a mood of deep cynicism and withdrawal. In the socialist state it is the past that is unpredictable.

Hua's position was now becoming very insecure and in the spring of 1980 there were public suggestions that Zhao might replace him as Prime Minister. He made an appeal for support from the army, always the last repository of Maoist values. But it did not avail and in September he announced his resignation as Premier.

His final demise as Party Chairman was preceded by bitter internal argument over the terms of a resolution giving the Party's final assessment on Mao, which was being circulated in draft. Hua naturally wanted it watered down. Deng wanted to make it clear that Mao's line, at least in recent times, had been wrong and that he had been guilty of something more than occasional errors. In the course of the dispute Hua's own record came under attack in the Politburo. He was replaced as Chairman at the end of the year, though the change was not formally announced until the following summer. The same document on Mao and the Party that had provoked the confrontation was finally to include a section on Hua's leftist faults.

The internal struggle for the leadership was now over. But there remained two formal acts to mark the reversal of verdicts. The first was the trial of the Gang of Four. At the National People's Congress in June 1979 the deputies had demanded, or had been prompted to demand, that the Gang should be put on trial. This demand was accepted and Peng Zhen, who had been placed in charge of the Legislative Affairs Commission, was given the task of supervising the preparations. The trial was held from November 1980 to January 1981.

A trial was an innovation. Hitherto in China losers had been disposed of expeditiously enough, but without publicity or legal pretence. Presumably Deng saw advantage in showing that the country was now less arbitrarily governed. But he also wanted to strike further at Mao's prestige and draw a line under the Maoist past. Another objective was almost certainly to hasten the departure of Hua Guofeng as the heir to Mao and his radical tradition. It seems possible that sections of the draft indictment, pointing to links between Hua and the Gang of Four, were used to blackmail him into resignation, then dropped from the final version of the document.

The accused, officially described as the 'Lin Biao and Jiang Qing counter-revolutionary cliques', were a heterogeneous collection. First came the Gang of Four, that is Mao's widow and her three Shanghai associates, who had risen to power in the Cultural Revolution and fallen in 1976, just after Mao's death. Then there were five military leaders, charged with involvement in Lin Biao's plans for a *coup d'état* in 1971. Finally there was Chen Boda, Mao's former political secretary, who fell from power in 1971.

They were charged with a variety of crimes, ranging from slander to torture, murder, conspiracy to assassinate Mao and carry out a coup, and the plotting of armed rebellion. The alleged victims included Party, state and military leaders and hundreds of thousands of ordinary citizens. The general indictment was of a gigantic counter-revolutionary plot to take over control of China.

Great efforts had been made to create the setting of a judicial process in a country ruled by law. There were judges, procurators, defence lawyers and ostensible reliance on verifiable evidence. There was an invited public audience of representatives of the people (no foreigners); edited excerpts were put out on television. The material was lurid: stories of secret meetings and lists of the proscribed (usually provided by Kang Sheng); recordings of interrogations under torture; confrontations between Cultural Revolution victims and their former tormentors. But the display could not conceal the fact that this was a political act and essentially a charade: the Party, or, more

precisely, the Party's current leaders, had drawn up the indictment, had written the script and would pronounce sentence.
Witnesses appearing independently produced identical statements. The guilt of the accused was publicly assumed from the
start.

Over the facts there was relatively little argument in court. But
the issue of the personal responsibility of the accused proved
extremely awkward. Though none appeared to have been brain-
washed in Soviet style, most of the defendants were enfeebled or
cowed and co-operated with the prosecution. Two, however, did
not. Zhang Chunqiao, the most able of the Gang of Four, maintained a contemptuous silence throughout. And Jiang Qing, the
principal defendant, defied the court in what was her last and
greatest starring role. She had to be forcibly removed three times
for denouncing the judges as reactionaries and shouting Mao's
slogan: 'To rebel is justified!' We watched the television extracts
fascinated.

Her defence was that all she had done had been in pursuance
of instructions from Mao and Zhou Enlai and in accordance with
collective decisions by the Party Central Committee. As she put
it, 'I was Mao's dog. I bit whom he told me to bite.' It was a
good line and highlighted the fact of Mao's ultimate responsibility. But the court drew back from this conclusion and after
some delay sought refuge in an unconvincing distinction between
Mao's acts, which were described as errors, and his wife's, which
were adjudged crimes.

She was, as expected, sentenced to death, but with a two-year
suspension allowing for commutation if there were signs of
repentance. The grounds were duly found: the Party did not
want a martyr, or to appear to be executing Mao by proxy.

The trial did not impress its international audience. At home,
in China, it was good theatre and fed the natural wish for
revenge. But even here there were qualifications. It was too obviously political, another round in the endless in-fighting. We
heard stories of students, gathered around television sets, cheer-
ing on Jiang Qing as the one participant who dared to expose
the hypocrisy of the proceedings.

Deng had achieved his objectives, but at a high price. Popular
cynicism about the Party, the law and the whole political process
was confirmed. The revelations about the Lin Biao clique and

the public humiliation of former military leaders deeply offended the PLA, who were in any event concerned at their declining prestige in a reformist China. In the end the finger pointed clearly at Mao, though the judges hesitated to make the responsibility clear. But it required little thought to conclude that it was not just Mao; it was the whole Communist system that was on trial and condemned.

The leaders were now ready, or as ready as they would ever be, to tackle the issue of a definitive judgement on Mao. A draft had been circulating for over a year and had been subject to much agonizing and revision. The final document, entitled a 'Resolution on Certain Historical Questions', was issued in June 1981 at the Sixth Plenum, which coincided with the sixtieth anniversary of the Party's foundation. It reviewed Party history and Mao's work since 1949. It trod delicately, distinguishing between early Mao (good) and later Mao (bad) and between the fallible Chairman on the one hand and the reliable Mao Zedong Thought on the other, the latter of course being a distillation of the experience of many revolutionaries, not just one man. As the painfully balanced clauses testified, it was, inevitably, a compromise.

The resolution broke new ground in blaming Mao for launching the Great Leap Forward and the Commune movement in 1958 without proper study and for purging Peng Dehuai in 1959. It also came clean in stating that Mao initiated and led the Cultural Revolution and, in a crucial passage, it described the movement as 'responsible for the most severe setback and heaviest losses suffered by the Party since the founding of the People's Republic'.

But such confessions were balanced by praise and evasions. Liu Shaoqi's death was ascribed to a frame-up by Lin Biao, Jiang Qing and their followers. Other leaders were blamed for acquiescing in Mao's decisions. A veil was drawn over the years 1949 to 1955, which were certainly not free from errors or purges. But the overall object was, while making a bow in the direction of the truth, to assert that Mao's virtues were primary, his faults secondary; also to show that the pain and the suffering of the years since Liberation had not been in vain.

A balance had been reached and it was neither practical nor

wise to press further. The primary constraint was that Mao was so bound up with the country's post-Liberation history that a thorough demolition job would have left a void. The leaders admitted as much in speeches and guidance material issued in advance of the Plenum. Mao Zedong Thought had to be upheld.

But there were other factors. The armed forces were getting restive. As has been noted, they did not relish the appearance of their former commanders in the dock beside Jiang Qing. They felt that they were not doing particularly well out of modernization. Along with many civilian cadres, they were not at ease with reformist ideology.

In particular they did not trust Hu Yaobang, the first of a new generation of leaders who were too young to have served at a senior level in the wars against Japan and Chiang Kaishek in the 1930s and 1940s. They had to be mollified. Press criticism of army attitudes was replaced by exhortation to emulate military heroes; an impressive series of military manoeuvres was held; and, significantly, Deng himself took over from Hua Guofeng as Chairman of the Military Affairs Commission, a post normally held by the Party Chairman.

The period 1980–1, which saw the trial of the Gang of Four and the judgement on Mao, was also, as it happened, one of political and economic strain. The economy was in serious trouble and had to undergo a painful adjustment. In addition, there was a political tightening up, designed no doubt to appease the more conservative cadres and reconcile them to economic experiment and the repudiation of Hua Guofeng.

It was also significant that the plans to hold 'Gang of Four'-type trials at provincial and lower levels were quietly shelved. Too many people had been involved in the Cultural Revolution. As an article at the time put it, during the Cultural Revolution 'some people fixed others, some were fixed by others, and some fixed others and were in turn fixed by still others . . . to settle all the scores accumulated in those ten years might be impossible, even with the aid of a computer.'

Deng had won his battles and had gone as far as he could go. But he was running into problems of a more lasting sort than those of correcting the verdicts of the 1960s and 1970s. How, among so much necessary revision, to maintain a respectable ideology? How to restore the Party's morale and prestige? How to avoid a destructive cynicism, especially among the young? He was also beginning to encounter the most critical question of all, namely how to invigorate the country's economy without losing Communist virtue.

CHAPTER THIRTEEN

The Seeds of Prosperity

CHINA'S ECONOMIC GROWTH has been so impressive since 1979 that we may be forgiven for thinking that it was bound to be a smooth advance once the Maoist chains had been cast off. But, for those of us watching in the early days, growth looked a much patchier affair, with many fits and starts; and even in the most successful sector, agriculture, the results took time to show.

The area of most immediate interest to foreigners was industrial development and here at first modernization seemed to offer glittering prospects. In his speech to the National People's Congress in February 1978, Hua Guofeng outlined a ten-year plan with a crash programme of construction. By 1980 China was to have a 'basically mechanized' agriculture. By 1985 one hundred and twenty new large-scale industrial projects (iron and steel complexes, coal mines, oilfields, harbours, etc.) were to be in operation. And so on. The plan had a whiff of the Great Leap Forward; indeed one of the ministers used those ominous words in presenting it. It also had some of the same faults, haste, over-ambition and the old-style, Stalinist concentration on heavy industry.

But, for the exporter, it was heady stuff. The business delegations poured in, were briefed at the Embassy, held their talks with the ministries and corporations, gave their return banquets at increasingly punitive prices, and left hopefully for home.

Sometimes they concluded contracts; but in most cases the Chinese would be non-committal though interested.

The Hua Guofeng plan was impracticable and at the turn of the year was seen to be so. At the Third Plenum in December Deng brought back to power the veteran Chen Yun, who since the 1950s had advocated measured economic development and had been responsible for the recovery policies after the Great Leap. Chen found serious imbalances in the economy. He also saw that the country was committed to far larger technology imports than it could afford. The target of sixty million tons of steel a year was dropped. Some big contracts were unilaterally cancelled. The ten-year plan had to go. And a general policy of 'readjustment' was introduced. This meant the abandonment of long-term planning in favour of a three-year period of more cautious advance, intended to permit the rectification of structural weaknesses and a later take-off into more balanced growth. The period was later extended.

'Readjustment' also meant a re-emphasis on agriculture and light industry at the expense of heavy industry, and, within heavy industry, stress on the infrastructure, that is, on energy, railways and ports.

Given the desperate nature of the underlying situation Deng inherited, the retrenchment was necessary and salutary: in 1979 one quarter of China's state-owned industries were making a loss; and the real earnings of staff and workers in the commercial and industrial sectors were lower than in 1965. But the move brought doubt and dismay to the visiting businessman.

I recall 1979 as a year of vast commercial efforts and modest returns, at least on the British side. Eric Varley came in February as Secretary of State for Industry, accompanied by a large group of senior industrialists. Certain general understandings were reached; but the visit coincided with China's border war against Vietnam and with the first pangs of readjustment. The Duke of Kent came in June to inspect the British Energy Exhibition with 700 businessmen and 364 stands, the first royal visit to China. My commercial staff, under the Commercial Counsellor, Trevor Mound, were indefatigable. Our exports rose; but the talk was increasingly of compensation-trading, buy-back and joint ventures; and we had to contend with the hesitations, revisions and sometimes total suspension of decisions imposed by the readjustment policy.

A controversial area, but one of particular interest to us and one where I myself was hopeful, was the sale of defence equipment. The Chinese military had their own modernization plans and Britain looked like being a favoured supplier. Vice-Premier Wang Zhen came to Britain in 1978, to date the most senior Chinese visitor we had had. A former guerrilla leader of legendary reputation, he became a notable hard-liner in subsequent internal struggles. None of this ferocity was apparent in our encounters; he was a charming old gentleman, who took to British life to the extent of acquiring a taste for smoked salmon and Stilton. He was interested in military purchases and made it plain that his government would like to buy Harriers.

In addition, the Chinese had plans for refitting fighter aircraft and destroyers. These were large and enticing prospects. But they acquired a mirage-like quality; they danced before our eyes; they kept changing; and they proved ultimately elusive.

The Harrier in particular caught the public and press imagination and became a symbol of our willingness to help China in the defence field. I worked hard to persuade Dr Owen of the case for sales; and was able to ensure that we reiterated our readiness to supply even during the Chinese hostilities against Vietnam, when Eric Varley made his visit. We also found that we faced high-level pressure from Mr Brezhnev to think again. I found this last approach a fascinating example of the kind of *droit de regard* the Russians would have liked to establish over Western Europe. Happily, it was brushed aside by Mr Callaghan and Dr Owen.

The real difficulties emerged, though slowly, on the Chinese side. They were becoming aware of the vast sums required if they were to re-equip their armed forces; it was also becoming clear that the PLA came last in the modernization queue. The talk began to turn away from sales of hardware and towards the transfer of technology. When Francis Pym visited China as Defence Minister in 1980 it was finally made clear that Harriers were not on the shopping list, though we were thanked for our steadfastness in the face of Soviet pressure.

The prospect of refitting fighters and destroyers remained. But even here, as time passed, substance diminished and doubts grew. In the end, in 1983, the contract for the destroyer refit was vetoed at the last stage by the State Council. It was mainly a matter of money; and even today the Chinese Defence Ministry, starved of hard currency, has had to resort to sales of dangerous technology in order to finance its purchases.

But while these revisions and retreats were in progress, the government was in fact conducting a series of experiments in an effort to tackle the underlying problems of its industrial base. It had two broad objectives: to shift decision-making power to smaller units; and to motivate the workforce.

In a socialist society with a strong Maoist legacy the problems were deep-seated and almost intractable. Industrial enterprises had virtually no powers of decision: they were the pawns of a bewildering network of central and regional government departments who, among them, disposed of such crucial matters as investment, prices, wages, the purchase of capital goods and the application of profits. Not only was there no real autonomy, there was no regard for profit or loss, no reward for efficiency or penalty for incompetence. The workers were assigned by the state rather than hired by the plant; they had a job for life, an 'iron rice-bowl'. Many were disaffected after the Cultural Revolution and nourished the resentments or feuds inherited from that time. Overmanning was endemic. To the Western observer the Chinese worker looked not industrious but idle; and the impression was not false.

Moreover, the larger economy was still infected by the virus of self-sufficiency. Mao, who thought in military terms, tended to see the country as a series of redoubts, with each province, regardless of its soil or climate, self-sufficient in grain, and every large industrial complex its own provider. This created something of a vicious spiral. Uncertainty of supply encouraged factories to manufacture their own spare parts and carry excessive stocks of raw materials. The lateral and inter-provincial links in the economy were meagre to non-existent and there was heavy duplication of effort.

To tackle these problems the government began to grant modest increases of autonomy to individual enterprises. Interestingly, the trials went furthest in Zhao Ziyang's province of Sichuan. Efficient factories were allowed to retain a percentage of their profits, once the state plan was fulfilled. Later, corporate taxation was tried, with the enterprise operating as an independent accounting unit. Even the idea of selling shares to workers was considered. Factories were allowed to advertise and to have direct contact with retail outlets. Those that could not sell their products were not automatically baled out. Links between industries and trades and, on the wider screen, between regions were encouraged.

The government now made it plain that it favoured light as against heavy industry: light industry demanded less raw material and energy supplies; it had greater export potential and could more easily mop up unemployment. Collectively owned businesses, frowned on in the past on ideological grounds, were now encouraged; privately owned restaurants and small service stations, like bicycle or television repair works, began to emerge. Street traders reappeared; hawkers sold toys and sweets; and, a great boon to us city dwellers, peasants were allowed to come into Peking and set up street markets. Their produce was more expensive than that in state outlets; but the quality was distinctly higher.

Much of this was experimental and tentative, with retreats as well as advances. Managers and Party officials were often cautious, if not hostile: if bonuses were earned by one group of workers in an enterprise, they would insist on bonuses for all; a venturesome entrepreneur might find himself on the wrong side of the law; and the more fundamental issues of prices and labour were not resolved; indeed the Chinese government is wrestling with them still. Industry was always a more complex area of reform than agriculture. But the trend was clear; and Zhao Ziyang, in a speech at the end of 1979, provided the ideological cover. He defined the essentials of socialism as public ownership of the means of production and a system of 'to each according to his work'. But public ownership did not mean owning all the economy, only the principal part; and outside these two basic principles, any system promoting production could be tried.

In accordance with this licence two measures were taken which were to have a profound and positive effect. The first was the law on joint ventures. This brought the socialist economy in direct contact with Western capital and management practices. The response from outside China was enthusiastic; but the first results were distinctly mixed. In many cases ventures foundered on the refractory nature of the Chinese workforce: lazy, untrained, negligent and unwilling. Or, if not the workforce, then the conservatism and inefficiency of the bureaucracy. But there were success stories as well as failures and gradually Western, and particularly Hong Kong, firms learned the tricks of the trade.

Even more important was the establishment of four special economic zones, in Guangdong near Hong Kong and in Fujian opposite Taiwan. Here a privileged regime applied: foreign companies were able to put up factories under their own ownership, staffed by Chinese workers. The zones had a particular appeal to overseas Chinese, many of whom had originated in those parts, and of course to Hong Kong and Taiwanese businessmen. For the government they were a conduit for the introduction of outside capital and technology. They were also designed to ease the political objectives of the eventual recovery and absorption of Hong Kong and Taiwan.

The zones were by definition discriminatory and seemed at first politically vulnerable, since they smacked of the treaty ports of the nineteenth century. But their success was striking, particularly in the case of Shenzhen. Further zones were later added along the coast and the result was growth which would critically affect the whole Chinese economy and could in the end influence the Chinese political system itself.

The main prize for the innovators, however, lay in agriculture and their success here became the distinguishing mark of Dengist reform.

For China, agriculture has always been of critical importance: seventy-five per cent of the people live on the land. A vast population has to be fed and kept contented, even though only a limited part of the country is actually suitable for farming. Chinese history is the story of a succession of dynasties terminated by peasant risings. For the Chinese Communists, the link was specially close: the peasants were the sea in which the Communist fish swam; and peasant support, based on a lively expectation of future benefits, was the key to the Communist victory against Chiang Kaishek.

When they came to power in 1949, the Communists expelled the landlords, and the peasants enjoyed their reward for that brief period which in the history of the Communist state comes between land distribution and forced collectivization. In China it was a shorter interlude than originally intended: Mao, as usual, was in a hurry and by the end of the 1950s almost the whole of the peasant population found itself pitchforked into advanced communes. The peasant was reduced to an almost landless labourer, retaining only a tiny private plot, which grew or dwindled according to the revolutionary temper of the times. Since he laboured for work points, which were secure if a certain number of hours of labour were completed, and were encashed only at the year's end, he had little inducement to produce more and concentrated his efforts on feeding himself.

Moreover, Mao's obsession with grain production meant that it was grown much too widely and at the expense of more appropriate crops and agricultural activities. In the model commune of Dazhai in Shaanxi province unsuitable hillsides were terraced with great labour and used as grain fields. The country was called on to emulate Dazhai and the obedient peasants of Inner Mongolia raised on their broad grasslands artificial hills, which they terraced in Dazhai style.

By the time of the Third Plenum in December 1978 the state of China's agriculture was dire. In 1977 the national average amount of food grain per person was slightly less than in 1957.

As in industry, the reformists began by devolving responsibility to smaller units. They instituted a system of contracts which provided that all produce over and above a certain quota could be sold by the peasants themselves, either to the state at a premium above the quota price, or in the free markets. The maximum size of private plots was doubled; and 'sideline' activities, usually pig and poultry rearing, workshops for agricultural machinery, or the processing of minor agricultural commodities, were encouraged, generally on a household basis. The new arrangements, which took a variety of forms, were known as 'responsibility systems'.

As time went on, the actual level of responsibility tended to move down, from the commune production team, comprising some thirty families, to smaller groups, around ten to fifteen adults, and then to the household. Originally it was intended that devolution to households should be confined to the poorer areas, but popular pressure ensured that it was applied much more widely.

At the same time the concentration on grain was abandoned; crops could be chosen to suit the land; and to facilitate this, the state announced its readiness to go on importing grain.

These relatively simple changes, small bows in the direction of human realities and economic sense, brought spectacular results. In 1980 and 1981, despite serious floods and drought, and despite a sharp reduction in acreage, grain production remained close to the record harvest of 1979. In the same period production of cash crops, such as cotton, sugar cane and oilseeds, rose dramatically. Vegetable supplies around the cities improved markedly, with produce of a quality city dwellers had not seen for years. In every town the free market became a scene of cheerful, bustling activity. And in the villages we began to see new housing, solid, impressive structures, which were the envy of city workers.

Ideologically, the cover was similar to that given industrial reform. It was pointed out that the land remained in common ownership; it could not be leased, sold or bequeathed. (In fact, after 1982 the authorities, in order to encourage investment, began to grant hereditary leases to peasant families for up to thirty years.) The principle of a unified agricultural plan, guiding the general strategy, was also retained. It was explained, correctly enough, that the new system was not a total departure and that its seeds were to be found in the early 1950s, or in the 'revisionist' interval between the Great Leap and the Cultural Revolution.

The peasants were naturally delighted, though many were uncertain how long the sun would shine and sought to cash in quickly, for example, by cutting down all the timber on the land assigned to them. The Party cadres, on the other hand, saw both their influence and their income diminished; some left their offices and went off to farm with their families; and conservatives of all kinds worried over the loss of Party control and the emergence of a new class of rich peasants.

Other difficulties emerged. The areas devoted to grain dropped too sharply and those given over to profitable cash crops grew too fast. In order to stimulate production, prices for crops were raised. But this meant higher subsidies to urban consumers in order to shield them from the increases; and the level of subsidies became the most thorny of economic and political issues.

As peasants went their own way, larger undertakings, such as irrigation, for which the collective had been well suited, proved harder to undertake. In some ways the responsibility system was better fitted for the rich south than the dry north of the country. And everywhere mechanization slowed down.

There were also social problems. Inevitably, some peasants did better than others. We had not yet reached the days of the rural millionaires, the 'ten thousand yuan households'; but the advantage lay with those with money to invest in the land and labour to exploit it. There were also disparities between one region and another: producers near cities, for example, flourished in a way that those in the deep countryside could not; and many areas of real poverty persisted. Military recruitment suffered. It was no longer a privilege to send sons to the PLA; they would be better employed in the fields. In some districts substantial cash grants had to be awarded to compensate families whose sons went for military service.

But the most serious long-term consequence was the clash between agricultural and birth-control policies. In 1982 the third national census revealed that there were a billion Chinese and that the population had virtually doubled since the Communist Party came to power in 1949. Mao, who saw strength in numbers, rejected any move toward population control and persecuted the academics and economists who advocated it, bore the main responsibility. The effect was a crippling economic strain: increased production would barely match the demands of the proliferating millions.

In order to meet the impending crisis the government introduced stringent family planning policies, backed by a draconian system of rewards and penalties. Each couple should have only one child. The aim was to keep the population to 1.2 billion at the end of the century.

This policy, if successful and maintained, would have meant a basic change in the social structure; it would also have required vast expenditure on welfare services to support the parents and grandparents of the one-child families. It was probably an unrealizable target at the best of times. In the cities controls could operate, though even here young couples worried about how they would be supported in their old age; in the countryside it was a different matter. The new responsibility systems made it unworkable: the traditional peasant preference for large families was heavily reinforced. The household wanted more field hands; sons were even more necessary; and the old practice of female infanticide revived.

These were all qualifications – some, like population control, very serious qualifications – on the success of agricultural reform. But success it undoubtedly was, recognized as such internationally as well as in China. It offered a precedent to Mr Gorbachev, which, unhappily, he was unable or unwilling to follow. At home in China it meant not only greater wealth but also greater stability. The new agricultural systems had come to stay; it is hard to see a reversal being tolerated. And though there was to be resentment in the late 1980s over new grain quotas and payment by letters of credit rather than cash, on the whole the peasants were to rest content with their holdings and new opportunities. This was to be a crucial factor in the disturbances of 1989: the peasants remained indifferent. Had a restive countryside then been added to student demonstrations and military doubts, we could have seen the end of another dynasty.

CHAPTER FOURTEEN

Hegemonists, Large and Small

THE FOREIGN OFFICE has a rule that at the end of the year the Ambassador addresses a short despatch to the Secretary of State, setting out the main developments within his country over the past twelve months. It is called the Annual Review. The Ambassador is also asked to devote his final paragraphs to the future and to tell ministers not only what has happened, but also what is going to happen. This last requirement makes it an impossible, but useful exercise.

I remember adding a paragraph about Vietnam to the Annual Review for 1978. I said I found the situation worrying. Since arriving in June I had listened to Chinese ministers and officials speaking about Vietnam in a curious way, both emotional and fatalistic; they had given it up and regarded it now as within the Soviet camp. I thought China's relations with Vietnam were bound to get worse; the only question, as I saw it, was whether there would be full-scale hostilities. On balance, I thought not. The Chinese would want tension on the border in order to check the Vietnamese in Cambodia; but a war would be a major gamble, in effect a proxy war with the Soviet Union; and it would be ruinous to modernization plans.

Though I drastically shortened the odds against war in the following weeks, that forecast at the turn of the year was wrong. On 17 February 1979 the Chinese government launched over 100,000 men into Vietnam in a punitive attack and kept them there for more than two weeks. The Chinese, who sometimes have a quaint turn of phrase, called it a 'limited counter-attack in self-defence'. Others preferred to call it the Sino-Vietnamese border war. It was the first upset to the sweetness and light which had attended China's early modernization efforts and it coloured our estimates of China's foreign policy over the next years.

The choice of antagonist was in many ways surprising. During the long American involvement in Vietnam the Chinese had repeatedly proclaimed their brotherhood and unqualified solidarity with Hanoi. 'As close as lips and teeth' was the way their spokesmen put it. Precious aid had been dispensed, even during the Cultural Revolution. Between 40,000 and 50,000 Chinese troops in Vietnam strengthened the anti-aircraft defences and kept the rail links with China in working order; and one of the Soviet charges that most nettled Peking was that they were interfering with Russian military supplies to Vietnam crossing China by rail.

But in fact the brotherhood was recent and the solidarity qualified. Historically, Vietnam had formed part of the Chinese Empire and Vietnam's traditional heroes and heroines had made their names in wars of resistance against the Chinese. China for its part did not want a strong power as its southern neighbour. During the long struggle against the French and the Americans the Vietnamese had detected a disturbing readiness on the part of Peking to contemplate the existence of two Vietnamese states, one, socialist, in the north and one, distinctly less so, in the south. Now America's departure had opened up the way for the Vietnamese to realize Ho Chi Minh's ambition, namely to bring all Indo-China under Hanoi's domination. From the Chinese point of view this was unwelcome; in particular it threatened the Khmer Rouge regime in Cambodia, which enjoyed Chinese backing. Moreover, Vietnam, impoverished by its wars, was becoming even more heavily dependent on Moscow for economic and military aid.

In these circumstances Sino-Vietnamese relations began to revert to the older historical pattern, with Vietnam resisting the great power to the north and China intent on preserving paramountcy on its southern flank.

During the summer I heard repeated outbursts from the Chinese about the persecution and expulsion of ethnic Chinese inside Vietnam. In July, Vietnam joined Comecon (Moscow's Council of Mutual Economic Assistance) and in November signed a friendship treaty with the Soviet Union. This last move must have convinced the Chinese that the situation was irretrievable; and Chinese aid to Vietnam was brought to an end. There were clashes between Vietnamese forces and those of China's client, Cambodia. Finally, the Vietnamese mounted a brief and successful invasion of Cambodia in December, occupied Phnom Penh and installed a puppet regime. This blitzkrieg was a painful blow to China's prestige and presented a challenge the government felt it could not fail to take up. We began to hear of incidents on the Sino-Vietnamese border and Chinese warnings grew increasingly stern.

There were good arguments why, despite the growing tension, we should see no more than sabre-rattling. Large-scale military action against Vietnam would be hazardous: the Vietnamese were better armed and had more recent battle experience. Soviet-Vietnamese links would be strengthened and the Russians would have pretexts for military intervention. Chinese relations with the West would be endangered and modernization plans, which were supposed to enjoy absolute priority, would be jeopardized.

On the other hand, the Chinese were deeply concerned at the spread of Soviet influence worldwide and at the West's apparent inability to stem it. Traditionally, they were extremely sensitive about hostile activity in countries on their periphery. In this case it conjured up the spectre of the Russians and the Vietnamese co-operating in a giant pincer movement, the one in the north, the other in the south-west. They no doubt felt that China's credibility as a major power was at stake. And they presumably judged that they could mount an attack strong enough to give Vietnam pause without provoking a serious Soviet military response, though it was a nice calculation. They seem to have had in mind the precedent of their war with India in 1962, when the Chinese armies inflicted dramatic defeats on the Indians and then withdrew.

Deng was warned of the dangers of military action when he visited the United States in January, but he was not very responsive. Both in America and in Japan on his way home he spoke of the need to punish Vietnam, as he put it, to 'shrink their swollen heads'. Presumably the final decision was taken shortly after his return. He would have wanted to have the visit behind him and its benefits secured before moving; and he seems to have given some advance warning to the Japanese government.

The Chinese leaders opted for action rather than threats. They no doubt judged that relations with the United States and the rest of their Western backers would be bruised, but would recover quickly. In this and in most of their other assessments they were right.

The invasion itself, however, was far from a model of the art of war and a long way below the standards of the Sino-Indian conflict. The Chinese prevailed by sheer weight of numbers. They captured and laid waste four provincial capitals and penetrated some fifteen miles into Vietnam. They then withdrew in good order. But they did not perform particularly well. Chinese weapons systems were shown to be outdated and their communications were faulty. They lost at least 20,000 killed and wounded. I asked the Foreign Trade Minister, Li Qiang, whom I was entertaining during Eric Varley's visit, whether they were not losing a lot of young men in Vietnam. He laughed his high-pitched laugh and said: 'We have a lot more.' It was a messy operation.

During the fighting the Chinese were careful to keep the temperature down: there were no great speeches or rallies; and, fortunately, the Russians played the part assigned them. They blustered, called on China to withdraw before it was too late and implied that there were limits the Chinese could not transgress without calling down direct intervention. But those limits were never set and it was at the same time made plain that in the Soviet view the Vietnamese were capable of looking after themselves, though of course with full Soviet material and moral support. The Chinese told me that the Russians probably found themselves in a dilemma: small-scale attacks, say in Xinjiang, would be easily dealt with; only a major Soviet conventional attack could make an impact. But this would sink large Russian forces in the Chinese morass and put undue weight on what was for the Russians a secondary front. I did not find this analysis entirely convincing; but the fact remains that the Chinese got away with it.

They could claim that they had achieved a number of their

objectives. They had inflicted heavy damage on Vietnam and had mauled Vietnamese forces, including some regular divisions. They had demonstrated the limits of Soviet power and had raised doubts about Soviet reliability as an ally. By stretching Vietnamese forces they had encouraged the Cambodian resistance and at the same time reassured Thailand and other ASEAN countries that Vietnamese expansion would not go unchecked. They had done all this without permanently damaging relations with the West or interfering with the modernization programme.

But the arguments were not all one way. Chinese forces had suffered heavy punishment. The government had taken high risks with the country's international relations and with international stability. And though China's record as a large but non-expansionist power is on the whole a good one, the operation revived fears in the outside world of a more militarist China. At the least, observers felt that Deng's China might be inclined to use military power too lightly. And the new Vietnamese empire did not fall apart: they maintained their control over Cambodia and strengthened their hold on Laos; their dependence on the Russians grew; and Soviet ships began regular use of Vietnamese naval facilities at Cam Ranh Bay. There were significant entries on the debit side.

Moreover, the prospects were forbidding. It was now clear that the border war was only a symptom of a broader and deeper clash of interests, the outcome of which the Chinese probably regarded as critical for their national security. They had shown that they were not prepared to tolerate the emergence of a united Indo-China controlled by a Vietnam closely aligned with the Soviet Union. A bitter struggle therefore impended. In Cambodia the Chinese would plan for a long and ultimately successful guerrilla war. On the Sino-Vietnamese border tension would have to be maintained and we could not rule out the possibility of further 'lessons'.

As will have been plain, the background to this crisis in the south was China's entrenched hostility to its neighbour on the long northern frontier. The Russians were the big hegemonists, the Vietnamese the little hegemonists; and the Chinese Foreign Ministry pressed for anti-hegemony clauses in all its treaties and communiqués. The statement in February 1979, after Deng's visit to the United States, affirmed that the two governments were 'opposed to efforts by any country or group of countries to establish hegemony or domination over others'.

A more vivid name than 'big hegemonist' was the 'polar bear' and in an interview with *Time* magazine during the same visit, Deng urged an anti-Soviet front: 'If we really want to be able to place curbs on the polar bear, the only realistic thing for us is to unite.'

We had come a long way from the China of the 1960s when, of the two superpowers, America had looked the more dangerous and American involvement in Vietnam seemed to presage an escalation and expansion of the war to include Chinese territory. Now the Americans were out of Vietnam and closely engaged in helping the four modernizations.

With the Russians, however, relations had gone from bad to worse. The old ideological dispute had by the late 1960s taken on a simpler and more brutal character, that of military confrontation. Soviet forces along the frontier (still disputed) had been substantially reinforced, and Czechoslovakia in 1968 demonstrated that the Russians had the will and, in the Brezhnev doctrine, the pretext to intervene in aberrant socialist states. The clashes on the Ussuri and in Xinjiang in 1969 underlined the point. The resulting sense of threat was a major factor in the Chinese *rapprochement* with the United States, and the assessment of the Soviet Union as the principal external danger became in practice the key judgement of Chinese foreign policy.

Chinese publicly proclaimed doctrine was rather different. According to Mao's Theory of the Three Worlds, the United States and the Soviet Union, the two superpowers, were denizens of the First World. China belonged to the Third World. Japan, Europe and other developed countries lay in between, in the Second World. The two superpowers alternately colluded and contended, seeking world hegemony. Their collusion could only be temporary and relative; their contention was permanent and absolute. China was not a superpower and would never seek to be one.

These were the sacred texts, but they seemed to me to bear little relation to China's practice. Its real concerns lay with Washington and Moscow and, though its officials would disclaim any interest in or indeed knowledge of triangular diplomacy,

Chinese leaders were, as Dr Kissinger observed, skilled practitioners in the art. What they thought about in the watches of the night were not the obscure feuds of Yemen or Chad, but their country's relations with the big power centres. China saw itself not as a Third World power but as a superpower *manqué*; and its object was by all means, but particularly with the help of rich Western states and Japan, to climb back to its proper position in the scheme of things. China too was prepared to collude and contend.

In this struggle the Chinese saw the United States as the principal counterweight to the Soviet Union, not only as a source of funds and technology, but also as a source of security, for example, against possible Russian nuclear threats to China and as a means of reducing US-Soviet collusion and preventing a US-Soviet condominium. They may also have hoped to erode Taiwan's position. It was a tactical move: they retained all their ideological reservations about the leading capitalist state; but, for the time being at least, the advantages of Sino-US co-operation were overriding.

They were anxious to engage other major powers in the same cause of unity against the polar bear. The Sino-Japanese Friendship Treaty ensured Japanese commitment. In Western Europe they advocated closer economic and political union and approved of NATO. They went further and were prepared to come to terms with 'imperialism' and 'colonialism': the residual US presence in the Far East was accepted; French and Belgian intervention in Zaire was applauded.

Meantime they dissected Soviet policy with the total realism reserved by one Communist government for analysis of the activities of another. They recorded the steady build-up of Soviet arms and the lengthening list of Soviet Third World interventions. When SALT II was concluded in the summer of 1979 they said they were not opposed; but the agreement would not stop the Russians. To them *détente* Russian-style was a fraud, a device to pursue Soviet objectives while lulling the West into inactivity and delusion. They were not impressed by President Carter: Deng thought Iran was lost through American weakness and feared that Saudi Arabia might be another casualty. Above all, they regretted the relative decline in American military power and, as they saw it, the erosion of the American will to use that power.

To China in such a mood, the Soviet invasion of Afghanistan in December 1979 came as a vindication but as no great surprise. In the presentations on the state of the world to which the Foreign Ministry treated the visitors I took to see them, there had always been a long section about Soviet activities in Afghanistan; it rarely evoked a response. Now they could watch as the scales fell from Western eyes.

They explained the invasion as part of long-laid Soviet plans to gain control of the Gulf, outflank Western Europe and extend hegemony into Asia. They noted, as we did, that a new, qualitative stage had been reached in Soviet expansion: the victim was not a bloc member, but a non-aligned Muslim country with which the Russians had a treaty of friendship and co-operation; surrogates were not employed; the war was waged and the country occupied and run by Soviet troops. China would have nothing to do with Western ideas of neutralizing Afghanistan like Austria; it demanded unconditional Soviet withdrawal.

Afghanistan brought a quickening in politico-military co-operation between Washington and Peking. Harold Brown, President Carter's Defence Secretary, came to Peking in January 1980 and spoke of American readiness to co-ordinate action with China in shoring up areas in Asia under Soviet or Soviet-supported threat, particularly Pakistan and Thailand. He also said that the United States was prepared to give China preference over the Soviet Union in the supply of advanced technology. A little later the administration indicated its readiness to supply selected items of military support equipment. There was also a secret agreement establishing a listening post, manned by Chinese, in Xinjiang to monitor Soviet rocket tests; this was designed to take the place of American facilities lost in Iran when the Shah fell. Co-operation was becoming a tacit alliance.

But, in the event, there was no substantial advance in relations beyond that point. China's relative weakness *vis-à-vis* Moscow and Washington limited the amount of great power business to be transacted in Peking. China was a regional, not a global power; agreements on nuclear arms and world stability lay between Washington and Moscow. Moreover, the Chinese before long took some small steps towards repairing state relations with the Soviet Union; they doubtless felt that the Americans should not have the sole run of the triangle. Above all, with the appearance of President Reagan, relations between the United States and Taiwan revived and flourished. US recognition of Taiwan was only narrowly averted; and US arms sales to Taiwan became a chronic problem, which was papered over from time to time rather than solved.

For the last two years or so of my stay in Peking, China's foreign policy took on a rather different style and tone, emphasizing China's links with the Third World. There was a steady flow of Third World rhetoric; Chinese leaders became diligent attenders at Third World functions; and there was a tendency to criticize the United States and the Soviet Union in the same breath.

I did not believe it amounted to very much in practice. Where matters were serious, as in South-east Asia, the opposition to Soviet influence remained the key. The main elements of China's world view had not changed: the awareness of the Soviet threat; the pursuit of friendly relations with Western countries; and the wish to preserve Sino-US ties, though not at any cost. A Third World policy was a convenient fall-back when relations with one superpower remained bad and those with another delicate.

Nor was China, a nuclear power with a permanent seat on the Security Council, entirely convincing in a Third World role. Set on a course of modernization with Western help, it could no longer stand as a shining example of radical purity, or offer the poorer countries an alternative course of development. The Chinese were cutting back their aid, taking the view that charity begins at home; and, as usual, they did not get on well with the Africans, whose diplomats and students in Peking continued to feel themselves the victims of lively racial prejudice.

The Third World approach certainly coloured the Chinese attitude to the Falklands War, when the government showed a strong partiality for Argentina. I was able to make little progress at the Foreign Ministry, and my analogies with Vietnam and Vietnamese claims to the Spratly Islands in the South China Sea failed to persuade. But public condemnation masked much quiet admiration for our military prowess.

It was a strange and worrying time for our small British community, as, I am sure, for many others like it across the world. We lived for the early morning broadcasts from the World

Service of the BBC, and as the fleet neared the Falklands and the losses mounted it took some courage to turn the set on. Diplomatic colleagues showed interest, but not always of a friendly kind. I recall the snide question: 'And how far has the fleet got today, Ambassador?' There was an audience waiting for our discomfiture. And, privately, one realized the risks were enormous. The historical parallels gave no comfort: would it be like the Russian fleet in 1904, sailing round the world to be destroyed at Tsushima? The thought that centuries of military glory might end in defeat at the end of the world at the hands of a South American republic was not to be borne.

So, with public composure, though some private nightmares, we went about our work. When the landing was achieved, however, there was no need to pretend. The Chinese Vice Foreign Minister, Zhang Wenjin, came to dinner to talk about Hong Kong. He asked about the war and I was able to tell him that we were ashore and that now it was only a matter of time. He was startled at the confidence. But it was instinctive and not misplaced. A little while later, we held a small party for the staff to celebrate a great feat of arms and the news of the birth of an heir to the throne, both happy events falling about the same time.

CHAPTER FIFTEEN

Five Years On

THUS WITH THE year seasons returned and the Embassy moved through its annual cycle of fixtures and festivals, half-Chinese, half-British: the Christmas pantomime; the Boxing Day lunch for the British community at the Summer Palace; Chinese New Year; June and the reception in the Residence garden for the Queen's Birthday; National Day in October.

And with the seasons came the visitors, flowing steadily in, reaching a peak in spring and autumn, but always plentiful. They were of all kinds, ministers and Members of Parliament, business leaders and bankers, actors and musicians, academics and soldiers, mountaineers and football teams. There was vast British interest in the country and a fund of goodwill, on which the Chinese, if they were not being deliberately perverse, could draw with confidence. A reforming and liberalizing China added to the appeal.

On the whole, the hosts handled their charges well. The tourists were despatched, under the care of China Travel Service, to the gardens of Suzhou, or the lake at Hangzhou, or to the first Emperor's tomb at Xian. Those more favoured could go down the Yangtze gorges or follow the Silk Road to Dunhuang. The marvels were all there; in fact there were so many archaeological treasures that the difficulty lay in housing them suitably once excavated; and it was thought better to leave a great number in identified sites below ground.

Strangely, for such a bureaucratic administration, programmes were remarkably improvised and sketchy, often rough outlines first produced at the airport with the welcoming party. For one of the most substantial ministerial visits, that of Francis Pym, there was, I recall, no written programme at all. On the day, of course, arrangements were always smooth and efficient; but there were heart-searchings beforehand, particularly in the case of royal visitors, who liked these things precisely mapped out in advance.

In Peking, more important delegations, after their normal business, would be accorded a meeting with a leader in the Great Hall of the People, or, more rarely, in the leadership complex at Zhongnanhai. These were heavily ritualized occasions. They would rarely be on the programme, such as it was, but left to be conferred as a mark of favour at the last moment. There would be a group photograph. Then the party, in precise protocol order, would be led in to take their seats on one side of a large horseshoe ring of heavily stuffed armchairs, with the principals at the centre.

Green tea would be served. The leader would often smoke heavily and spittoons would be available and sometimes used. The Chinese spoken might be of an unfamiliar kind, with a heavy provincial accent, causing difficulties even to the home side. The higher one moved up the hierarchy, the greater the problem of interpretation.

The leader would be well briefed: the machine worked efficiently and he would be aware of the detail of lower-level discussions. But his own disquisition would usually be bland and generalized, a benevolent exposition of certain principles of Chinese policy. There would be little give-and-take and a marked absence of curiosity about conditions or policies on the visitor's side. Only the delegation heads would speak; the rest would listen in respectful silence. The didactic tone, the sense of condescension, of a favour being conferred, was reminiscent of audiences in imperial China given to tribute-bearing envoys. But the guests normally went away well pleased.

Some were so taken with what they saw on their visits, and the ease and affability of their hosts, that they would tell me that the Chinese had found the secret of modern living. When I thought of the pressures of Chinese life and the Chinese I knew

1. The Office of the British Chargé d'Affaires festooned, June 1966. The slogans read 'Down with British Imperialism!' and 'Down with Soviet Revisionism!'

2. Meeting the masses, summer 1966. Scene outside the Chancery building, Tony Blishen and Len Appleyard on duty

3. The Halls of Diplomacy: the British Mission, August 1967

4. Donald Hopson and staff, October 1967. The background is the Registry door where the masses came in and we came out.

5. 'The Rogues Gallery'. Cultural Revolution art: in the sedan chair and litter, Liu Shaoqi and Deng Xiaoping; on the bicycle, Wang Guangmei; Yang Shangkun with headphones; Luo Ruiqing in the basket

6. The Queen's Birthday Party, June 1980. Ambassador and wife engage the senior guests: Ambassador with Liu Shaoqi's widow, Wang Guangmei; Birthe with Vice Foreign Minister Han Kehua. The Trade Minister, Li Qiang, momentarily neglected

7. Ambassador and staff, Peking, summer 1983

8. Hong Kong: the first soundings. Deng Xiaoping and Sir Murray MacLehose, March 1979

9. Hong Kong negotiations, the first encounter. Deng Xiaoping and Mrs Thatcher, September 1982. In the background, Ambassador Ke Hua and Vice Foreign Minister Zhang Wenjin

10. Hong Kong negotiations, second session, July 1983. The first photo-call. On my right, Sir Edward Youde and Robin Maclaren; opposite, Yao Guang

11. Hong Kong negotiations, the London team, September 1984. *Left to right*: Jonathan Powell, Olivia Walker, Christopher Hum, Tony Galsworthy, author, Trevor Mound, Richard Hoare, Jane-Ann Klowek and Anthony Forester-Bennett

12. Hong Kong negotiations, a celebration toast. Zhao Ziyang and Mrs Thatcher, December 1984

13. Signature of the Joint Declaration, December 1984. Behind Mrs Thatcher, David Blunt, author, Sir Richard and Lady Evans, Lady Howe

14. The Adviser's lonely road.
Exercise at the Summer Palace
during the 'secret visit' of
December 1989

15. Hong Kong Airport Agreement, June 1991. Discussion with General Secretary Jiang
Zemin. To the left, Sir Robin Maclaren; to the right, Lu Ping

well, in their private moments, watchful, chain-smoking, hag-ridden by memories of past purges and fears of purges to come, ceaselessly manouevring for small material advantages in conditions of deprivation and tight surveillance, I confess I wondered at the judgement. But it was a tribute to the Chinese people, to their resilience, good humour and adaptability, their capacity to enjoy simple pleasures; and, in a more general sense, it was evidence that the country could still cast its spell.

Of the procession of visitors who passed through the Embassy the vast majority were a bonus, stimulating and accommodating, opening up new areas of information or access to the Chinese. Only one or two felt that their importance had not been recognized and that they had not been appropriately received. To the last category belonged Robert Maxwell, who wanted me to secure him an immediate interview with Deng Xiaoping and felt that there had been inadequate Embassy attendance at the exhibition in Peking held by one of his many firms. Since I was simultaneously entertaining Norman Tebbit and a government delegation celebrating the opening of the British Airways route to Peking, I had had to ration my time with him and he left, after an angry scene, full of complaints to ministers.

But against this tiny deficit entry, there was a long list of satisfied guests.

Harold Macmillan came, insisting that he was doing so as a publisher, not an ex-Prime Minister. The Chinese drew on their deep experience of men of that seniority and provided an attendant nurse. When he arrived and stood swaying at the head of the aircraft steps, I confess I had a moment of doubt. But I should have known better; that was just part of the deliberate act of frailty; he proved perfectly spry. I gave a lunch for him, attended by Liu Shaoqi's widow, Wang Guangmei, and by all the previous Chinese Heads of Mission in London. As the Chinese speeches ran on he pulled at my sleeve and asked whether he was not going to have a chance to say something. I assured him that was the whole purpose and he gave a brilliant little speech, which bore all the marks of careful improvisation.

Edward Heath was a regular visitor. As the Prime Minister under whom we had upgraded relations to ambassadorial level and vacated Taiwan, he had a permanent tick against his name in the Chinese books. In April 1982 Deng used him to pass on important messages about Hong Kong.

James Callaghan, who visited us in May 1980, was entertained by Hua Guofeng and was naturally unwilling to believe that by this time his host, like Lord Goderich, his English predecessor in the 1820s, was 'a transient and embarrassed phantom'. But so it was. Soon after the guest left and after a final visit to Japan in the summer, Hua went his way and was replaced by Zhao Ziyang.

In September 1980 in Shanghai we had the first fleet visit since 1949 and Birthe and I were entertained by Rear-Admiral Jenkin on board the light cruiser *Antrim*, which was later to figure in the Falklands War. Also in the flotilla was HMS *Coventry*, one of the tragic victims. The East China fleet and the Shanghai garrison put on a splendid theatrical performance and acrobatic show for all ranks, complete with excellent renderings in English of traditional British songs and shanties. 'Oh! No John, No John, No John, No!' brought the house down. I was anxiously asked by the Chinese director whether I could understand the words. Puzzled, I said: 'Of course.' It was only then that he explained that the singers knew no English; they had simply memorized the sounds.

Sino-British cultural relations flourished. English was the language in demand, and, if possible, English English, not the other varieties. There was endless scope for our language teachers. The British Council, back in China after some decades, and operating from a reconstituted shed at the rear of our shabby premises, did wonders under Keith Hunter and later Adrian Johnson. There were British films at the cinemas, *Jane Eyre* and *Oliver Twist*, 'the orphan of the foggy city' to the Chinese. The Festival Ballet and the Old Vic came and Derek Jacobi starred in *Hamlet*. Many Chinese companies gave their own interpretations of Shakespeare, to which I was regularly invited. Lord Carrington, after a gruelling day of talks on his visit in 1981, was entertained with *Measure for Measure* in Chinese, not the easiest of plays in its native tongue. But he took it in his stride. Indeed he struck back, by thanking the assembled company at the end for their excellent Japanese rendering. Even the imperturbable interpreter paused for a fraction of a second. There was yet more exotic fare for Sir Kenneth Cork, the former

Lord Mayor of London and great company doctor, who found himself with a free evening in Shanghai. His hosts, who had done their homework, had discovered his links with the Royal Shakespeare Company; and he was carried off to a performance of *Romeo and Juliet* in Tibetan.

One visit I remember with special pleasure. Hugh Thomas came to China in 1982 and since he was a distinguished historian, as well as an old friend from Cambridge days, I took him on a tour of the old Chinese capitals. He saw not only Xian and Loyang, but also the Song tombs at Gongxian. We went further back in time, to the Shang capital at Anyang and to the even earlier one at Zhengzhou, with its grim relics of human sacrifice. We enquired about the traces of the first dynasty, the Xia, for which the Chinese archaeologists felt there was good evidence. In the icy little museum at Anyang we gazed on the oracle bones, on which, in the first known forms of Chinese writing, are preserved the questions the Shang kings put to the gods, and sometimes their answers. One in particular held our attention. It was simple and poignant: 'Will there be a disaster in the next ten days?' We experienced a strong fellow feeling with the questioner. The world had not changed much over the intervening millennia; nor had the business of prediction.

What was the state of Deng's China at the end of 1983, more than five years on from my first encounter with it? At the most obvious visual level it was of course vastly changed. As the visitor drove from the airport he saw that the great hoardings that had carried the words of Mao were now covered by advertisements for Japanese fridges or Hennessy cognac. On billboards or on television, pictures of seductive Chinese ladies proclaimed the virtues of soaps and cosmetics. Foreign and local consumer goods were available in quantity and the message was that there was virtue in selling and buying them. Big new hotels were going up, one or two with foreign management and run in the Hong Kong fashion, not as the old Russian barracks. In Peking there was even a branch of Maxim's.

Dress had radically altered. Louche young men in T-shirts and sunglasses belonged to a new, non-revolutionary world. The girls had taken to high heels, smart dresses, curls and make-up. Even the PLA and the police were out of their workmanlike fatigues and arrayed in elaborate uniforms, with much gold braid. There was Western-style dancing, Taiwan or Hong Kong hit-tunes, portable radios and ghetto-blasters. The noise was still there, but its content was very different.

There was greater access and openness. There were now direct flights into Peking from Western capitals and from Hong Kong. On television every evening there would be ten minutes of straight international news, provided by Viznews in Britain and ABC in the United States, to balance the heavily slanted domestic product. There were many more foreigners about, not just official delegations and tourists, but resident businessmen and experts. China was now a member of the international financial organizations and in receipt of Western aid. Western oilmen, prospecting in the South China Sea, congregated in Canton and there were usually visiting Japanese businessmen in any sizeable provincial town.

In the countryside the communes had gone, the cash crops increased and the peasants, or most of them, grew richer. They could hold contracted land for a period of at least fifteen years and that land could be transferred from one household to another. Enterprising peasants were setting up small factories or transport businesses and were praised by the government for doing so. The advice was: 'Get rich by working hard. Have no fear of becoming prosperous.' With greater freedom, old beliefs and superstitions were reviving. There were reports of shrines to local deities and spirits being rebuilt and of renewed worship of the God of Wealth and the Goddess of Childbirth.

In the towns the street markets flourished and the street traders, condemned in the past as 'the tails of capitalism', were back in strength. There were privately run restaurants and inns and even agencies providing cooks and nannies for better-off families. Most important, the non-state sector of the economy, that of the collective and private enterprises, was assuming an ever larger role in the overall scene and growing much faster than its state-run counterpart.

Education and learning were again officially respected and the authorities were out to woo the intellectuals, recognizing them as the key to modernization. Mao had condemned intellectuals as 'the stinking ninth category', below landlords, capitalists and reactionaries; and the Cultural Revolution had left them all spiritually and often physically scarred. Now they were classed as 'theoretical workers' and Hu Yaobang offered them better status and salaries. These were encouraging moves, though the intellectuals, who had been courted in the past only to be savagely repressed, remained very wary; and the authorities themselves were determined to keep this volatile element in society on a tight ideological rein. They were kinder to scientists than to artists and writers, whose work brought them nearer the fault-line between literature and politics.

The backdrop to these material and social changes was of course the radical transformation of the political scene. Deng was now supreme. The Party Secretary, Hu Yaobang, and the Prime Minister, Zhao Ziyang, were his men. Hua Guofeng, the 'What-everists', the Gang of Four had all been dealt with. Mao himself had been judged and substantially devalued; his victims had been formally rehabilitated. There was political correction as well as economic reform and, as usual in China on the accession of a new dynasty, history had been rewritten.

In many ways it was an easier, more comfortable China – freed from Maoist dogma, given greater rein to exercise natural enterprise and instincts for self-enrichment. But one Maoist legacy, the extra hundreds of millions born since 1949, could not be shrugged off. A billion Chinese, sixty-five per cent under thirty, made necessary draconian and unpopular birth-control policies, which agricultural reform was making even less workable.

Modernization had other dark sides. There was more street crime; it had never been absent, but had seemed so to the foreigner. Now there were admissions of serious official concern at the crime wave and reports of gangs operating, not only in individual cities, but across the country. There were also highly publicized 'prosecution rallies' and exemplary punishments. At one of these occasions a grandson of Marshal Zhu De was executed.

There was a great increase in smuggling: antiques and stolen cultural relics on the outward journey; watches, tape-recorders and television sets on the inward run. Money mattered, perhaps too much. The visitor discovered that there were two kinds of prices, one for the Chinese, one for the foreigner, with the latter set as high, or a little higher, than the market would bear. The mountaineers hiring their yaks or the businessmen giving their banquets encountered the same hard-faced pursuit of foreign currency. In the same cause beauty spots were being disfigured by some of the grosser touches of modern commercialism. Prostitution was returning to the cities; and pollution, which had been growing for many years, now, with rapid economic development and greater visibility, had become a recognized and acute danger.

Corruption had become widespread and was believed, on good grounds, to involve the families of the highest cadres. There were campaigns against it, but somehow they never reached beyond middle-level officials. 'Swatting flies, not catching tigers' was the popular comment.

Behind the corruption and the nepotism lay an even more serious problem, in effect a crisis of faith. The wholesale changes of line over the past years, the reversal of verdicts and the attendant revelations had destroyed the idealism and spirit of dedication that had been a mark of the early Communist regime. 'The homely beauty of the good old cause' was gone. In its place, patriotism apart, there was a void, or rather a corrosive cynicism, plus a lively wish to do well out of the new situation. This was particularly true of the young. The Party had become merely the necessary adjunct to a successful career, the established church in a non-believing age. Who now believed in the superiority of the socialist system? It was an article of faith, but it was conceded officially that there were doubts among all ranks. There was talk of a 'Three Belief Crisis' (belief in the Party, confidence in socialism, trust in Party cadres). Campaigns to restore discipline and morality were of no avail and attempts to invoke once again the spirit of Lei Feng, that selfless and improbable soldier hero of the early 1960s, made no impression.

Nor was it, despite the brighter surface, a thoroughly new China. The fundamentals had not changed; the essential features of the socialist state were still there. Though my visitors usually overlooked these aspects, and were meant to do so, it remained a ruthlessly authoritarian regime, as the brave voices of the Peking Spring had discovered. The familiar apparatus of the Party, the secret police and the labour camps was still there to ensure order. Democracy meant democratic centralism. The individual was still under tight supervision, pinned down between his work unit on the one hand and the local street committee on the other, trying to exploit the reforms and the new contacts with foreigners so as to achieve a slightly greater measure of comfort or freedom for himself and his family. Deng's object was economic growth, but always within a frame-work of tough political discipline.

There were also older continuities, those imposed by history and geography. Between China and the outside world there was still a great gulf of culture and perception, independent of the distortions imposed by Marx and Lenin and Mao. Despite the ritual assurances of openness and readiness to learn from the West, I was often struck by the resemblance to the experiences of my first predecessor, Lord Macartney, when in 1793 he tried to establish meaningful relations with Qian Long and his offi-cials. My colleagues and staff, penned in the modern equivalent of the Barbarian Hostel, would have readily agreed. It was partly the bureaucratic formalism, partly the hierarchy and secrecy; but occasionally, and most revealingly, the tone, showing that for many Chinese, and among those the most important, China was still a sufficient world to itself and, conceptually at least, still the centre of things.

Change, then, was spectacular, but not yet basic. The tide of political reform had reached a certain point, then paused, or even perhaps ebbed a little. The reservations in the judgement on Mao marked the water-line.

There were plans for more political reform to go hand in hand with the economic changes, just as there were plans for rectifying the Party so as to remove the large number of unqualified or leftist members who had enlisted during the Cultural Revolution and the time of troubles. But they did not get very far. The great mass of middle-level cadres were opposed to change and wanted only to enjoy the perquisites of their station. And the military remained a powerful conservative force.

The balance that had been struck in judging Mao was there-fore delicate. Even more delicate was the balance sought in the key Dengist formula: economic vigour but political obedience, or, to give it its approved name, socialism with market char-acteristics. Many would have called it not a balance at all, but a contradiction in terms. Every move in economic liberalization, and there were many to come, carried its political fall-out and stepped up pressure for corresponding political freedoms. Every advance in modernization seemed to the conservatives to carry greater dangers of spiritual infection. Where should the line be drawn? Over this ground from 1981 onwards a protracted battle was waged between conservatives and reformers, with fortunes shifting from one side to the other. This was the true internal struggle in the later years of Deng's rule; it was largely covert and, like many Chinese political battles, it was fought indirectly and often via cultural channels.

In 1981 a film appeared entitled *Bitter Love*, with a script by the army writer, Bai Hua. It told the story of a patriotic overseas Chinese, who returned to China after Liberation to help build socialism. Through various political movements, in particular the Cultural Revolution, he lost his job and family and, after escaping to a barren steppe area, died in the snow. He had loved the motherland; but had the motherland returned his love? The film provoked an angry chorus of denunciation for what was seen as its bourgeois egotism. But there was rather more to it than that. The film was probably a deliberately chosen target in the 1981 campaign against 'bourgeois liberalism', one of the conservative swings in the continuing internal struggle. The criticism reflected dissatisfaction in sections of the army with the reform movement and, more particularly, military doubts about the credentials of the new Secretary-General, Hu Yaobang. The army was reproved, but army dissatisfaction with the political trend simmered and was to burst out again against Hu Yaobang in 1986, with fatal results for his career.

In 1983 there was another, more obvious sign of reaction against reform. A campaign was launched against 'spiritual pollution and cultural contamination'. Deng Liqun, once Liu Shaoqi's secretary and now the head of the Central Committee's propaganda department, who was the leading spirit in the campaign, gave a comprehensive definition of the evil:

> Spreading things that are obscene, barbarous, treacherous, or reactionary;
> Vulgar taste in artistic performances;
> Efforts to seek personal gain and indulgence in anarchism and liberalism;
> Writing articles or making speeches that run counter to the country's socialist system.

This was partly a reaction to the Western influences now penetrating the country, particularly from Hong Kong; but it was also an attempt to recover the Party's lost faith; and, most important, it was an attack on reform and modernization. It was in the direct line from innumerable similar calls by Chinese officials from imperial times onward as they faced Western encroachments; the message now, as then, was: Return to orthodoxy and expel the foreigner.

For a while the campaign gathered strength. The *People's Daily* attacked intellectuals whose work prompted 'mistrust of socialism'. More disturbing, there was criticism in one or two Peking department stores of staff who indulged in strange hair-styles and used cosmetics. In Sichuan and the north-east youths donned red arm-bands and invaded homes to crop long hair and break off high-heels on shoes. There was a whiff of the summer of 1966 and fears that a big anti-rightist campaign might be brewing. The intellectuals, who had been through this experience only too often in the past, began to go to ground.

But then Deng intervened and the tone of official guidance altered. We were told by the *People's Daily* that 'Pollution should be eliminated, but life should be beautified' and by the end of the year it was made clear that the campaign had gone too far. There was naturally no popular enthusiasm for it: people were too busy trying to live their own lives and if possible make money. It was probable that, in order to win support for his plans to purge the Party of leftists, Deng had countenanced some criticism of unhealthy bourgeois influences, of which he was, in any case, genuinely suspicious, and that his approval had been misused. But it was a distinct wobble and illustrated the fragility of the governing compromise, economic but not political reform.

It was then a mixed scene. But when I left Peking at Christmas 1983 it seemed to me that we had about as good a China as we in Britain could reasonably expect. It was stable and reformist; it provided strategic balance against the Soviet Union; and its government was increasingly ready to discuss with us matters of common interest. It was Communist rule certainly, but not of the militant variety. I did not fear a reversion to such extremes as in the Cultural Revolution: Chinese of all kinds had suffered too much then to forget it.

There were of course worries. Too much hung on the health

of one old man. His two lieutenants had not yet dug themselves in. One in particular was impulsive, unpredictable and apparently commanded no confidence as yet among the military. We were also reaching a point when, by the mere efflux of time, the seamless web of Party and army was beginning to unravel. Finally there was always the underlying contradiction of reform within a Communist state.

But we could not have everything. On the whole the situation was encouraging. It was as propitious a time as we could find to settle with Peking the major issue between us, that of Hong Kong.

PART THREE

Hong Kong

CHAPTER SIXTEEN

Hong Kong: The First Steps

UP TO THIS point Hong Kong had been only one refrain in the sometimes dissonant music of Sino-British relations. Never absent, and, on occasion, as in the Cultural Revolution, harsh and threatening. But still a secondary theme. From 1979 onwards, however, it gathered strength and from 1982 became the main motif, drowning virtually all others.

Before continuing the story, a little background is necessary.

Britain formally acquired Hong Kong Island in 1842 by the Treaty of Nanking, which concluded what in Britain was called the First Anglo-Chinese War, in China the First Opium War. Hong Kong was the 'barren island with hardly a house upon it' of Lord Palmerston's reprimand to Captain Elliot, the British representative who negotiated the original agreement. The island was ceded in perpetuity. In 1860 the tip of the Kowloon peninsula and Stonecutters Island were added on the same terms by the Convention of Peking, which ended the second 'Opium War'. The remainder of the colony, the New Territories, passed to Britain by a lease signed in Peking on 9 June 1898 by the British Minister, Sir Claude MacDonald, and the veteran Chinese diplomat, Li Hongzhang. MacDonald had originally been instructed to seek a cession of territory; but the other European powers were accepting leases at the time and the Minister deferred to the Chinese argument that cession would prompt Germans, Russians and the like to press for conversion of their leases into permanent transfers. This further partitioning of China would have been highly unwelcome to Her Majesty's Government. In London, Balfour, the Foreign Secretary, accepted the change, though the Colonial Office complained privately that Hong Kong was being subordinated to the wider China policy of the Foreign Office.

The lease was for 99 years, expiring on 30 June 1997. It was this lease, covering 92 per cent of the territory, which determined the nature and timing of the negotiations on Hong Kong's future.

When, in 1949, the Communist armies overran the mainland, surprisingly, they stopped short of the Hong Kong border. The new Communist government seemed content to let the situation rest for the time being, though they pressed, without success, for the appointment of a Chinese Commissioner in Hong Kong. The official Chinese position was that the treaties were 'unequal' and of no effect; Hong Kong had always been part of China. But Hong Kong was a question left over from history to be settled when the time was ripe; this would be done peacefully and through negotiations.

Even in 1967, despite the riots and the violent rhetoric of the Cultural Revolution, this policy did not change in its essentials, though Zhou Enlai made it clear that the territory belonged to China and that its future would be determined by patriotic Chinese, not by a few British imperialists. In 1972 the Chinese further made plain to the United Nations Committee on De-colonization that Hong Kong and Macao were not on the 'colonial territories' list and not subjects for self-determination.

The firmest indication of Peking's thoughts on timing came in remarks by Zhou Enlai to Malcolm Macdonald (the former Commissioner-General for South-east Asia) in 1971, to the effect that China had no intention of seeking to recover Hong Kong until the expiry of the New Territories lease and that Kowloon and Hong Kong Island would not be viable without the New Territories. The implication was clear that 1997 would be the watershed. Though the Chinese government took the line that the leases were invalid since they had been signed under duress, they knew that Britain regarded them as valid and the expiry of the New Territories lease was therefore a critical date, and a convenient one.

With the death of Mao and the coming of modernization, the way was clear for more practical co-operation between Hong Kong and the mainland. I remember there were still endemic problems over illegal immigrants who continued to pour into the territory; and it was not until 1980 that the flow was stemmed. But bilateral trade and communications expanded; mainland Chinese investment in Hong Kong went up sharply; and Hong Kong was recognized in Peking as an invaluable source of expertise and capital for the modernization drive. Li Qiang, the Chinese Minister for Foreign Trade, emphasized these points when he visited Hong Kong in December 1978. Li issued a return invitation to the Governor, Sir Murray MacLehose, to visit Peking.

This summary recital of events neglects, however, a more elusive and influential factor, namely the emotions, ambitions and prejudices of the two sides, or, more accurately, the three sides, for Hong Kong in this respect held strongly individual views.

In London, the most detached point in the triangle, the New Territories lease was seen in the 1970s as an issue that would have to be faced and eventually settled amicably with Peking. But it was not as yet the most urgent or the dominating issue in Sino-British relations and there was no clear view of the likely terms of any such settlement. It was acknowledged that the long-term trend was probably unfavourable to Hong Kong's continued existence as a colony. But there was always the chance that the status quo might be quietly maintained, particularly if there was some bow in the direction of Chinese sovereignty. I remember seeing optimistic forecasts by one senior official at the end of the 1960s that it should be possible to renew the lease. I thought the view unrealistic; but it was not my business at the time; and the fact that it could be advanced suggested a considerable openness of mind on the question.

In Hong Kong attitudes were less relaxed and more complex. The question of the lease was in the minds of all officials and many businessmen; but it was extremely delicate material; it would crop up briefly at dinner parties and then be pushed out of sight. It was still a distant threat; and Hong Kong money was made or lost on short time-frames. Hong Kong was also in those days a much more isolated place, an insular culture: there was little direct contact with the mainland, particularly for officials. London too was distant and often unsympathetic, seeing China in a wider perspective and always it seemed, inclined, as in that first choice between lease and cession in 1898, to subordinate the territory's interests to wider foreign policy considerations.

There was, very properly, immense local pride in the territory's achievements and a greater readiness than in London to reason that Peking would acknowledge the value of Hong Kong's economic contribution and be reluctant to interfere. Well-informed journalists in Hong Kong wrote of the irrelevance of 1997 and laid weight on China's reforms as a mark of common sense and statesmanship.

Finally, Peking, where apparently there was least reflection on detail, but certainly the deepest reservoir of feeling. There was a vivid memory of humiliations suffered at foreign hands, a determination to reassert sovereignty and recover lost territory, an abiding suspicion of foreign capitalists and their devious ways, plus a formidable ignorance of the working of the Hong Kong economy and the territory's connections with London. This was a powerful emotional charge, to be neglected at our peril, but which was, nonetheless, insufficiently appreciated by most of the actors until well into the negotiations and which from time to time is underestimated even today in London and Hong Kong.

It was against this background that we considered the agenda for Murray MacLehose's visit, planned for late March 1979.

The obvious subjects would be links between Hong Kong and Guangdong and the wider topic of Hong Kong's role in China's modernization. But the interesting question was whether we should also use this opportunity to broach the issue of Hong Kong's future.

There were a number of strong arguments in favour of doing so. The first was that time was running on and, though Hong Kong flourished enormously, there would shortly come a point when fears of the future would begin to overshadow that prosperity. The normal duration of Hong Kong mortgages on land, we were told, was fifteen years. If there were no clarification of the future by 1982 or 1983, prospective purchasers might feel they lacked security and business confidence could rapidly dwindle. This was the Governor's considered judgement and it was naturally accepted. There were supporting arguments. We now had, in the person of Deng Xiaoping, a Chinese leader who was rational and pragmatic. The senior official in charge of Hong Kong and Macao matters, Liao Chengzhi, was similarly flexible. Moreover, China was bent on modernizing rapidly with outside help, a policy which maximized the value to the mainland of a stable and prosperous Hong Kong. We could not be sure how long this situation would last. We would be wise to exploit it while we could.

There was also the fact that visits by senior ministers to Peking would be natural occasions to discuss future arrangements for Hong Kong; failure to do so would be increasingly difficult to explain and might seem irresponsible. In particular, Dr Owen, the Foreign Secretary, was expected in Peking in the spring. He wanted to raise the Hong Kong issue; some preliminary soundings would be in order.

On the other hand, we were all wary of tackling the matter head on. It was felt that a useful approach to the subject might be by way of the technical question of individual land leases in the New Territories. The practice was for the Hong Kong government to grant such leases up to a date three days before the expiry of the New Territories lease itself. The terms were now getting shorter. If we were able, with Chinese agreement, to grant individual leases going beyond 1997, we would be able to sustain confidence. We would also be doing something to blur the 1997 deadline. The idea came from Hong Kong, either from the Governor or from one of his advisers. I thought it worth a try.

If the Chinese agreed, we would have to legislate by an Order in Council, making it possible to grant individual land leases valid for so long as the Crown administered the territory. To this a further idea was added, namely that the legislation would amend the original Order in Council, under which Britain administered Hong Kong up to July 1997, by removing the terminal date. This was a more ambitious step, but it followed logically from the first and avoided a possible challenge to the validity of leases exceeding June 1997 as *ultra vires*.

Since the Governor was likely to have an audience with Deng Xiaoping, the approach would be at the highest level. But it would be presented as a technical and commercial matter, as a means of sustaining investment; there would be no grand *démarche* on the political issue. It would also have to be highly confidential in view of the impact on the Hong Kong stock market of any rebuff.

I think we all felt some trepidation on the eve of the visit. We were moving into unknown territory. But some soundings had to be taken and we were taking them in the most oblique and confidential way possible. I was not particularly optimistic on the outcome and was sure the Chinese would not accept unilateral changes. I also differed from the Hong Kong view that the Chinese were concerned primarily with economic reform and that nationalist considerations came second: I thought it was the other way round. Otherwise, ministers in London, the Governor in Hong Kong and the Embassy in Peking were at one on the tactics.

In the event, the meeting with Deng took an unexpected form. It preceded the meetings with Liao Chengzhi of the Hong Kong and Macao Office and with Huang Hua, the Foreign Minister. Normally in Peking one moves in ascending order up the hierarchy to the leader, giving him the chance to be briefed beforehand. The effect was that a complex, technical point had to be put to Deng without preparation. The other surprise was that he himself took the initiative and raised Hong Kong's future.

He explained that China had a consistent position that sovereignty over Hong Kong lay with China. But China recognized that Hong Kong had a special status. The end of the New Territories lease was eighteen years off. This was not a long time, but there could be discussions before then. And, whatever the political solution, it would not affect investment. Just as the return of Taiwan would not change the social system or the living standards there, so China would respect Hong Kong as a special case. China needed Hong Kong, and a flexible policy, such as he had outlined, helped socialist reconstruction.

The Governor now had his opening and put his proposal on the land leases. Deng, however, may not have understood it, or may not have appreciated the distinction between the head-lease and sub-leases. He contented himself with saying investors should put their hearts at ease. When Murray pressed the point, Deng became cautious and advised against any reference to British administration. He could not confirm that the political situation would remain unchanged. By 1997 China might take over Hong Kong; or it might 'recognize present realities'; but, either way, in this century and into the early years of the next the capitalist system would continue there. The key point was that investors should feel easy.

This was far from satisfactory, but there the matter had to rest. Huang Hua would not discuss it further, as was natural once Deng had spoken. He added, rather grandly, that it was in any case a matter for the Foreign Secretary and himself. Liao Chengzhi was encouraging but vague. The Governor explained to the press on his return to Hong Kong that it had been a good-will, not a negotiating visit. He laid stress on the assurance that investors should put their hearts at ease. Dr Owen's visit did not materialize, for the Labour government fell; we received the telegram of cancellation at the dinner I gave in the Residence for Murray MacLehose and Li Qiang.

There was, however, still some clarification to undertake. We had made a suggestion which Deng had probably misunderstood, at least the first time round. We should explain ourselves more clearly and give the Chinese government time to think. I was accordingly instructed to pass the Vice Foreign Minister for Western Europe, Song Zhiguang, a written statement of our ideas.

We received a reply in September. It was distinctly negative. The Chinese government thought the legal steps we were proposing to take were unnecessary and inappropriate. They hoped we would not persist, since the effect could be adverse for both British and Chinese interests. Song added that the matter had wider implications, extending beyond Britain and China. The Chinese were presumably thinking of the reactions of other powers with whom China had 'unequal treaties'.

That was the end of the indirect approach. The Hong Kong government still hoped that economic realities would press upon the Chinese and bring them round to a more co-operative attitude. I was much less hopeful. It was now clearer that for them political goals came before market forces and that any solution was likely to require a recognition of Chinese sovereignty. We would also have to take account of China's model for Taiwan.

On the other hand, despite the rebuff, I wanted to keep up the dialogue. The main danger, as I saw it, was that Peking would now unilaterally formulate and perhaps impose its plan for Hong Kong, without our having an opportunity to bring our influence to bear. But both London and Hong Kong were now nervous, and authority to talk further with the Foreign Ministry was withheld.

Though there was disappointment at the time, the Chinese response had been informative and not really hostile. We now knew a little more about their timing: 1997 would be the critical date, though even here there were suggestions of possible action before that time ('by 1997'). Quite what would happen in 1997 was left vague, whether a complete take-over or a continuing degree of British control. Clearly, they were not ready. They were, however, thinking about Taiwan and they seemed to envisage considerable autonomy in both the Taiwan and Hong Kong contexts. This was encouraging, though it did not follow that continuing capitalism in Hong Kong would necessarily mean continuing British rule. Realistically, we could not have expected much more in the way of information: if, as they now would recognize, the Chinese were approaching a major negotiation, they were unlikely to give away tricks in advance.

It has since been suggested, mainly in Hong Kong, that we made a great mistake in stirring the Chinese into life in 1979; that if we had not been overactive, we could have passed smoothly through the 1997 barrier without anyone being the wiser. I think this a mistaken view. For the reasons given above, the Chinese were alive to the significance of 1997 and unlikely to let the opportunity pass. While there could be differing views on the precise timing, it was incontestable that anxieties among investors would increasingly undermine confidence as the deadline approached. There would have been growing questions on our own side. Above all, we could not administer the territory beyond June 1997 without amending the Order in Council from which the Governor drew his authority; and no such legislation could have been undertaken without the agreement of the Chinese.

In fact, the sidelong approach of 1979 was the most we could do to blur the deadline without tackling the main issue head on. As has been seen, it was rapidly identified and rebuffed by Peking.

The next two years were punctuated by a series of unsatisfactory exchanges between Chinese and British ministers on the subject of Hong Kong. Hua Guofeng, as might have been expected, conveyed nothing new when he came to London in the autumn of 1979. Huang Hua, the Foreign Minister, was also unforthcoming. Lord Carrington saw both Huang Hua and Deng on his visit to Peking in April 1981. Huang Hua said nothing significant and Deng, who normally radiated authority, was on this occasion curiously constrained, speaking for once as if from an agreed brief and suggesting that we study Taiwan.

In fact, during this interregnum the Chinese leaders had been thinking hard, not so much about Hong Kong as about Taiwan. They announced a nine-point plan for Taiwan in September 1981 and clearly had been preparing it when Lord Carrington called on Deng. This plan provided that, after reunification, Taiwan would become a special administrative region, enjoying a high degree of autonomy. It would be allowed to retain its existing social and economic systems and lifestyle, together with its economic and cultural relations with foreign countries. Private property, enterprises and foreign investment would be protected.

It was a document which bore a striking resemblance to the eventual solution in Hong Kong. But it seems that Taiwan was, at least initially, the prior Chinese objective. It was, after all, larger and potentially more threatening, the major prize in the reunification stakes. And Mao was reported to have said on one occasion that Hong Kong should not be tackled until Taiwan was recovered.

It is possible, as Robert Cottrell suggests in his book on the Hong Kong negotiations, *The End of Hong Kong*, that the Chinese leaders originally entertained high hopes of engaging Taiwan in negotiations after the normalization of Sino-US relations in December 1978, the repeal of the US-Taiwan Mutual Defence Treaty and the closure of the US Embassy in Taipei. They may have calculated that this lessening of American support would induce a receptive frame of mind on the part of Taiwan's leaders. Certainly Chinese thinking on autonomy, special administrative regions, even the concept of 'one country, two systems' first evolved in the Taiwan context.

The theory continues that, by the time the doctrine was

formally promulgated, the glow was fading from the Taiwan prospect. The Taipei government were proving unreceptive to Peking's overtures and Ronald Reagan, who thought as much of Taipei as of Peking, had come to power in Washington. Deng then decided to switch his attention to Hong Kong, a lesser objective certainly, but one important economically as well as politically, and one which, if all went according to plan, could provide a valuable precedent for the bigger game of Taiwan.

The theory is plausible, if unproven. Certainly, about the end of 1981, after several fallow years, there was a sharp increase in official Chinese interest in Hong Kong. Successive delegations of Hong Kong Chinese were invited up to Peking; and, after having carefully evaded British enquiries for two years, the Chinese government suddenly became forthcoming, not to say expansive, about their plans for the territory.

The main occasion was the visit of the Lord Privy Seal, Humphrey Atkins, who, as a junior Foreign Office minister, was responsible for Hong Kong. He came to Peking in early January 1982. He had instructions to put a low-key enquiry to the Chinese on their intentions over Hong Kong. He was also preparing the ground for the visit of the Prime Minister, a return engagement for Hua Guofeng's visit to London in 1979, which it was felt should take place later in 1982.

Mr Atkins saw not only Ji Pengfei, the State Councillor and former Foreign Minister, who was to succeed Liao Chengzhi as head of the Hong Kong and Macao Office, but also the Prime Minister, Zhao Ziyang. In both interviews he was told that China had evolved general plans for Hong Kong which would preserve the interests of industrialists and businessmen. The measures would be very reasonable; there would be no confiscation. China would safeguard her sovereignty, but Hong Kong's prosperity would be maintained. It would remain a free port and a commercial and financial centre. We should study China's plans for Taiwan. As regards timing, China would not leave the problem on the shelf until 1997.

I found these comments encouraging, in that the Chinese were beginning to apply their minds to the subject. But they were only beginning: there was a lot of detailed work to be done and a lot of detailed instruction to be conveyed by our side, provided we were given the chance. It would, for example, be extremely important that we should be able to tell them how Hong Kong worked and what were the foundations of investor confidence there.

It was also significant that the Chinese were talking about changes to Hong Kong in the context of Chinese control. They had not said so explicitly, but the clear implication of their remarks was that they intended to take over the territory in 1997. We should therefore be thinking of a solution which recognized Chinese sovereignty, while retaining British administration. Without that, it was hard to see how confidence could be preserved. Finally, it seemed to me important that, when the Prime Minister came, she should welcome the suggestion of talks and seek to have them soon. Otherwise there was a danger that we would be presented with a cut-and-dried solution.

Having decided to open up, the Chinese were now becoming embarrassingly frank. We began to encounter the practice to which we became inured in the course of the negotiations, of Chinese official briefings, or leaks to journalists, and important messages conveyed, not directly to our Embassy, but to various visiting dignitaries. When Edward Heath came to Peking in early April, Deng spoke to him very openly. Fortunately, I was there. He asked whether we could agree to a solution for Hong Kong along the lines of the nine-point plan for Taiwan. Sovereignty would pass to China, but Hong Kong would remain a free port and international investment centre. It would be run by Hong Kong people and would become a special administrative region of China.

I saw this as a high-level message which called for an official answer. It was not perhaps incompatible with the idea of continued British administration, but we would have to move quickly if we were to leave our mark on Chinese thinking. I also advocated study of the Taiwan plan as a fall-back position, in case it proved impossible to secure British administration after 1997.

Unfortunately, London and Hong Kong thought Deng's message, not being addressed to the government, required no formal acknowledgement. To be fair, it also raised major issues, calling for ministers' attention; and at the time, in the midst of the Falklands War, it was virtually impossible to gain their attention. Francis Pym, the new Foreign Secretary, held a meeting of officials, but Mrs Thatcher was unobtainable. I was told to be patient and to fend off Chinese enquiries. I was also assured that we could leave it to Chinese businessmen from Hong Kong, who were now travelling to Peking in droves, to educate their compatriots in the realities of Hong Kong's prosperity and the need for continued British administration if that prosperity was to be preserved.

I found this a frustrating and unsatisfactory answer. It was true that there was now a steady flow of Hong Kong personalities to Peking. Moreover, they were being received by senior leaders and spoken to very frankly about Chinese plans. For example, Dr Rayson Huang, the Vice-Chancellor of the Hong Kong Chinese University, had a session with Deng Xiaoping, who told him the issue had to be settled in the next year or so. If China did not recover her sovereignty, the people would rise up and strike down the Communist Party. There could be no modern Li Hongzhangs (Li had signed the 1898 lease on behalf of the Chinese government). Other visitors were being served other portions of the blueprint and on this basis pro-Peking journals in Hong Kong were able to set out extraordinarily detailed pre-scriptions for life after 1997, as seen by Peking.

But it was, unhappily, a one-way traffic. The leaders of Hong Kong opinion no doubt sincerely believed that only British administration could ensure lasting prosperity and stability, and certainly told us so. But before the dragon throne their resolution faltered and they invariably failed to make the crucial point. They listened and reported; but they did not intervene and instruct, let alone dispute. The education of the Chinese in the economic realities as we saw them was left to be attempted much later by the British negotiators. Unofficial messages were not to be relied on. There were two occasions later when Hong Kong delegations bravely spoke up, to be met with an angry response from the leaders in Peking: Alan Lee's group of young indus-trialists and Sir S. Y. Chung's delegation of Unofficial Members of the Executive and Legislative Councils. But in this formative period nothing was said.

So the Falklands War ended and we found ourselves on the eve of Mrs Thatcher's September visit. The two sides, like figures in a formal dance, had by now exchanged positions. In 1979 it was the British who were pressing, the Chinese who were reluctant. Now, in 1982, it was the Chinese who were voluble, the British who were silent and constrained. The Prime Minister had not been briefed. Planning papers in London still ranged over a variety of options, mingling the realistic and the unrealistic, and bearing little relation to the emerging Chinese blueprint. There was general agreement that the Chinese plan would not command business confidence. For that British administration was essential. It was also accepted among British officials that in order to retain British administration we would probably have to concede sovereignty. But no ministerial decisions on strategy had been taken. Nor could they be until Mrs Thatcher had had time to apply her mind to the issue.

CHAPTER SEVENTEEN

Mrs Thatcher's Visit

THE HISTORIANS OF the Thatcher years tend to pass over Hong Kong as an issue that never fully engaged the Prime Minister, something she was content to leave to the diplomats, who handled it, or mishandled it, as diplomats do.

For those who know the lady, it is an unlikely story; and it is, of course, untrue. The Prime Minister was intensely interested in Hong Kong, readily discussed its various aspects and made, or endorsed, the key decisions on its future, sometimes after punishing investigations.

She approached the question, however, in a combative and uncooperative spirit. She was fresh from the Falklands experience, in which, as she saw it, her will and the courage of the armed forces had with difficulty retrieved a situation created by Foreign Office lack of foresight and overreadiness to yield to foreign pressures. Hong Kong bore some superficial similarities to the Falklands scene: another distant colonial possession was threatened; our legal and treaty freehold base in at least a part of the territory was sound; again the diplomats were canvassing ideas for pre-emptive surrender. Moreover, the Chinese were involved; and unlike most political leaders who had been feasted in Peking, she was not enamoured of her hosts. They were Communists; and, at least at the time of her first encounter with them in 1977, they ran an economy of a peculiarly wasteful and unsuccessful kind. Hua Guofeng, their Prime Minister at the time of the London visit in 1979, had been entertained by her without enthusiasm and had left a faint but distinctly negative impression.

Her approach, therefore, could be called one of free, not to say hostile, enquiry, with a predisposition to solutions based on legal or even military strength. Admitted that the lease of the New Territories would expire in 1997. Could we not stand on the ceded land of Hong Kong Island and the southern extremity of the Kowloon peninsula? What was the military advice? Was the position really indefensible? Could not the United Nations be involved? Could there not be joint rule after 1997? If the Chinese dismissed some treaties as unequal, what assurance could there be that they would honour any agreement we made with them? And so on. The concept of a settlement based on some concession to Chinese sovereignty, if not entirely excluded, was to be approached only as a last redoubt, after a series of intermediate defensive positions had been obstinately fought over.

Despite the suffering involved in this approach, it was in fact a healthy intellectual exercise. Alternative theories were all tested to destruction. We could be sure in the end that nothing had been taken for granted and that all avenues, particularly the stoniest and least rewarding, had been exhaustively explored.

The front-line troops in this exercise were the officials of the Far Eastern Department of the Foreign Office, headed by Dick Clift, the Head of Department, and Alan Donald, the Assistant Under-Secretary for the Far East. It fell to them, with the assistance of the Legal Advisers, to draft the papers and to bear the ferocious comment they commonly elicited. Sir Edward Youde, from 1982 Governor of Hong Kong, and I would be brought back for important meetings to give the view from our separate vantage points. This was not too difficult: we spoke, as it were, for our clients. But the work of synthesis, of providing the concluding paragraphs of the policy documents, was more contentious; and here all Alan Donald's considerable resources of flexibility and good humour were in demand.

Casting about at the time for adjectives to define our discussions, I hit on two: 'unstructured' and 'abrasive'. Abrasive certainly. Unstructured, because the Prime Minister's mind moved in unusual ways. We were accustomed to a frontal approach to the topic in hand, logical and step-by-step, as in eighteenth-century pitched battles. The Prime Minister recognized no such rules and conducted a species of guerrilla warfare, appearing suddenly behind the lines, or firing from unconventional angles. She also often operated behind a smokescreen of her own making, a series of remarks which were commonplace or even off the point and which induced a false and fatal sense of security on the part of her listeners. Then, amidst the dross and the chaff, would come the missile, a question or comment of such relevance and penetration that it destroyed the opposition. I have seen many redoubtable visitors and seasoned Whitehall warriors emerge worsted and reeling from such encounters, with a vague sense that there had not been fair play, or that they had been somehow prevented from doing themselves full justice.

The Foreign Secretaries of the day played little part in these preliminary war games. Lord Carrington, sadly, was never given a chance to grapple with Hong Kong: he was active only in the phoney war period between the MacLehose and Thatcher visits to Peking; and his contribution was to tell Teddy Youde and myself, when we approached him in the course of his 1981 visit, to go away and think up a good wheeze. I suppose in the end we thought up several, but something more was needed to secure the continuance of British rule.

Francis Pym, who succeeded Lord Carrington as Foreign Secretary, had been, as Defence Secretary, one of my most successful and agreeable guests in Peking. I recall how, on revealing that he had been a real soldier, a tank commander in the Second World War, he had won the hearts of the dour PLA generals who entertained us in Shanghai, with the result that the *maotai* flowed in even greater quantities. I had great respect for him. But he had had serious differences with the Prime Minister during the Falklands War, and at the meetings I attended with them both on Hong Kong he would sit constrained and almost silent.

Geoffrey Howe played a much larger role, but his time was not yet. He was not appointed Foreign Secretary until the summer of 1983, when the battle was already joined. He was a skilled and patient negotiator. His approach to the issue was very much as my own, that we would need to make serious political concessions if we were to guide the eventual outcome, and it was easy

to co-operate with him. My only difficulty arose from his oblique
mode of expression and, more serious, the low volume, so that
it was often very hard to make out just what it was he was saying.
He was the note-taker's despair. In this respect he was outclassed
in my experience only by Bill Casey, the former head of the CIA;
and while Casey's whispers were frustrating at the time, I
sometimes used to think afterwards that it was perhaps as well
one had not heard everything he said.

The dialogue therefore was mainly between the Prime Minister and officials. I proposed, and it was accepted without too
much difficulty, that we should set ourselves a modest and
attainable objective for the visit itself, namely an agreement to
begin talks. The visit would raise great hopes; it was essential
that we should have something to show at the end of it. In a
sense, the question of substance was secondary: we would be
returning to that many times in the future. I would have liked
to obtain Chinese agreement in advance to this goal of opening talks; but when I returned to Peking they refused to be
drawn.

On substance, there was also some progress, though it was
hard to be sure that the Prime Minister was always convinced:
I suspect that the heart, or was it the viscera, supplied reasons
of which the head knew nothing. As a result there were frequent
relapses; ground that had seemed to be secured at one session
had only too often to be fought over again at the next. There
was resolution in plenty at those meetings; but it tended to be
resolution of a one-dimensional kind, with little or no sense of
the other side in the struggle, their prejudices, strengths and
likely reactions; and in such an embattled setting it was not
always easy to supply the missing elements in the equation, in
other words to give a realistic assessment of the prospects,
without sounding negative or even faint-hearted.

It was accepted, however, that Hong Kong was militarily
indefensible. The New Territories lease covered 92 per cent of
the land; the remaining 8 per cent was not viable on its own.
The boundary line between leased and ceded territory cut
through Kowloon; if we stood defiant, there would be an
unmanageable influx of refugees into the ceded portion; the
reservoirs and utilities were in the wrong segment; and all
this neglected the total dependence of Hong Kong on food and

water from the mainland, and the presence of overwhelming Chinese military force. The conclusion was not surprising, but it was fundamental. It meant that there had to be a negotiated settlement; that, whether we liked it or not, there would be a reversion of the whole territory in 1997; and that what would matter would be the terms of that reversion.

It was common ground that the Chinese plans offered no satisfactory basis for business confidence and that this would have to be explained to Peking. It also seemed that the best hope for reconciling the positions of the two sides was a recognition of Chinese sovereignty, together with some form of management contract under which Britain would administer Hong Kong. The Prime Minister made it plain, however, that sovereignty in this context meant only titular sovereignty.

On her way to China Mrs Thatcher visited Japan and I received a summons to meet her in Tokyo to go over the Peking plan of action. I remember arriving at the Tokyo Residence to find the Ambassador, Hugh Cortazzi, and his staff in a state of some disarray, scattered about the house rather as if playing a game of hunt the thimble. In fact what they were hunting for were Japanese proverbs for use in a speech the Prime Minister was delivering the next day. It was a demanding process; successive gems of Japanese wisdom were dug out and offered, only to be peremptorily rejected. But eventually the *mot juste* was discovered and I had an opportunity to talk with her about the people she would encounter in Peking. As usual, the preparation was careful and the brief was mastered.

She also presented it skilfully in her first meeting on Hong Kong with Zhao Ziyang, the Chinese Prime Minister, in the Great Hall of the People on 23 September. She concentrated on the need to sustain prosperity; she feared that the plans outlined by Deng Xiaoping to Mr Heath would not meet that requirement; there would in fact be a flight of capital and economic and financial collapse. Indeed, anything less than British administration would inflict similar damage. Britain had a moral obligation to the people of Hong Kong. On the other hand, she understood the Chinese position on sovereignty. She held out the hope that, if suitable arrangements for the administration and control of Hong Kong could be worked out, and if they commanded confidence and were acceptable to the people of

Hong Kong and to the British Parliament, she would consider the question of sovereignty. It was a highly qualified sentence, but it dangled the possibility of a concession.

Zhao replied at length in what was clearly a prepared statement. Although quietly delivered, it was unyielding, denying almost all the British propositions. China would recover sovereignty in 1997. No other country would be allowed to administer the territory on China's behalf. Deng's proposals would be sufficient to maintain confidence. It was, I think, here that he added the significant remark that prosperity came second to sovereignty and that, if it came to a clash, China would put sovereignty first. But he hoped for British co-operation.

This was not only a negative statement from our point of view; it was also virtually a public one. Before going in to the meeting Zhao had announced to reporters China's intention to recover sovereignty in 1997 and to take a series of measures which would ensure prosperity and stability within this framework. It was one of the more blatant examples of the Chinese practice of publicizing their intentions and of treating the British government as simply one member of a wide audience. Indeed, in the days preceding the visit virtually the whole of the Chinese position had been published in selected Hong Kong newspapers. This became known as the Chinese Twelve Points.

There remained Deng, with whom we had two and a half hours the next day. This was a more abrasive meeting, rehearsing in sharper fashion the contradictions that had emerged with Zhao Ziyang. The principals were not altogether at their best. Deng, whose hierarchy had room for only token women, was uneasy arguing with a leader of the opposite sex and of Mrs Thatcher's resolution. For her part, the Prime Minister was, despite herself, impressed by this short, barrel-like figure, with bruised face and dismissive gestures and almost limitless authority, chain-smoking and spitting, a product of a totally alien political environment. She remarked to me afterwards how cruel he was. It seemed to me an odd observation: anyone who had risen to Deng's position, and fallen and risen again, more than once, in that setting and with such comrades, would require very remarkable qualities, a degree of cruelty, not to say savagery, among them. But the remark accurately conveyed an instinctive recoil.

The Prime Minister spoke with eloquence and charm. She repeated her willingness to consider the sovereignty issue in certain conditions and explained the distinction in her mind between sovereignty and administration. Deng countered by emphasizing the absolute necessity of recovering sovereignty; there could be no more Li Hongzhangs. He was prepared to wait one or two years for consultations; then China would announce its decision.

The Prime Minister said we accepted the termination of the lease; but the other two treaties were valid in international law; if they were changed it must be by agreement, not by unilateral abrogation. Without the assurance of British administration, investors would not commit money.

Deng took issue with this and the temperature rose. China's policies, not British administrators, would decide Hong Kong's prosperity. There might be a little turbulence when China announced its decisions, but that would soon pass. If, however, there were serious disturbances in the next fifteen years, China might have to consider an earlier take-over. The Prime Minister, in her strongest intervention, replied that serious disturbances would not be of Britain's making; but, if China intervened, the world would know what to think.

After this clash, the two leaders turned to the question of a communiqué and Zhang Wenjin, the Vice Foreign Minister, and I went into a corner to prepare one. I had a draft in my mind and managed to get something like it accepted. The important point was that it committed the two sides to talks to ensure the stability and prosperity of Hong Kong without including preconditions. (Deng's earlier remarks had referred to discussions on the premise that in 1997 China would recover Hong Kong.) The draft was approved by the leaders and we adjourned to lunch. As we did so, the omission seemed to strike Zhang Wenjin. He said to me that of course we would recognize that the communiqué was drafted on the understanding of the Chinese premise. I said it was not; there was no mention of such a term. We were to argue round this point for many months.

That night the Prime Minister hosted a return banquet in the Great Hall of the People. It was a rather subdued occasion. She herself was tired and was developing a cold. She had slipped and fallen going down the Great Hall steps at the end of the morning session. While still in London she had given detailed attention to the menu and arrangements for the evening; but the smoked salmon we had brought sat rather uneasily with the sea-slugs and other native delicacies from the Great Hall kitchens. There was also a quantity of regimental silver which the Prime Minister had had specially transported in order to decorate the tables; but these splendid trophies, redolent of past military glories, struck a slightly incongruous note among the chinoiserie; and I doubt whether the Chinese, in so far as they understood them, relished their presence. Zhao Ziyang, as the Prime Minister's opposite number, was the principal guest; but at the same time, in another room in that house of many mansions, the most senior Chinese leaders were carousing with Kim Il Sung, the North Korean dictator, whose visit happened to coincide with Mrs Thatcher's.

The next day, on her way out of China, the Prime Minister stopped briefly in Shanghai, where she launched a ship for Sir Y. K. Pao and was entertained by the Mayor at a banquet. I recall we ate to the strains of Auld Lang Syne, Home Sweet Home and the Last Rose of Summer. Then to Canton and Hong Kong.

In Hong Kong at a press conference Mrs Thatcher, in answer to questions, rehearsed her view of the three treaties. They were all valid in international law. They could be changed by agreement, but should not be abrogated unilaterally. She had said as much in the private talks, but repetition in public went down badly in Peking. What was worse, she went on to say that if a country would not stand by one treaty it would not stand by another. This seemed to impugn Chinese reliability and provoked an angry reaction, which had the effect of complicating the already arduous task of getting negotiations started.

Not surprisingly, it had been a tough visit. It had conveyed very forcibly the strength of Chinese feeling and their determination to recover what they saw as their territory in a limited period and with the minimum concessions. Summing up the situation at the time, I described the prospect as bleak. We had won on points over the communiqué, but would certainly face a prolonged struggle over the Chinese claim that talks could only be held on the understanding that sovereignty and administration were to pass to them in 1997. Even if that obstacle were to be overcome, any talks were sure to prove painfully difficult. There would no doubt be Chinese press campaigns. We faced the dangerous Chinese thesis that they were pronouncing on their own territory; as a kindness and for a time, they were prepared to consult, but they would then issue their decrees. In other words an unequal negotiation, even if we got into it; and so far, we were still on the outside.

But we had a few cards. We had achieved our objective of agreement to open talks. We would have a chance of instructing the Chinese in the economic realities of Hong Kong. In the light of that it might be possible to squeeze concessions on administration, though we had to recognize that sovereignty would certainly pass. We still had everything to play for.

CHAPTER EIGHTEEN

The Negotiations: Premises and Preconditions

THE NEGOTIATIONS TO which we were now committed occupied the next two years and demanded, and received, immense infusions of industry, ingenuity, imagination and patience. Their outcome was a considerable triumph and a significant strengthening of Hong Kong's position and confidence; but there were many times when they seemed mired in incomprehension, or poised on the verge of angry breakdown. I shall not attempt a blow-by-blow account: it is a long and complex story. Though at the time we agreed they were to be secret exchanges, the Chinese in one way or another have revealed most of the proceedings; and books are now appearing that give a not too misleading report of what went on. I shall content myself with broader impressions and some comment on the turning-points.

There were three main phases: first, the struggle to get into talks at all, which lasted from October 1982 until July 1983; then the fight to retain British administration, from July to October 1983; finally the stage of conditionality, that is the detailed examination and improvement of the Chinese proposals, on the understanding that, if we could make them satisfactory, we would be prepared to commend the result to Parliament. This final and most intensive stage of negotiation occupied us for the last year and culminated in the initialling of the agreement, the Joint Declaration, in September 1984. After that there was a period in October when Hong Kong opinion was tested on the question whether the product was acceptable. Finally, the Joint Declaration was signed in December 1984.

Phase one, the approach to negotiation, was an extended Kafkaesque episode, in which we wrestled with the Chinese demand that we begin by accepting their precondition, in effect that we should give the game away before we ever got on to the pitch. I made a series of calls at the Foreign Ministry, pressing for an early opening of the talks our leaders had decided on, to be consistently told that we had only to accept the premise and the path would be smooth; otherwise, there would be, to put it mildly, 'difficulties'. The Chinese showed no interest in discussing practical details of the talks, or any supplementary matters. We were confronted with a large issue of principle, which we could not in any circumstances accept and which for long proved impossible to circumvent.

My interlocutor in the first weeks was Zhang Wenjin, the Vice Foreign Minister for Western Europe. He was an old friend. He had been the first senior Chinese official to meet Dr Kissinger in Pakistan on his way to Peking on the celebrated secret visit of July 1971. Kissinger likened him to a Spanish cardinal. He was courtly, austere, intelligent, a professional. But he had his instructions and was obdurate. Unfortunately, he was sent as Ambassador to Washington at the end of the year and personnel changes added to the delays on the Chinese side.

His replacement, Yao Guang, came from a different background. He was an administrator, a solid Party man with links to Zhao Ziyang. He did not pretend to be master of the complexities of the subject and had reportedly been dismayed at the appointment. But he was amiable, secure in his position and reliable as a channel for Chinese views. I came to value him.

We had long and exhausting arguments about the premise, in which I would offer him a prize for any word about preconditions he could find in the joint statement. It was a debating point and gave me some private satisfaction; but, as usual with the Chinese, it did not affect the response. Their statements were opaque but stubborn. It was all rather like trudging through mud and after one particularly trying session, I likened the experience to a wet day on the Western Front. We were not making progress.

The situation in those early days, as we pressed and the Chinese stalled, was both frustrating and worrying. Time was passing and we were now aware there was a deadline. There were also reports of a preliminary Chinese announcement to be made in June. Though we had agreed that the talks were to be kept secret, Chinese leaks and statements in Hong Kong were proceeding apace. Our lips were sealed; in any case we did not want to get into a public argument, which would only have the effect of carving the Chinese position in stone. In November, Liao Chengzhi, the head of the Hong Kong and Macao Office, receiving a Hong Kong delegation, produced the seductive slogan, '*Gang ren zhi gang*' ('Hong Kong people running Hong Kong'), as the mark of the post-1997 era. It had considerable international appeal, with its suggestion that Hong Kong would be liberated from the colonialists and become virtually independent.

These further elaborations of the Chinese plan reminded me of the weakness of our position and the danger that we could be locked out of meaningful discussion, while Hong Kong's fate was decided, and promulgated, in Peking.

In the end we overcame this first major obstacle by a small adjustment in the language about sovereignty. Mrs Thatcher had originally spoken of being ready in certain circumstances to 'consider' making recommendations to Parliament on sovereignty. Tony Galsworthy, my extremely able Head of Chancery, and I together evolved the idea that we might strengthen that clause, making it: 'would be prepared to recommend to Parliament'. We were now stressing to the Chinese that sovereignty was not in the government's gift; it could only be surrendered by Parliament. The whole offer would of course be subject to the condition that suitable administrative arrangements for Hong Kong could be worked out. I carried the proposal back with me to a meeting with the Prime Minister in London in March 1983.

It was as well I did so. Some explosive ideas were being canvassed in the frustration of the time: a public statement by the Prime Minister; a UN-supervised referendum for Hong Kong; bringing the ceded territories, Hong Kong Island and a portion of Kowloon, nearer independence. At one of our meetings Michael Heseltine, then Minister of Defence, was called in.

But the Prime Minister was eventually persuaded to delay, if not abandon, these more dramatic moves and to try the effect of a personal message along the lines I proposed. I returned to Peking with it. She made plain to me, however, that this was her last word, a point I was happy to convey, since it added force to the letter I carried.

The letter did the trick. I called it the first finesse. We had given nothing substantial away. But the Chinese are good at reading between the lines; indeed, their most important reading has to be done in just that way. They saw in the change of wording, slight though it was, a sign of the British government's readiness to move towards a transfer of sovereignty and thereby to make a nod in the direction of their premise, if not a full obeisance. Of course, they sought to present it as an outright acceptance and I had constantly to remind them of its highly conditional nature; but even then they did not draw back. Slowly we were able to move on to settling the agenda, the composition of the delegations, the place and timing of the first formal meeting. The Prime Minister commented that we were treading on eggshells; true, but we were at last inching forward.

A new character emerged on the Chinese side in those days, Assistant Foreign Minister Zhou Nan. He was just back from New York, where for twelve years he had been on the Chinese delegation to the United Nations. Intelligent, cultivated, a great man for quotations, whether in Chinese or English, a great man for toasts in *maotai*, he had acquired some of the Western habits of transacting business: it was even possible to get authoritative answers out of him by telephone; and he accelerated the delicate manoeuvres on the agenda for the talks, which occupied us in the early summer of 1983. But, if less ponderous than Yao Guang, he was also less reliable. I would guess also less secure in his position: he seemed always afflicted with an uneasy need to justify himself to his superiors. He was ambitious and, if given a chance, he liked bullying. He took over from Yao Guang as leader of the Chinese delegation from the end of 1983 and was later to serve as head of the New China News Agency in Hong Kong, in effect China's unofficial representative there. I found him lively and a challenge, sometimes amusing, more often exasperating.

Our first formal negotiating session was held on the morning of 12 July 1983 at a Foreign Ministry guesthouse in Peking. Appropriately, it was in the old Legation quarter and had originally been the home of the Austro-Hungarian Legation. I had with me Teddy Youde, Governor of Hong Kong, but on this and subsequent occasions attending simply as the number two in the British delegation. The Chinese insisted on this veiling of his Hong Kong attributes. There had been a row when he, not unnaturally, told the Hong Kong press that he was going up to Peking to represent the interests of Hong Kong, just as earlier there had been an outcry when a Foreign Office minister spoke of the three-legged stool of Peking, London and Hong Kong. For the Chinese this was a purely bilateral negotiation between London and Peking; they, not the British, would answer for their compatriots in Hong Kong.

Teddy was accompanied by his Political Adviser, Robin McLaren, who was to play an important role in the later detailed negotiations and to serve with distinction as Ambassador in Peking. From the Embassy there came a group of clever young sinologists, Tony Galsworthy, William Ehrman, Nigel Inkster and Bob Pierce. I was well supported.

The Hong Kong press were also there, and in strength, pursuing us from the Embassy to the guesthouse, lying in wait outside and popping up at intervals from behind the bushes in the Residence garden. The Foreign Ministry were unused to this hyperactive style of journalism, but realized quite soon that there were tricks to be won and learned to provide the expected facilities and photo-calls.

We met for two days at a time and only in the mornings. When we protested at this dilatory approach, the Chinese said the afternoons were too hot. In fact they needed to consult their superiors, who kept them on a tight rein; and we too came to see advantage in free afternoons, which gave us time to handle the mass of recording telegrams.

The proceedings were formal, with set speeches and presentation of papers, followed by slightly less rigid rejoinders and rebuttals. (There were less formal contacts, where much business was done, at delegation dinners and bilateral meetings between the heads of delegation.) It was easy for us to score debating points, but they had little impact on the Chinese juggernaut. The talking was confined almost entirely to the delegation leaders.

Sometimes the Governor would speak, whereupon the Chinese, with their fine sense of symmetry, would call on Li Zhusheng, a genial lightweight from the New China New Agency in Hong Kong, whom they had brought up to be a foil to Teddy Youde and to show that they too could speak for the people of the territory.

At the end of each round of talks the two sides issued a short agreed communiqué. This was closely negotiated and when released anxiously analysed by the waiting press. The rather tired adjectives we used to describe our proceedings came to acquire inordinate political, and economic, significance.

Our main concern during those days was to convey to the Chinese how Hong Kong worked and to demonstrate that its remarkable prosperity and investors' confidence were organically linked to British administration, British law and British freedoms. By contrast, there could be no assurance that a socialist country, particularly one like China, with its record of instabilities and upheavals, would be capable of absorbing a capitalist economy without doing fundamental damage to it. The abrupt change could be fatal; unilateral assertions or general expressions of good intent on the part of the Chinese would not suffice to steady the markets and hold investors; continuity of administration was essential. We urged the Chinese to approach the matter objectively, and, to quote from Deng, 'to seek truth from facts'.

The Chinese rejected these arguments in statements which, as session followed session, grew increasingly emotional. They could not accept any division between sovereignty and administration. (In fact their concept of sovereignty embraced administration and from the outset they had been nonplussed by the distinction we drew.) To allow continued British control would be tantamount to another unequal treaty. They repeated that their plan for Hong Kong, the Twelve Points, would certainly assure prosperity and confidence and they set out their proposals in more detail. In any event, China was not prepared to subordinate its political imperative, namely recovery of sovereignty, to arguments about prosperity. There could be no progress in the talks until we acknowledged that both sovereignty and administration return to China.

As the summer wore on, the tone grew shrill and the communiqués no longer contained reassuring adjectives, like 'useful' and 'constructive'. After our August meetings I was reporting that there was little prospect of a move on the Chinese side and that, barring changes in my instructions, we would probably face a breakdown in September.

We adjourned for a short recess and the British side assembled in London in early September to review the situation. It was plain that we faced a crisis. The Chinese would not retreat and we assessed that they were wholly committed to this stand. We therefore had the choice of either accepting a breakdown, or negotiating for the maximum degree of autonomy for Hong Kong that we could get. Breakdown would bring a collapse in confidence and do serious economic damage to the territory. It would not prevent reversion to China in 1997, but would simply mean that such reversion was unqualified, without any of the safeguards we were intent on adding. This would be the worst of all worlds; negotiation for something short of British administration would be preferable.

The Foreign Office and the Governor agreed. But the rest of the Hong Kong government were not ready to draw this conclusion. From an early stage the Governor's Executive Council (Exco) had been fully informed and consulted at each step in the negotiations; and the British officials on the Council and, even more important, the Chinese members, the Unofficials, represented a critical element in the balance of power on the British side. The Chief Secretary, Sir Philip Haddon-Cave, opposed any concession. The Unofficials, led by Sir S. Y. Chung, were also obdurate. A majority took the view that the Chinese were bluffing, that they depended on the Hong Kong economy and that, faced with the prospect of economic collapse, they would draw back. Even if there were to be a breakdown, it was argued, its effect could be softened and it could be turned into something like a gentlemanly adjournment.

We were therefore divided as well as in crisis. The Prime Minister was worried, but felt that we should hold our position for the first meeting after the recess, to see whether our persuasions and papers had had any impact on the Chinese. I accordingly took a firm line when talks resumed on 22 September in Peking. I repeated that the Chinese proposals would not command confidence since they lacked the crucial element of British administration.

Yao Guang's response was intransigent and threatening. He angrily rejected the 'dream of British administration', enlarged on Chinese suffering at the hands of imperialism and formally stated that if there were no agreement by September 1984, the Chinese would announce their decisions for Hong Kong. Ominously, he also revived Deng's threat that if there were disturbances in Hong Kong, China might have to intervene earlier.

Outside the negotiating chamber, Chinese propaganda pressure was mounting. The Hang Seng Index fell sharply and, more seriously, the Hong Kong dollar was slipping. I pressed Yao to agree to some encouraging words in the communiqué so as to prevent further falls. He refused and accused us of manipulating the dollar for political ends. In fact, about this time there was evidence that the Bank of China itself had been speculating against the dollar, which lost 8 per cent in one day, following the issue of the communiqué. There was panic buying of essential goods in Hong Kong; and at home in London the Treasury feared that British reserves might be called on to support the Hong Kong currency.

Eventually, the Hong Kong dollar was linked to the US dollar and the panic subsided. But the markets remained very uneasy and the fragility of the underlying situation had been made apparent.

Further meetings were summoned in London and I called in Hong Kong on my way home. In discussion with Exco I urged them 'to look into the pit', in other words to think hard about the consequences of breakdown. Deng was not bluffing and would let the Hong Kong economy go to the wall if he had to. There was no possibility of a polite stand-off if the clash continued: a breakdown would be rough and there would be no second chance. I recall I won little support, except from the Financial Secretary, John Bembridge, and the Commander British Forces, Derek Boorman.

During the summer I had been thinking about the crisis which would inevitably develop if, as seemed likely, the idea of continuing British administration was rejected. I had drafted a formula, which I called the second finesse. It was a statement that the British view on administration remained unchanged, but that, since the Chinese did not accept it, we were prepared, on a strictly conditional basis, to explore the Chinese proposals in order to see whether on that foundation arrangements might be constructed to ensure lasting stability and prosperity for Hong Kong. If this exploratory process was successful, the government would consider recommending to Parliament a bilateral agreement enshrining such arrangements.

As I saw it, if such a formula could be approved, we would have moved round the obstacle presented by the Chinese insistence on the transfer of sovereignty and administration and would be able, without prejudice, to examine, and no doubt improve, the detail of the Chinese proposals. We would not be totally committed, but confrontation would be avoided.

Again I carried the formula to London and was able to win over the Foreign Secretary and, with slightly more difficulty, the Prime Minister. The Exco Unofficials, who arrived in London with the Governor, proved at first less amenable. They came firm in the conviction that no concessions should be offered. The Foreign Secretary and his Minister of State, Richard Luce, argued persuasively that it would be folly to embark on a confrontation without having first explored the Chinese position fully. Geoffrey Howe had just returned from an interesting meeting with his Chinese opposite number, Wu Xueqian, in New York, in which the latter had spoken of fifty years of capitalist society in Hong Kong after 1997 and a large role for Britain there even after the handover. There were prospects there that deserved further clarification.

The Unofficials wondered aloud whether there was any means of conducting such enquiries without commitment. I said I thought a formula could be found, without at that time revealing the wording. That was left to the Prime Minister the next morning; she produced the form of words and spoke eloquently in its favour. In the end Sir S. Y. Chung, on behalf of his colleagues, accepted that the formula was an excellent basis for exploring the Chinese position without giving anything away. We had restored unity in our own ranks and the negotiations were saved.

It is worth pausing at this moment, a turning-point in the process, to see just what had happened. We had given ground, there was no doubt of that. But we had retreated in good order from what had been shown to be an untenable position. We had carried the fight for British administration as far as it could be carried without fatally damaging, not just the bargaining process and our capacity to influence the outcome, but also the business confidence and economy of Hong Kong itself. The effect of confrontation and the size of the stakes had been demonstrated in late September as the Hong Kong dollar fell. The illusion that China would be restrained by fears of the economic effects had also been exposed. The Prime Minister, who combined a shrewd tactical sense with rigidity of principle, had rapidly realized the choice we faced and had drawn her conclusions. Her arguments to the Unofficials about the damage that would flow from confrontation had nothing artificial or induced about them; she was personally alive to the dangers.

The formula we deployed allowed us to reiterate our unaltered view of the ideal solution, while offering the best chance of exploring and improving the Chinese framework. We retained, at least in theory, the option of drawing back and saying it was not good enough. But, inevitably, as time passed, this option grew more theoretical. Whatever the reminders from Hong Kong or London, and the Prime Minister naturally clung to conditionality to the end, we had accepted the transfer of sovereignty and administration and were negotiating for the best we could get, short of that. As I saw it, that had always been the most likely outcome, though it had been essential to fight the preliminary battles and to show that we had done so. Everything would now depend on what we could inject into the final document in the way of binding and detailed legal obligations defining the structure and way of life of Hong Kong after the hand-over.

The Chinese reception accorded our conditionality proposal was at first cautious, even suspicious. They noted that, while making our proposal, we repeated our views about British administration. They looked for unqualified acceptance of their preconditions. In a radio interview the Prime Minister spoke of enduring British links with Hong Kong and they wondered what lay behind that. A further assurance by us in November, that, in the context of the explorations we were conducting, we intended no link of authority between Britain and Hong Kong after 1997, was necessary before they began to open up and permit an enquiry into quite what their plans entailed.

Here a surprise awaited us. We had been pushing at the door of a locked room, containing, as we thought, treasures of Chinese planning. Now the door was open and the room was found to be virtually empty. There were some broad prescriptions, little else. This offered us an invaluable opportunity to fill the void with our essentials for post-1997 Hong Kong. But we found we had to be very careful how we described them. The Chinese still tended to object to the style and language of our offerings and to shy away from talk about practical matters. They were particularly allergic to the word 'details'. Probably somewhere in the Foreign Ministry there was a minute from on high, specifying a general agreement without detail and they were responding to it. But we learned to rechristen our details as principles and found we got along much better.

There was also at first a disposition on the Chinese side to refuse discussion of any aspects not directly bearing on British economic interests. This they saw as our only field of legitimate concern after the hand-over. If persisted in, this would have excluded us from influencing vital tracts of the post-reversion scene. Happily, after a while, this distinction fell away. There was still a marked reluctance to admit that there was any give-and-take in the process. The best we could expect was that passages from our working papers would appear without acknowledgement and be presented to us as part of the Chinese blueprint. But we had no great pride of authorship; and by the end of the year we were at last through the thickets of premises and preconditions and grappling with the issue of how Hong Kong might best be run after 1997.

CHAPTER NINETEEN

The Negotiations: The Breakthrough

I LEFT PEKING at Christmas 1983 and was succeeded as Ambassador and leader of the British delegation by Sir Richard Evans.

Before leaving, I had had interviews with Zhao Ziyang, with Wu Xueqian, the Foreign Minister, and with Ji Pengfei, Director of the Hong Kong and Macao Office. The message I tried to convey was that Britain was sincere in trying to give the Chinese plan the best chance of success and that our experience in running Hong Kong made us uniquely qualified to help. The Chinese should listen carefully to us and take full account of our advice in developing their plans. In general, they should avoid changing existing arrangements except where it was absolutely necessary. It was essential that civil servants, local or expatriate, should be able to stay on. I also urged them to act with immense care over the issue of stationing troops in Hong Kong. We did not dispute their right to send them; but the effect could be seriously to impair at least the impression of autonomy.

The question of troops had surfaced a little earlier and had about it the extra rigidity evident whenever Deng was personally involved. I was not able to dent their determination here, but on the other issues they were receptive.

Back in London, I became Mrs Thatcher's Foreign Policy Adviser and moved into Downing Street in early January 1984. Characteristically, the Prime Minister had said I must be given ample time to settle back in England and sort out my affairs, but had added that she would like to see me at work in January. In addition, the Foreign Office gave me a post, and a handsome room, as Deputy Under-Secretary in charge of the Hong Kong negotiations. So that I shuttled between two offices and two piles of telegrams.

The focus inevitably changed. I found, for example, that in the first days I was having to turn my mind to the predicament of Western forces in Lebanon and the question of the succession in the Soviet Union. But the negotiations remained an imperative.

For this, the final stretch, I had round me in the Foreign Office a remarkable assembly of talents. The Office were very alive to the importance of the negotiations and, under Antony Acland's kindly direction, did their utmost to supply my needs. Alan Donald, the Under-Secretary, sadly was going off to Indonesia as Ambassador; as replacement I asked for David Wilson, who was to play a crucial role in the detailed work on the text and eventually to serve as Governor of Hong Kong. He was highly intelligent, a first-class Chinese speaker, whom I had known since language-student days in Hong Kong; and he had in addition that feel for the workings of the Chinese mind which I regarded as the negotiator's irreplaceable attribute. He had had experience as the China desk officer in the Far Eastern Department, as Editor of the *China Quarterly* and as Political Adviser in Hong Kong.

To replace Dick Clift, who, as Head of the Hong Kong Department, had borne the heat of the day in the earlier stages of the negotiations, I brought back Tony Galsworthy, my Head of Chancery from Peking, and relied heavily on him. I also secured Christopher Hum, who had earlier served as a gifted Chinese Secretary on my staff in Peking, and William Ehrman, a rising star. As general moderator and purveyor of wisdom I had Trevor Mound, my former Commercial Counsellor. There were others, whom I do not detail for reasons of space. Their faces are in the group photographs I turn over from time to time. *The Times* carried such a picture, over the caption 'Cradock's people'. I should like to record my debt to them all, to their intelligence, resilience and good humour, qualities which were greedily drawn on.

The final months naturally involved major struggles with the Chinese; but, interestingly, the focus was almost as much on the internal debates on our own side. The arguments over conditionality had been an earlier instance. As the negotiations wore on, it was natural that Hong Kong should see itself under pressure and should sometimes feel its case was not given due weight in London. Sir S. Y. Chung, the leader of the Unofficials, was a man of absolute integrity, whom I liked and respected. But he often felt, as did his group, that we should take a harder line and face the Chinese down. He and they held to the view that economic factors would weigh with Peking and induce a retreat on their part. I could not accept that view, which was contrary to all our experience in September and October 1983. Nor did I believe that the Unofficials, or their allies among the British officials, had any way of retrieving the situation and getting back into talks if, as was all too likely, their theory proved wrong and we found ourselves facing a breakdown and unilateral Chinese decrees on Hong Kong. As a result, I too often saw the Unofficials as poised uneasily on the window-ledge, threatening to jump, with myself desperately clutching their coat-tails. The trouble was that Mrs Thatcher, who was instinctively drawn to their extreme ideas, would urge me to listen to the Unofficials, who, she pointed out, were after all Chinese and must therefore know the minds of their compatriots in Peking. Very respectfully, I had to disagree.

As I have said, the British officials of the Hong Kong government were also unyielding; and the Governor himself was driven to move from the centre position to one more nearly corresponding to that of his constituents. He handled them with great skill and was uniquely able to bring home to them the wider considerations; but, inevitably, he and I found ourselves more frequently at odds and having to argue out our differences before ministers. These were to my mind the most difficult encounters of the two years; Cradock's First Law of Diplomacy was proving itself again; but success in them was crucial to the success of the whole process.

The first instance, which fell to be decided in the early months of 1984, was whether we should comply with the Chinese timetable and try to conclude an agreement in September; or refuse and aim only for an interim agreement, or even a broad outline, a series of headings to be filled out later. Hong Kong were strongly in favour of an interim agreement only and, to be fair, they had been encouraged to think that this was also the Foreign Office view. As Hong Kong saw it, Deng's deadline should not be accepted as final. The quantity of work to be done was daunting and, a point the Governor stressed, the Hong Kong public would not accept an agreement before they had had warning of the kind of deal likely to emerge and had had some opportunity of expressing their views. The fact that we were no longer insisting on British administration, for example, was known only to Exco members, though it was to be deduced from any intelligent reading of the press.

On the other hand, I had been coming more and more to the view that our only chance of extracting concessions of substance from Peking and enshrining them in a binding agreement was by working within the Chinese timetable. If we did so, the pressure of time would in the end work for us as well as for the opposition. If we rejected it, there was little chance of inserting our substance and details into the outline Chinese principles. Moreover, we would face the considerable risk that they would make their announcement in September and would then have small incentive to offer more.

This view prevailed, though there was some ill-feeling in Hong Kong in consequence. Looking back, I am sure it was right. Deng was set on his deadline and, if we had not met it, would have announced China's decisions *tout court*. As it was, in the final months the timetable helped to drive both parties to agreement.

But the Governor had a point in pressing for greater communication with the Hong Kong public and this was one of the considerations prompting the Foreign Secretary's visit to Peking and Hong Kong in April 1984. In the course of this visit, at a press conference in Hong Kong, Sir Geoffrey took the opportunity to reveal that we regarded the goal of British administration as no longer attainable. He said it would not be realistic to think in terms of a settlement along those lines. He went on to stress the various Chinese assurances that Hong Kong's society and systems would remain substantially unchanged. But it was an emotional moment.

In Peking he was able to establish a sympathetic working

relationship with the Chinese Foreign Minister, Wu Xueqian, a relationship which significantly helped the progress of the talks. He also obtained Deng's agreement to the timetable, that is, initialling in September. He made some progress on the nature of the agreement. We wanted it binding and detailed. The Chinese hankered after parallel declarations, or declarations of intent. Eventually, they accepted the concept of a binding agreement, but characteristically explained that this could not cover their plans for Hong Kong, which was their own territory. We were to be bound; they were to remain free. They also recoiled from detail.

But the most troublesome issue was the Chinese proposal for a Joint Commission stationed in Hong Kong to oversee the last years of the transitional period leading up to 1997. There had been immediate alarm in Hong Kong when this idea first emerged: it looked very like an excuse for an alternative administration and, in the Governor's view, it would make the territory ungovernable. But in Peking during the Foreign Secretary's visit it became apparent that this was very much Deng's idea. One virtue he saw in it was that it might deter the British from removing the family silver from Hong Kong before they themselves left: Jardine's decision in March 1984 to move their legal domicile to Bermuda had fed this primitive suspicion; and, in rather more sophisticated forms, it is still with us today.

The Joint Commission, or, as it came to be known, the Joint Liaison Group, dominated discussion for the next three months. Coolly considered, it was not an unpractical suggestion: after signature a group of some kind would be needed to deal with the fine print of the agreement and handle consequential issues. As regards its malign effect, if the Chinese were so disposed, they could readily interfere in Hong Kong, with or without a group. But to Hong Kong, that was no reason why we should give it our blessing; the proposal spelt premature surrender; and it was just one more issue on which, as they saw it, London was showing itself rather less than solid. The crux for Hong Kong was not so much the establishment of the group, though that was bad enough; it was the proposed location in the colony. This they bitterly resisted.

We should of course have realized that the idea's origin made it immune to veto, but at the same time of enormous leverage.

Instead of resisting it *à outrance*, the right course was to examine it, emasculate it, delay the date for its entry into force, then sell our acceptance at the highest possible price. In the end we did something like that; but our responses were perhaps slower than they should have been.

One area where we were able to move forward in those frustrating summer months was the setting up of a working group to draft the detailed text of an agreement and to begin work on the annexes which would define post-1997 Hong Kong. These annexes would be vital: the main agreement would be generalized; the meat would be in the fine print. Geoffrey Howe wanted some eminent legal figure to lead our contingent. I resisted this. I had no doubt of the learning he would bring to bear; but the Chinese are not a people of profound legal tradition; and, above all, I feared it would take weeks and months of frustrating, and perhaps fatal, experience to educate our QC in the hard reality of Chinese political sensibilities and negotiating style. We could not afford the time; besides, we already had an excellent legal adviser in Fred Burrows from the Foreign Office. I pressed the case for David Wilson. Happily, this was accepted; and he and Burrows, plus Robin McLaren from Hong Kong, began work on 21 June in sweltering conditions in a room at the International Club in Peking.

About the same time I began pressing for another visit by the Foreign Secretary to Peking. This would accelerate work on the pile of major issues confronting us; and it would enable us to settle the dispute over the Joint Liaison Group at the highest level and, we hoped, at the highest price. We were prepared in the last resort to accept location in Hong Kong rather than see the talks break down. But we had to make progress.

The Foreign Secretary was at first a little hesitant about a visit; and I recall Len Appleyard, his Private Secretary, and myself talking to him and arguing that history would not excuse us, by which we meant him, if we were not seen to have made every effort to reach agreement in the few remaining months. He readily took the point.

Teddy Youde strongly opposed the proposal. He was not prepared to see the negotiations founder over the location issue; but he regarded the concession as so damaging to Hong Kong that it must be withheld until early September, when we would know whether it was indeed inevitable. Until then we should sit tight. A visit in July would be a sign of weakness; we would be running after the Chinese.

So once again the protagonists assembled under the Prime Minister's chairmanship. It was our last and fiercest passage of arms, once again against a background of financial turbulence in Hong Kong. I argued, as did Richard Evans, that postponement of the visit would carry excessive risk of a harsh Chinese reaction during the period of deadlock. That might well prevent constructive discussion in the few months available to us. Even if that did not occur, postponement would make it impossible to complete our outstanding business by the deadline of the end of September. We just did not have the time. We needed every day, in order to cover the agenda and construct an agreement if all went well, or, if not, at least to demonstrate to Parliament that before the breakdown we had thoroughly explored the Chinese position.

It was agreed that the Foreign Secretary should make his visit, but should carry a firm message in the form of a letter from the Prime Minister, emphasizing that we could only accept an agreement that we could honourably commend to Parliament and suggesting that both sides should put aside the location question for the time being. They could return to it when they had settled other aspects of the group's constitution and work, and other matters in dispute in the negotiations. It was in some respects a compromise, but it got the Foreign Secretary to Peking.

On the eve of the visit I became worried that the authority we had been given for negotiation might prove too narrow and might tie our hands in Peking. I minuted to the Prime Minister, suggesting contingent authority for the Foreign Secretary, particularly if we found ourselves in a situation where the Chinese refused to discuss other aspects of the Joint Liaison Group before its location was settled. She refused, saying we would have to refer back. As it turned out, she was right. The Foreign Secretary, making the same request a few hours later, received an even firmer refusal. But she agreed to a change in her letter, hinting that postponement of the group's location in Hong Kong might make things easier for us.

We stopped in Hong Kong on the way to Peking and the Foreign Secretary outlined our tactics to British officials. They made it plain that they opposed any concessions over locating the Joint Liaison Group in Hong Kong and said the British line was generally much too pliant. I warned them that breakdown would bring much worse consequences. They remained unconvinced, but I recall David Akers-Jones, a lone voice, saying that if the Foreign Secretary did not make this trip to Peking, Hong Kong people would never forgive him.

At the Exco meeting the next morning the Unofficials urged that we should insist on extending the life of the Joint Group beyond 1997 in order to balance the fact that it would be in operation well before British rule ended. This was a clever idea, which I think originated with Maria Tam, an able lawyer on Exco; it had been about for a little while and we had had varying reactions to it from the Chinese side. My only concern was that the request should not be put on paper, lest it find its way to Deng, who was showing himself increasingly irascible and unpredictable, and be struck out for good. Subject to that, it was added to the brief.

So to Peking. I had a private lunch with Zhou Nan on the first day. We had had a similar meeting during the Foreign Secretary's April visit and found it useful. On this occasion I was not looking forward to it. I had not slept much: the first night out from home had been mainly spent at the back of the plane with Geoffrey Howe and Tony Galsworthy, drafting and redrafting revised terms of reference for the Joint Liaison Group; and the prospect of a bibulous lunch, with repeated toasts in *maotai* with Zhou Nan, was not appealing. But his message brought me sharply awake. He said that there were important meetings of leaders impending on the Chinese side. They would affect Hong Kong. That meant that outstanding issues had to be resolved in the next two to three days. Otherwise the Chinese would withdraw their offers and the talks would fail. They were prepared to accept our terms of reference for the Joint Liaison Group, also prepared to accept postponement of its siting in Hong Kong and its extension for three years from 1997. But they wanted a rapid answer and, he hinted, the issues had to be resolved before the Foreign Secretary saw Deng Xiaoping. He seemed nervous about Deng's possible reactions.

It was clear to me, and to Tony Galsworthy, who accompanied me, that this was the moment of truth and that the offer was to be taken very seriously. I returned to the Diaoyutai guesthouse, where we were all accommodated, and asked Geoffrey Howe if I could talk to him in the garden; that seemed a more discreet setting. We stood under a flowering tree on that blazing July afternoon, a small, rather tense group, and I told my story and made my recommendations. The Ambassador, the Governor and the Private Secretary, Len Appleyard, all agreed that we were at the Chinese bottom line. The Foreign Secretary likewise agreed. It was left that I should draft a telegram to the Prime Minister, helped by Galsworthy and Appleyard, while the rest of the delegation returned for the afternoon round of talks with the Chinese Foreign Minister.

The telegram, slightly amended in the light of information from Wu Xueqian that afternoon, was duly sent and a reply arrived the next morning. Essentially, it approved the proposed strategy but asked for more. It gave encouragement, but not *carte blanche*.

It was just the reply we needed. On that basis we were able in the next two days to enjoy maximum leverage and to settle issues over which we had haggled fruitlessly for months. The Joint Liaison Group was dealt with, its powers curtailed, its operation from Hong Kong postponed until 1988 and its life extended until the year 2000. The Foreign Secretary moved quietly and skilfully through these thickets, pocketing gains, pressing for more, recognizing when the limit was reached. At the same time, in another part of the forest, decisive progress was made on the agreement itself: it was accepted that the annexes were to be of equal force with the main agreement; and that the policy set out in the main agreement and annexes would be stipulated in the Basic Law (the constitution for Hong Kong which the Chinese would draw up). The objectionable language about history and the transfer of sovereignty in the Chinese draft was struck out. Finally, and most important, language was included which tied the declarations of intent by each side into a legally binding international commitment.

In *David Copperfield*, it will be recalled, the amiable Mr Spenlow, Dora's father, finds it convenient to transform his part-ner, Jorkins, into a hard man, an ogre, to whom he can attribute refusals of any inconvenient request. We operated on the same principle in those few days; with the difference that our Jorkins, in London, needed no invention. It was not until the evening of 29 July, on the eve of the Foreign Secretary's meeting with Zhao Ziyang, that his, or rather her, authority to settle arrived. But in the interval the main work had been done.

On 31 July the Foreign Secretary and his party were received by Deng Xiaoping, who had travelled back specially from Beidahe, the seaside resort beloved by Chinese leaders. It was well understood that this was an act of benediction, not a negotiating session. He would not have come unless we had succeeded.

Deng noted with pleasure that the two sides had virtually reached agreement on Hong Kong: only small points remained. He congratulated Mrs Thatcher on bringing to an end British colonial rule, just as General de Gaulle had brought to a close French colonial rule. He accepted the Foreign Secretary's compliments on the value of his concept of 'one country, two systems'. But, as in April, he revealed his concern that there might be asset-stripping in the territory before the hand-over. Geoffrey Howe gave his personal assurance that the prudent management of Hong Kong would be maintained; and at the end of the interview Deng made the interesting remark that the Chinese had now come to the conclusion that, in the matter of Hong Kong, they could trust us. He concluded by inviting the Queen to visit China.

The Governor, who was worried about premature disclosure, had arranged that our reporting telegrams from Peking should not be repeated to Hong Kong. Exco were therefore in the dark when they were summoned to Government House on the afternoon of 31 July to hear our report. It was received in almost total silence. But at the formal Exco meeting the next morning Sir S. Y. Chung was warmly appreciative and paid a handsome tribute to the negotiators. At the meeting with Umelco (the Unofficial members of the Executive and Legislative Councils) there was spontaneous applause; and, following the Foreign Secretary's press conference, the Hong Kong press were enthusiastic.

There were a number of turning-points in the negotiations: the Prime Minister's message of March 1983, which allowed us to move from preliminary discussions to formal negotiations; the message of October 1983, in which we dropped our insistence on maintaining British administration and showed a readiness to examine what could be built on the basis of the Chinese Twelve Points; and the decision, in February 1984, to meet the Chinese deadline and attempt an agreement by the end of September. These were all critical episodes. But there is no doubt that the July visit to Peking was in many ways the most dramatic. Before it took place the prospects of a tolerable agreement were doubtful; breakdown seemed possible and there was considerable anxiety, particularly in Hong Kong. After the visit, although there were still delicate and difficult matters to settle, the back of the problem had been broken and we were within sight of an historic agreement.

Looking back, the decision to proceed with the visit in July was vindicated. It gave us the last chance of a resolution of key issues before the Chinese leaders reviewed the Hong Kong question in what would have been a hostile atmosphere, and it left us just enough time for the remaining detailed work before the September deadline. The key was the location of the Joint Liaison Group in Hong Kong: as we had expected, we had to give way on that; but the timing proved negotiable and the way to a compromise. Finally the need to refer back to London proved an advantage: for two days of maximum leverage Spenlow and Jorkins fought on our side.

When we got back to London the Cabinet recorded their formal thanks to the Foreign Secretary, Sir Richard Evans, Sir Edward Youde and myself. On my report to her, the Prime Minister added her personal thanks and congratulations, going on to say, 'It was an excellent result – progress beyond all expectations.' From that quarter, praise indeed. But there was an immense amount still to do; and it is unfair to those who laboured in the last six weeks to treat their work as a kind of anticlimax.

The Ambassador was still condemned to struggle with Zhou Nan, who seemed unmoved by the new spirit of compromise and regularly added his own touch of hostility to Chinese instructions which in any case remained discouragingly negative. Increasingly, we had to have recourse to personal messages from Geoffrey Howe to Foreign Minister Wu.

After a short break, David Wilson's working group was again in full cry, treating questions of crucial importance, such as the legal system and constitutional arrangements after 1997. To deal with the highly technical matters of land, civil aviation and nationality, another working group was established under Robin McLaren and performed wonders. Robin had to deal with Lu Ping, the ablest member of the Chinese team, and one we were to hear much of later. We owed a great debt to these small bodies of front-line troops, wrestling with intricate and sensitive questions in parallel English and Chinese texts under ever more demanding timetables.

Their reports and recommendations, as well as the telegrams relating Richard Evans' encounters with Zhou Nan, flowed in mounting streams to London and were repeated to Hong Kong, where officials sat up most of the night to despatch their comments and improvements. In London serious work began in the late afternoon with the arrival of the Hong Kong telegrams and continued into the night. Rapid decisions were required. It was usually a choice between the Wilson text (relatively short, though distinctly longer than the Chinese draft) and the Hong Kong text (very long and detailed). I tended to come down more on the side of David Wilson's recommendations: he could judge best from his position how much detail the Chinese could take without revolt. In the end we got a surprising amount.

Finally texts were ready. The work drew to an end in the third week of September, though not before Zhou Nan had vainly tried to substitute 'will' for 'shall' throughout the main annex, in an attempt to make it less binding. Exco came back to London to pronounce on the documents. The agreement was initialled in Peking by the Ambassador and Zhou Nan on 26 September 1984.

In October the Hong Kong public were given a chance to express a view on the outcome, by an assessment process, which was the nearest we could come to a full-scale vote without Chinese resistance. The choice was stark: Do you favour acceptance or rejection of the agreement? Amendment was not a realistic option. Only a small minority of the opinions favoured rejection.

In December, just before Christmas, the Prime Minister flew out to Peking to sign the agreement. I have very little recollection of that visit. I like to think that is because little that was new or of great substance was said, though there were of course the customary ceremonial statements. At home our minds had been turning to other things; Gorbachev, still not the Party leader, had just been for lunch at Chequers; and there was much debate about President Reagan's Strategic Defence Initiative (Star Wars). I do, however, recall the flight out. We had provided Mrs Thatcher with a speech which ended with a quotation from Tennyson's 'Ulysses'. She liked Tennyson and knew the passage. I remember her sitting over dinner and, in concert with Robin Butler and myself, intoning the final lines.

> . . . . for my purpose holds
> To sail beyond the sunset, and the baths
> Of all the western stars, until I die.
> It may be that the gulfs will wash us down:
> It may be we shall touch the Happy Isles,
> And see the great Achilles, whom we knew.
> Though much is taken, much abides; and though
> We are not now that strength which in old days
> Moved earth and heaven; that which we are we are;
> One equal temper of heroic hearts,
> Made weak by time and fate, but strong in will
> To strive, to seek, to find, and not to yield.

CHAPTER TWENTY

The Joint Declaration

THE AGREEMENT EMERGING from these labours was brief in its main provisions but long and detailed in its annexes.

It began with two balanced declarations, one by the Chinese government, that China would resume the exercise of sovereignty over Hong Kong with effect from 1 July 1997; and one by the British government, that Britain would restore Hong Kong to China on the same date. These declarations recognized and gave effect to a situation which was already inevitable as a result of the approaching expiry of a lease covering 92 per cent of the territory. Another statement, this time in the name of both governments, later in the agreement declared that Britain remained responsible for the administration of Hong Kong up to July 1997 and that China would give its co-operation in this respect. Thus the framework of control was laid down without upsetting the position of either side on sovereignty.

There was then an abbreviated statement in China's name on the principal policies to be followed in Hong Kong after the hand-over. These were in effect China's Twelve Points. At the end of them was a statement that these policies, plus their elaboration in Annex 1 of the agreement, would be stipulated in a Basic Law for the territory to be passed by the National People's Congress and would remain unchanged for fifty years.

This was a very important provision, since it brought in the detail in the annexes and undertook its incorporation in the new

constitution for post-1997 Hong Kong. It also gave the assurance
of fifty years' duration. This was later interpreted by the Chinese
as 'at least fifty years'.

There were references to the annexes on the Joint Liaison
Group and on land leases. Following these came the critical
sentence that both governments agreed to implement the
preceding declarations and annexes. This gave legal force to the
undertakings. Until late in the day the Chinese had wanted no
more than a declaration of intent.

The meat of the agreement lay in Annex 1, which was the
elaboration, nominally by both sides, but in fact by the British,
of the broad Chinese plans for Hong Kong set out in the main
agreement. It was extensive, detailed and cast in the precise,
lawyer-like language that we wanted. It covered virtually every
aspect of Hong Kong life, beginning with constitutional arrangements and the legal system and passing on to a variety of other
sectors.

Among the key provisions were the following:

- after 1997 Hong Kong would become a Special Administrative Region (SAR) of China, enjoying a high degree
  of autonomy;
- within this Special Region Hong Kong's capitalist system
  and lifestyle would remain unchanged for fifty years;
- the legislature would be elected (it was not specified how)
  and the executive would be accountable to the legislature;
- the existing legal and judicial systems would be
  maintained;
- Hong Kong people's rights and freedoms under Hong
  Kong law would be maintained, as would those under the
  International Covenant on Civil and Political Rights and
  the International Covenant on Economic, Social and
  Cultural Rights;
- Hong Kong would enjoy autonomy in the economic,
  financial and monetary fields. China would not tax Hong
  Kong. The Hong Kong dollar would remain convertible
  and there would be freedom to move capital. Hong Kong
  would remain a free port;
- existing land leases would be recognized after 1997;

- the existing educational system would be maintained;
- Hong Kong residents would remain able to travel and move freely in and out of the territory; and
- members of Hong Kong's public service would retain their employment, and their pension rights would be safeguarded.

It was as comprehensive protection as could be devised and agreed. On foreign affairs and defence, which were to be the responsibility of the central government, the provisions were necessarily more restrictive. But it was established that the SAR government would manage certain aspects of its external relations, for example, in the economic field; and in the difficult area of defence, where we did not get all we wanted, it was agreed that the maintenance of public order would remain a local responsibility, that military forces from the central government sent to Hong Kong would not interfere in its internal affairs and that their expenses would be borne by the central government.

On perhaps the most sensitive subject of all, nationality, it proved impossible to reach agreement on all issues and there was therefore an exchange of memoranda, setting out the British and Chinese positions.

This was as good an agreement as we could realistically have hoped to obtain. It was always possible to imagine circumstances in which something better would have been forthcoming, say a totally compliant or powerless government in Peking. But this was the world of fantasy. The British negotiators faced something quite different: a regime enjoying vastly superior power, imbued with nationalist sentiment, determined to recover lost territory, and impatient to issue its decrees to that end. The fact of a lease with only fourteen years to run completed the picture. The choice was always between reversion on the best terms we could obtain and breakdown plus unqualified reversion, that is, without any protection for Hong Kong. At each crisis the British side had to remind itself of this decisive fact and choose with care. Against this background, the Joint Declaration was a considerable achievement.

Would the Chinese honour their undertakings? There could be no absolute guarantee of this, any more than with any other international agreement. But compliance was entirely in accord

with their interests and that was the best safeguard. They had
entered into a solemn legal commitment, a treaty registered with
the United Nations. To breach it would destroy their international standing and any prospect of inducing Taiwan to enter
into similar arrangements. Having opted for the legal rather than
the military solution to the problem, they could be relied on to
adhere to such a course.

The process of negotiation which eventually brought the two
sides together also revealed how remote were their starting
points, their preconceptions and their negotiating styles. The
critical objective from the Chinese point of view was the recovery
of national territory, control of which had been lost to Britain
in humiliating circumstances in the nineteenth century. This
imparted a special sensitivity and rigidity to the Chinese
approach and in consequence to the whole proceedings. It meant
that the basic concept of negotiating with a foreign power over
Hong Kong was objectionable to the Chinese: how could they
do so over what was Chinese territory? It meant that the Chinese
not only rejected out of hand proposals for continuing British
administration under Chinese sovereignty, but also that they
would only negotiate on the basis of their Twelve Points. The
final arrangement, though legally binding, had to be expressed
in large part as a unilateral Chinese declaration and the crucial
annexes as an elaboration on that declaration. Throughout there
was deep suspicion of anything that might seem to derogate from
or qualify the Chinese assertion of full sovereignty, including
administrative rights.

The negotiations were more coloured by these nationalist
emotions than by Chinese Marxist, or Maoist, preconceptions.
But the difficulties inherent in the subject were compounded by
the differences between the British and Chinese political philosophies and analysis. As the Chinese saw it, we were in Hong
Kong to exploit the territory and extract revenue from it. The
British government exercised control over British businessmen
there and manipulated the local currency for political ends, as,
for example, in the financial crisis of September 1983. The
negotiation would be a struggle in which the British as colonialists would prove both obstinate and devious. Deng warned
against their tricks. In the end, British commercial and financial
interests would need to be satisfied; on this point they were

prepared to talk. Our assurances that we sought only the well-being of the people of Hong Kong and recognized a moral responsibility for them were found both baffling and hypocritical.

It followed from this that the Chinese were particularly touchy about the role of the Hong Kong government in the proceedings. Anything suggesting an independent function, such as talk about a 'three-legged stool', was anathema. To them the negotiations were strictly bilateral. They objected to us citing Hong Kong opinion, insisting that they knew its people better than we did. Public debate in Hong Kong about the negotiations invariably sent the temperature up in Peking. There were deep suspicions that we were seeking to give Hong Kong true independence rather than a high degree of autonomy as part of China. This sensitivity and suspicion persist today.

On the British side, the negotiations were not bilateral but triangular, with Hong Kong as the third party. We made it clear from the outset that any arrangements reached had to be accept-able to the people of Hong Kong; the clause was in all our formulations. At each stage we had to bring Hong Kong along with us. At the end we had to test Hong Kong opinion as thoroughly as we could without provoking violent Chinese reaction and endangering the agreement. For us, many of the critical debates were internal and strong Hong Kong opposition had to be overcome before certain moves could be made, for example, compliance with the Chinese timetable and the Foreign Secretary's visit to Peking in July 1984. For the Prime Minister, the real criterion throughout was what was best for the people of Hong Kong; and she would pause and respond to this point in the midst of the most abrasive debate.

It was a highly unequal negotiation. The Chinese held virtually all the cards. They had only to wait until 1997, when, under a treaty we recognized, 92 per cent of the territory would pass to them, the remaining 8 per cent not being viable on its own. They possessed overwhelming military force, in addition to the capacity to cut off essential supplies. At an early stage they took up, in their Twelve Points, a position that was interna-tionally presentable, namely that Hong Kong should be governed by Hong Kong people and that the capitalist system should survive there. They sought the economic benefits of

Hong Kong, but were confident that their plan would secure them; and, if it came to the crunch, they were prepared to sacrifice economic benefits for nationalist and political objectives.

The British cards were that Hong Kong under the existing system undoubtedly worked well; that if possible the Chinese wanted to have their cake and eat it, that is, achieve their nationalist aims without economic loss, and feared that in certain circumstances we might sabotage Hong Kong's prosperity; that China, for international and presentational reasons, preferred to recover Hong Kong by agreement rather than seizure; and that Chinese unilateral action or a clear failure of prosperity in Hong Kong would adversely affect Peking's plans for Taiwan. We enjoyed one further advantage, that the Chinese had already made the imaginative leap of 'one country, two systems': they were not seeking a socialist regime in the territory. Imperfect though the base was, we had something on which to build.

The Chinese approach, as in many other negotiations, was to set up principles and make acceptance of them the precondition for further discussion. Since the principle invariably involved the whole point at issue, finesses had to be devised permitting continued discussion and exploration without irrevocable concessions. As has been seen, these were delicate and time-consuming manoeuvres; but, to be fair, it should be noted that in the end relatively small changes of language were sufficient to open the door. There was throughout an underlying Chinese wish to have an agreement, naturally on terms they thought acceptable, and in consequence a willingness to look positively at formulae that would save face and allow work to go on. They pressed hard for unconditional acceptance of the premise but did not make it a sticking point. As the talks wound on there was increasing movement on their side; at first, in other meetings or in the public elaboration of their plans new material emerged; later there were explicit concessions, as in the Foreign Secretary's July visit. In the final stages there was open horse-trading.

On the question of detail, there was again a vast difference of approach. From an early stage the Chinese made it clear that they did not want much in the way of small print. What they hankered after was a bland, generalized statement, rather in the style of an imperial edict. The reason was in part unfamiliarity with Hong Kong conditions; in part a wish to leave detail to be worked out in the Basic Law and so give themselves a freer hand. But there was also probably a cultural obstacle, an instinctive recoil from the lawyers' language in which we were accustomed to deal.

For our side it was crucial to have detail covering every important aspect of Hong Kong life, to have precise language and to have a provision that all this would later be stipulated in the Basic Law. Eventually the device of annexes of equal validity to the main agreement helped us over this obstacle. But even now, looking at the annexes, I am surprised at the degree of detailed prescription for what they saw as their own territory the Chinese were brought to accept.

It was agreed that the negotiations should be secret and we stuck to that. The Chinese did not. From early 1982, through remarks to eminent visitors, or to journalists, or in meetings with Hong Kong Chinese, they gradually made known their plans for the territory after 1997 and continued to do so in face of our protests. There were probably two reasons. First, they asserted a right to communicate directly with their compatriots in Hong Kong, probably seeing this as a way of exerting pressure on them and outflanking the British position. Second, for reasons given above, they did not recognize Hong Kong as a proper subject for negotiations with a foreign power. The statements were a means of developing their own thinking and sometimes taking account of British concerns without admitting that there was any give-and-take.

Despite this deliberate breach of the rules, I am sure that the confidential or secret framework was essential to success. It allowed exploration without commitment and retreat without loss of face. A more public process would have been foredoomed. The Chinese required discretion, at least on the part of their interlocutors; they also demanded respect. This did not mean affection for China – sentiment would have been ruthlessly exploited – or subservience. What they sought was a recognition that China was a major power, whose views and co-operation counted, particularly on a semi-domestic matter like Hong Kong, and whose history and outlook demanded careful attention. Given such an approach, they were accessible and sometimes rewarding, though never easy. *Per contra*, anything that smacked of imposition, or edict, or what they saw as 'old colonial attitudes' could be guaranteed to alienate and inflame.

In the end, progress and eventual success in the talks depended on a series of judgements as to how far the other side could be pressed, how much traffic a flimsy bridge would bear. These judgements were not blind: they were informed by knowledge of the other side's habits and attitudes, and by a sense of the 'correlation of forces'. But they were all to some degree acts of faith, leaps in the dark. And they were not capable of subsequent proof. We were not in a laboratory, able to repeat the experiment with a series of samples; we were given one shot in each case. If the judgement was wrong it would probably mean a breakdown, when, by definition, knowledge would come too late. The only criterion for the success of a particular move was its contribution to a satisfactory final outcome.

I am confident that more could not have been extracted; but I cannot indisputably demonstrate the fact. Perhaps the only measure of how far we got and how near to the edge of tolerance we were operating was the violent Chinese reaction to later limited attempts to extend the bounds of Hong Kong's autonomy.

The agreement was received with relief and acclamation in Hong Kong, Britain and further afield. In the House of Commons all parties were complimentary. Enoch Powell called it a remarkable achievement. The United Nations Secretary-General spoke of it as 'one of the most outstanding examples of effective quiet diplomacy in contemporary international relations'. The Hong Kong press were jubilant; the British papers were more cautious, but still overwhelmingly favourable. The *Sunday Telegraph* called it 'a pretty good deal in the circumstances'. For *The Times*, 'Given the limits on what could be achieved, it comes close to being as good as Britain and Hong Kong can expect to get.' Only *The Economist* struck a sour note, drawing a parallel with Hitler's Anschluss of 1938. The *Sunday Times* noted there was nothing in the agreement to stop a perfidious China reneging on the deal:

But there is no way the British negotiators could secure Hong Kong against such risks. No way that is unless Mrs Thatcher was prepared to break international law, tear up the treaties that leased the colony to Britain and prepare to fight (and lose) a war against China.

In practice, the only alternative open to Britain was to reject an agreement with China and wash its hands of any interest in events after 1997. That might have removed the guilt some Britons now feel about Hong Kong's future, but it would have done nothing to help the luckless people of Hong Kong.

For Britain the negotiations have been a triumph of realism over woolly hopes.

It is interesting to read these comments today against the background of the criticism routinely evoked by any proposals for further agreements with China over Hong Kong.

CHAPTER TWENTY-ONE

The Road to Tiananmen

THE SIGNATURE OF the Joint Declaration inevitably brought a change of tempo and, to some extent, of direction. There was no longer the compulsion of the negotiating process and the deadline, or even the preparation for the final exchanges between the two leaders. The great effort was over. There was some consequential business, but it flowed smoothly: the Hong Kong Bill passed through Parliament in the early months of 1985 and, after the exchange of instruments of ratification on 7 May, the agreement entered fully into force.

With the signature, my work in the Foreign Office was done and I could close my office there and concentrate on No. 10. In addition to the post of Foreign Policy Adviser, I took on new duties as Chairman of the Joint Intelligence Committee. It was in some ways an odd combination; and once again it was a case of two offices and two piles of paper. But I found that in practice it worked well. In the second role I had responsibility for a powerful intelligence and assessment machine, with a worldwide reporting function; and while the thoughts of an unsupported Foreign Policy Adviser might have weighed lightly against the numbers and experience of the Foreign Office, they were not so easily dismissed when drawing on the collective judgements of the Assessments Staff and the Intelligence Committee. It was a crisis post, with the impossible task of foreseeing and warning against every international contingency affecting British interests; but it provided a solid base of information and at least the illusion of knowing what was going on in the outside world.

Even so, our arrangements in No. 10 were odd and par-simonious to a degree. Only two men on her immediate staff helped the Prime Minister over the whole range of foreign affairs, her Foreign Policy Adviser and the Private Secretary on the foreign affairs side. And though the Private Secretaries were picked men of outstanding ability, in my time John Coles, Charles Powell and Stephen Wall, it was, and indeed is, a typically British, shoestring arrangement, depending more on devotion beyond the call of duty and a certain sleight-of-hand than on any inherent logic or practical sense. Our allies, par-ticularly the Americans, who work in more lavish ways, admired the result but wondered at the organization.

Given such domestic economies, it was natural that my eye should stray from China from time to time in the years imme-diately following the Joint Declaration. Gorbachev, Star Wars, nuclear weapons generally, the Iran-Iraq War, South Africa, terrorism, these all now could claim priority. And at first it seemed we could relax a little on China. The two governments basked in unwonted good relations. Zhao Ziyang, the Prime Minister, paid an official visit to Britain in 1985. Hu Yaobang, the General Secretary, followed the next year. In 1986 the Queen visited China.

But there were already concerns, even anxieties. The Chinese had undertaken to pass a Basic Law, which would be the con-stitution for the Special Administrative Region of Hong Kong after 1997 and would repeat, in its own language, the provisions of the Joint Declaration and its annexes. A Drafting Committee was set up in June 1985, with fifty-nine members, twenty-three from Hong Kong. Its product would be a Chinese document and strictly Britain had no *locus standi*. But it was obviously essential that the Basic Law should faithfully embody the result of the negotiations. It would also break new ground by adding detail; and this had to be watched carefully. The Joint Liaison Group was also holding its first sessions, meeting in Peking, London and Hong Kong in rotation; and there were the first signs of differences in interpretation, for example, over the issue of representative government.

There was also the question of political development. Were we preserving, as in amber, Hong Kong society as it existed on 26 September 1984? Or were we allowing for development between 1984 and 1997? If so, what degree of development? It was very much in the interests of both sides that there should be a smooth transition; and there were now legal obligations in that sense.

From this grew the principle of convergence, namely that major changes in government during the transitional period should be agreed so that they should remain in force beyond the hand-over. This meant having them enshrined in the Basic Law. The principle had advantages for both sides: it gave the Chinese an influence in the remaining period of British rule; and the Chinese came to see convergence as an arrangement whereby they would decide what to put in the Basic Law and the British would converge with it. But, by the same token, it offered Britain a further opportunity of shaping the scene after the transfer and of ensuring that evolution in the final years would survive the transition. In practice there was consultation on the Basic Law and to some degree British views were taken into account. It was recognized that there was no point, and much danger, in developments that would be abruptly terminated on 1 July 1997.

These were delicate issues. In the public domain, the press had by now recovered their equilibrium after the welcome for the agreement in September 1984 and were beginning to pick at Hong Kong's worries. Would China keep its word? What assurance could there be? The figures of those emigrating rose and were duly highlighted. Some returned, having set up an alternative base and acquired the necessary papers; others went for good. Hong Kong flourished enormously: gross domestic product was up 30 per cent between 1985 and 1988; but for the press, particularly the British press, the negative aspects held greater attraction.

The factor with the greatest and, as it turned out, the most malign influence on the Joint Declaration and on Sino-British relations as a whole was the course of Chinese politics. During the years 1984–8 the internal and often covert struggle between reformers and conservatives on the mainland swayed to and fro. Bouts of economic reform would be interspersed with backward-looking campaigns against 'spiritual pollution' or 'bourgeois liberalism'; deals by which veteran leaders were retired or army influence reduced would be paid for by checks on liberalization and a hardening of the ideological line. Political reform was the most sensitive field of all. In September 1986, at its Sixth Plenum, the Party committed itself to reform, both political and economic, and Deng stated in June of the same year that 'in the final analysis all our other reforms depend on the success of political reform'. But moves on this front remained extremely cautious. The battle illustrated the underlying contradiction between economic reform and tight political control. It revealed the abiding strength of 'old thinking', particularly among the Party elders. But it also revealed the vigour of the subterranean stream of political dissent, breaking out on the surface from time to time, usually under the encouragement of dissident intellectuals.

In the autumn of 1986 relaxation of the political constraints on cultural work prompted a new popular debate on political reform. The prominent astro-physicist, Fang Lizhi, not without some support from senior Party officials, encouraged his students at Hefei University in Anhui to campaign for genuine elections to the local provincial people's assembly. But the campaign, once launched, did not stop there and broadened out into a repeat of the 1979 Democracy Movement, involving universities across the country and calls for Western-style democracy, political pluralism and human rights. It culminated in demonstrations by Peking students in Tiananmen Square on 1 and 2 January 1987 in defiance of a ban on marches and rallies.

This outburst and Deng's sharp reaction to it cost Hu Yaobang his post as General Secretary (he resigned on 16 January). It also brought lasting damage to the reformist cause. There was, inevitably, a rectification campaign, condemning bourgeois liberalism. It went hand in hand with an austerity budget and reductions in capital spending. Zhao Ziyang took over as Party Secretary and endeavoured to keep up the liberalizing momentum. But it was an uneasy compromise, even in 1988, by which time the force of the conservative backlash had somewhat dissipated. The promotion of the hard-line Li Peng to succeed Zhao as Prime Minister in November 1987 showed how frail it was; and behind Li Peng stood the 'Gang of Elders', people like Chen Yun, Peng Zhen, Wang Zhen, Zhou Enlai's widow Deng Yingchao, and the ex-President, Li Xiannian. To these could be added the new President, Yang Shangkun, who had strong military connections. The longer-term effect of Hu's downfall was fatally to weaken the reformist wing of the leadership for the rest of the decade.

In the main internal debates of 1988, which turned on prices, whether they should be set by the state or by market forces, Zhao's proposals, after an initial, illusory success, were effectively sabotaged by the conservatives, helped by a series of crop failures, severe floods and marked social discontent in the cities. Deng was quoted as saying: 'We have been bold enough. Now we need to take our steps in a more cautious way.' The mood of resurgent conservatism was reinforced by unrest on the borders of China, in Tibet and Xinjiang. The disturbances there were put down by force and the events used to discredit the more tolerant minorities policy of the past, associated with Hu Yaobang.

In this tense atmosphere a renewed outburst of pro-democracy agitation came with explosive force. In January 1989, Fang Lizhi, now based in Peking, wrote an open letter to Deng Xiaoping seeking the release of Wei Jingsheng, the principal spokesman and victim of the 1979 'Peking Spring'. Fang also sought an amnesty for other political prisoners. Similar appeals, together with calls for political reform, were submitted by many other prominent writers and intellectuals. Preparations were made on campuses for rallies against corruption and in support of more democracy to coincide with the anniversary of the 4 May student movement in 1919.

As if this was not enough, there was one further event which had a determining effect, namely the death of Hu Yaobang on 15 April. This transformed what could have been a narrowly based and transient pro-democracy agitation into a national movement. It provided a figurehead, a 'lost leader' of liberal inclinations, on the pattern of Zhou Enlai in 1976. It also prompted early, and damning, political comment directed at the existing leadership, along the lines of 'The wrong leader has died'. Massive demonstrations followed, in part mourning Hu, in part demanding a freer political system, and increasingly in defiance of the instructions of the authorities. For many weeks Tiananmen Square was effectively occupied by the protestors, at first as normal demonstrators, later as hunger-strikers.

The remaining acts of the tragedy are reasonably well known

and there is no need to recount them here. In the end the demonstrations were bloodily suppressed. Between 3 and 7 June, mainly on 4 June, very large numbers of students and other civilians were killed by troops in Peking; precise figures are still disputed; there were disturbances and a significant number of deaths in other cities; some soldiers and policemen also lost their lives.

It is clear that from an early stage the movement was seen by a substantial majority of the leadership as a threat to Communist rule, which would have to be suppressed, by force if need be. The *People's Daily* editorial of 26 April, itself based on Deng's secret speech the day before, reflected this position. Deng flew to Wuhan to consult with army commanders. At senior Party levels Zhao and fellow reformers were throughout in a small minority.

The final acts were postponed until after the visit by Gorbachev from 15 to 18 May, though the humiliations attendant on that visit, the hastily revised programme, the entry into the Great Hall by back doors, must have reinforced Deng's determination to liquidate the protest at whatever cost.

Several features of the crisis must have deeply alarmed the leaders and convinced them that they had their backs to the wall. It was not simply the proliferating student protest, with its widening political agenda, repeated in cities across the country. It was also the fraternization of students and workers and the support for the demonstrators from the Peking populace, revolutionary combinations common enough in the textbooks, but extremely rare in reality. The cities were full of discontent caused by inflation, unemployment, declines in real income and a general sense of cynicism about the system. Then there was the PLA. Troops from several armies were ringing Peking; but there were audible misgivings about the use of force among army leaders, including Long March veterans and a recent Defence Minister and a Chief of Staff. Finally, there was a split in the Party, with Deng's anointed successor, Zhao Ziyang, openly dissenting from him and declaring that there was no great turmoil and that the students were 'in no way opposed to our fundamental system'.

To those of us watching from abroad, events had the quality of a slow-motion tragedy. I say slow-motion, since the drama was prolonged by the Gorbachev visit, the apparent readiness at one stage to hold a dialogue with the protestors and the repeated repulse of the troops by a friendly population. As always, the picture was murkier at the time than now appears with benefit of hindsight. There was, for example, much uncertainty about Deng's health and reports that he was terminally ill. It was, however, clear that there would be tears before evening and that blood would probably be shed. We got the Prime Minister to issue an appeal against violence, but in reality there was little we, or other governments, could do. It was evident that Hong Kong would be badly affected. Instability on the mainland always upset the territory and at an earlier stage of the crisis, when the students seemed to be winning, the Hang Seng Index fell sharply. Sudden change, from whatever quarter, was unwelcome.

The massacre traumatized Hong Kong. There had been much sympathy for the students. There were big support rallies and Hong Kong funds provided the tents for the encamped demonstrators in Tiananmen Square, a fact Peking did not let us forget. The Executive and Legislative Councils passed a motion in support of speedier democracy in Hong Kong. After the news of the killings there was an immense, silent march. Hong Kong people suddenly discovered they were Chinese. Their feelings were primarily sorrow for the crushing of their compatriots' hopes on the mainland; but there was also a deep anxiety about what this could mean for the future of the territory itself.

In London the Prime Minister issued a statement expressing her outrage and condemnation. At my suggestion a passage was added about the need for Chinese adherence to the Joint Declaration. We put off the next meeting of the Joint Liaison Group, due to be held in London in July. We also supported a European Community decision to take various measures against the Peking government, including a suspension of high-level contacts.

The British press were naturally less restrained and, while properly condemning the massacre, moved on to the more doubtful ground of questioning the value of any agreement with such a bloodstained regime. I recall an editorial in the *Spectator*, under the heading, 'A Titanic Betrayal', calling for us to denounce the Joint Declaration, though it was never made clear how that would help Hong Kong or what we should put in its place. *The Times* was not far behind, proposing that the government should announce its intention of reviewing the Joint Declaration and suspending all negotiation on the Basic Law. There was an impulse, though not so strong as in the United States, to suspend all dealings with Peking and to ostracize the regime. We began to read more about the British decision in 1984 to 'hand over Hong Kong to China', as if there had been a free choice and as if any alternative to the Joint Declaration would not have been infinitely worse. Even among the commentators who remembered the rationale of the agreement, there was a growing tendency to criticize those responsible for it as having been far too accommodating to Peking. The words 'betrayal', 'appeasement' and 'kowtow' became fashionable, usually in remarks about Foreign Office officials. Ministers tended to come off more lightly.

The events of 4 June were a tragedy for China and, in consequence, for Hong Kong and for Britain in their relations with China. On the mainland the protests and their suppression were the sharpest expression to date of the contradictions inherent in Deng's China. True, they were not the final word: the internal struggle would continue between liberalizers and reactionaries. But they meant an enormous setback to the cause of reform; and by a sad irony the students destroyed their chief supporter, Zhao Ziyang, and with him the hopes of political liberalization for years to come. There were wiser heads among them, warning of the dangers; but they were overborne.

In the context of Hong Kong, Tiananmen revived all Peking's neuroses about British duplicity and the external threats to their socialist system. It imported a renewed element of 'struggle' into a relationship where co-operation was slowly beginning to grow. It became a more obvious Chinese goal to extend a dominant influence over the territory as rapidly as possible, whatever the undertakings that British rule would continue undisturbed until 1997. Joint Liaison Group meetings reverted to a gladiatorial pattern. Democracy in Hong Kong in particular became a neuralgic issue.

In Britain and, more understandably, Hong Kong the massacre meant that the rational calculations underlying the 1984 agreement were clouded by a rush of emotion, a search for dramatic gestures and even for scapegoats. The atmosphere bred an easy cynicism about the value of China's word in any context. It also bred a growing impatience with the compromises and accommodations inseparable from a policy of co-operation over Hong Kong. There was a search for a chimerical alternative policy, which would somehow be tougher with Peking and at the same time more beneficial to Hong Kong. It could be said that this impossible quest for something between co-operation and confrontation still continues.

I found the Prime Minister deeply disturbed by what had happened, even though it had been foreseen, and briefly even disposed to ask herself whether she had been right to conclude the 1984 agreement.

In my advice to her I stressed the need to keep our heads and to avoid rapid, emotional responses, which might only worsen the situation for Hong Kong people. We would be dealing with a harsh, repressive regime in Peking, which had been badly frightened and would be highly suspicious and defensive, particularly under international reprobation. We had to strike a fine balance between the need, on the one hand, to express our revulsion at the recent barbarities and, on the other, before long to resume dealing with Peking in the interests of Hong Kong. We must avoid getting ourselves into a position of saying that normal relations were impossible until aspirations towards democracy on the mainland were met. If we wished to serve Hong Kong we had to remain able to talk to Peking.

We must cling to the Joint Declaration. Without it, Hong Kong would be anchorless and adrift on a stormy sea. The territory would revert to China without any safeguards. Fortunately, Peking were showing no disposition to abandon or infringe the agreement.

We needed also to be clear on the rationale for our signature. We had not concluded the agreement with Deng Xiaoping because we thought he was a liberal. We had no illusions on that score. We had concluded it because he ruled China and had in consequence the power to harm or help Hong Kong. That reasoning still applied. The validity and justification of the Joint Declaration were not dependent on the moral tone of the government in Peking, or the continuance of reform on the mainland. We should avoid giving colour to the media theme that in some way they were. One country, two systems meant what it said. Communism on the mainland would always mean dictatorship and repression there. What mattered was that the Chinese should keep their word over Hong Kong. If we confused the two cases and treated recent events as the end of the world, we could precipitate the very situation we feared.

But, when all that was said, Hong Kong's emotions and fears were political facts which we would now have to address and, so far as we could, allay. This would mean examining the scope for more representative government, looking at the prospects for more immigration from the territory into Britain, and doing what we could to help over the Vietnamese boat-people now congregating in a crowded colony.

This work would not be easy in the new political climate. There would be many new points of political friction between Hong Kong and Peking, for example, Hong Kong demonstrations and other activity in support of the dissidents, plus probable Hong Kong willingness to accept political refugees. Peking would also now be specially ill-disposed to arguments in favour of greater democracy in Hong Kong.

For the immediate future there was little to be done with Peking. But we must keep the lines open and be ready to move back to business, despite our abhorrence of the regime's internal policies. We had to keep our nerve and recognize that for a long time to come China and Hong Kong would need handling with even greater care than usual. We should ask of each policy move, not whether it made us feel better, or appealed to British sentiment, but, as we did throughout the negotiations, whether it would help the people of Hong Kong.

This was the tenor of the advice I submitted. Happily, most of it was accepted and after a necessary interval we were able to take up again the work of reassuring Hong Kong, which inevitably also meant talking to Peking. There were two areas of special importance – democracy and passports.

CHAPTER TWENTY-TWO

Democracy and Passports

THE TIANANMEN EPISODE had the effect of greatly intensifying pressures in Hong Kong and in Britain for a more rapid development of democratic government in the territory. At the same time it made it much harder to win Chinese agreement to any such step.

The pressure had been growing for some time before 1989, but it had been a relatively recent growth. In Hong Kong, before the negotiations, democracy was rarely sought and scarcely heard of. The conventional view was that it would prove a source of instability, provoking clashes between Communist and Nationalist adherents, alarming Peking and distracting the territory from its main preoccupation and skill, making money. And it was a fact that Peking had let it be known that the introduction of Westminster-style democracy in Hong Kong would be seen by them as movement towards independence. Government in Hong Kong took the form of a benevolent autocracy, answerable in the last resort to Whitehall and Westminster. The Governor was assisted by an appointed Executive Council. The Legislative Council was also appointed. The only infusion of democracy came in 1981, through the introduction of elections for a minority of seats on 18 newly created District Boards, the lowest level of local government.

During the negotiations there was little Hong Kong interest

in securing a more representative system. It was far from the top of Exco's priorities. The phrase in the Joint Declaration, 'the legislature of the Hong Kong Special Administrative Region shall be constituted by elections', was one of the last concessions wrung out of the Chinese and had required a special message from the Foreign Secretary to his Chinese counterpart, Wu Xueqian. Exco would have preferred us to use our last shots on a nationality point. The Chinese were very unwilling; their resistance to democracy was at least consistent; but in the end they gave way. Even so, there was no reference to direct elections; nor was there any chance at the time of securing agreement to such a phrase.

There was more interest in elections when the Joint Declaration was debated in Parliament in December 1984. A Hong Kong White Paper published in November had announced plans for 12 'functional constituencies', composed of trade and professional groups, and for a further 12 seats to be returned by an electoral college made up of local government bodies. The White Paper spoke of introducing a small number of directly elected seats in 1988, with the longer-term prospect of 'a significant number' of directly elected members of the Legislative Council by 1997. It noted a public preference in Hong Kong for a cautious approach to direct elections.

In the House of Commons opinion was mixed: several members stressed the importance of stability and the risks of adversarial politics in the special conditions of Hong Kong; others wanted more rapid progress. In replying to the debate, ministers were rather more positive than the White Paper and spoke of the prospect of building toward a firmly based democratic administration in Hong Kong by 1997.

There was a further review of the situation in 1987; and in 1988 it was decided to introduce 10 directly elected legislature seats in 1991. Hong Kong public opinion was in favour of a directly elected element; but views were divided about the timing of any move; and at senior level the attitude remained very cautious. The figure of 10 accorded with the figure published in the first draft of the Basic Law in 1988. There was Sino-British understanding on this point, supported by the Hong Kong government and by Exco. The figure represented a considerable advance on the initial Chinese position, which was no directly elected element at all. The draft also envisaged an increase to 15 directly elected seats in 1997. The plan was that we would introduce the 1997 arrangements in 1995, the last election before the hand-over, and that the Legco members then elected would serve until 1999, thus ensuring continuity through the 1997 barrier. This was the famous 'through train'.

Such was the situation when Tiananmen burst upon us. It was a modest programme; but it accorded with Chinese plans and would thus survive; and it ensured progress, an upward gradient, to 1997.

In the face of the crisis on the mainland, Hong Kong opinion, hitherto hesitant, rapidly shifted in favour of earlier democratization. This was seen as a necessary safeguard against possible pressures from Peking. There was a demand for 20 directly elected seats in 1991 and no less than 30 in 1997. The Governor saw a move in this direction as essential if we were to maintain a credible administration in Hong Kong. There were also demands in Parliament and in the British media that we should accelerate direct elections and, a new element, that if need be we should do so in disregard of Peking's views.

I found this a difficult situation. As I saw it, we needed to think carefully about the value of a more rapid move to democracy in Hong Kong. It was desirable in itself; it had acquired great symbolic significance; and, to sustain confidence in the territory, we had to show we were responsive to opinion both in Exco and amongst the public at large. But more democracy was not, as increasingly claimed, an infallible protection against Chinese pressure if the Chinese were bent on that course. In fact, if it provoked such pressure it could do more harm than good. To be of real worth, our arrangements had to stick after 1997; that required Chinese acquiescence. To act unilaterally would mean confrontation; and, given the weapons at China's disposal, to embark on confrontation with Peking over Hong Kong, however good the cause, would be doing the territory no service at all. I saw little chance of extracting agreement for 20 directly elected seats in 1991 from Peking in their ugly mood at the time. But we had to try.

There was the further consideration that time was short: the Chinese would finalize the Basic Law in February 1990; and after that, argument would be useless. Attractive though it would be to let the months go by and the passions of June 1989 cool, we could not afford to wait.

It was against this worrying background that the Prime Minister decided that I should go as her personal representative to Peking to pick up the threads of business with the Chinese leaders and to open the case for more democracy in Hong Kong. To be effective, our gesture had to be at the highest level: I would carry a message from her; and I had to be sure of access to senior Chinese leaders. It would also have to be a secret visit: it would be a long shot; publicity and speculation would be damaging; and a public approach would be one way of ensuring a hostile Chinese response.

I travelled to Peking on 4 December 1989, flying direct and avoiding Hong Kong (though the Governor, of course, was privy to the plan). I asked Robin McLaren to go with me. He was by now the Assistant Under-Secretary in the Foreign Office dealing with the Far East. He was also an old friend and great expert, on whose judgement I could place complete reliance. On the spot we would also have the guidance of the Ambassador, Sir Alan Donald.

It was all managed very discreetly and I had meetings with the Chinese leaders from the General Secretary, Jiang Zemin, down, including the Prime Minister, Li Peng, the Foreign Minister, Qian Qichian, the head of the Hong Kong and Macao Office, Ji Pengfei, and our old friend, Zhou Nan, now Deputy Foreign Minister. Our initiative and the Prime Minister's personal involvement ensured a friendly reception and the discussions were civilized, though tough. We agreed on the need to look beyond recent events, to maintain contact and to restore a degree of co-operation, both in the wider international sphere and, more particularly, over Hong Kong. Both sides reaffirmed their commitment to the Joint Declaration.

So far so good. But the Chinese were, as expected, extremely touchy and resentful about the British and Western reaction to the events of June, what they called the 'counter-revolutionary rebellion'. They claimed that China had done nothing to harm Britain; but we were one of the first to impose sanctions in response to a purely internal affair. I also had to answer repeated attacks on the role of Hong Kong in that period. Jiang Zemin, the new Party Secretary, told me he had hard evidence of funds from Hong Kong being used to provide tents and general support for the demonstrators in Tiananmen Square. More generally, there was a feeling of anger, and a complete failure of understanding, over the reactions of Hong Kong people to the student movement and its suppression.

I could not refute the charge about Hong Kong funding for the students: it was true enough. But I could repeat the assurance the Chinese had already had from our ministers that we had no intention of allowing Hong Kong to be used as a base to subvert the authority of the Chinese government. Hong Kong had to be administered in accordance with its own laws, but no group would be given greater tolerance than the law allowed. The Governor had already called on Hong Kong people to exercise their freedoms in a responsible fashion. Community leaders had spoken similarly.

This argument was a recurrent theme throughout twelve hours of talks. But, despite our assurances, we detected a strong disposition, possibly already a decision, on the Chinese side to add a prohibition against subversion to the Basic Law. We argued strenuously against, but, as it later transpired, to no avail.

Another charge, though one that proved a little easier to handle, was that we were seeking to internationalize the Hong Kong issue by involving other powers, particularly the United States, on our side. I assured them, with the Prime Minister's authority, that we continued to regard Hong Kong as a bilateral issue between London and Peking. We had no intention of allowing third parties to intervene. But Hong Kong was a great financial and commercial centre, with links with many countries. Both Britain and China recognized this and, indeed, were committed in the Joint Declaration to preserve and promote this aspect of the territory. It was natural that third countries should approach us to enquire about economic and commercial prospects in Hong Kong and the future of their investments there.

The hardest exchanges, inevitably, were over representative government. In return for the assurances on subversion and internationalization, I asked for Chinese help in rebuilding Hong Kong's confidence. Their chief contribution would be a final version of the Basic Law which would command support in Hong Kong and which the British government could sincerely welcome. There had been a big change of opinion in Hong Kong over the last two years on the subject of the composition of the future legislature. As the Chinese government's own sources would confirm, there was now a widespread desire for a substantial proportion of the legislature to be directly elected when the Hong Kong Special Administrative Region came into being. The British government had to respond to the wishes of Hong Kong people.

But at the same time we were committed to maintaining stability and we wanted convergence between any arrangements we made and the provisions of the Basic Law. We therefore needed Chinese help in the form of sufficient flexibility in the Basic Law to accommodate the new situation. More specifically, we needed to reflect Hong Kong opinion by providing at least 20 directly elected seats in 1991 (in place of 10) and a correspondingly larger number in 1995 (in place of 15).

The Chinese were tough and unyielding. They did not understand and deeply mistrusted our wish to double the number of directly elected seats in 1991, in disregard of the figure in the 1988 White Paper. They reminded me that there had been an understanding on that point, which should not be overturned by sudden fluctuations of opinion in Hong Kong. They saw such changes as related to the events of 4 June and, as such, particularly suspect, in fact a sign of a conspiracy to exert pressure on China.

They would not give way on the number of seats for 1991, though towards the end there were some faint signs of flexibility. They were prepared to envisage 20 seats, no more, in 1997, but they would move to that from a lower starting point than we proposed. For good measure, they added the warning that if we acted unilaterally, they would impose their own conflicting arrangements in 1997, the 'through train' would break down and there would be, as they put it, 'big trouble'.

We argued back and forth for many hours, but made no headway. Behind the detailed exchanges, the proposals and rebuttals, lay a profound suspicion on the Chinese side of Western-style democracy as a force for political change and instability, even chaos. For them it was associated with the threat to their rule in the past months and with interference from Hong Kong. These fears had been sharpened by the recent news from Eastern

Europe, where Communist governments were falling like ninepins. At the time of my visit Ceausescu, a close friend of China, was still in power; but East Germany, Czechoslovakia, Hungary and Poland were already an ominous list of casualties. The Chinese leaders were clearly uneasy: they would refer, apropos of nothing, to these European revolutions and hasten to differentiate China's case: those were governments set up by the Red Army; their Communism was imposed from outside; in China it was a native and vigorous growth. There was something in the distinction; but the constant need to draw it argued a certain lack of confidence.

I had had only moderate success. We were back in communication with Peking and working within the same framework of the Joint Declaration. We had perhaps dissipated some suspicions. On the central issue, directly elected seats, there was agreement on 5 more seats for 1997; but there was no movement for 1991; we still had a way to go.

Fortunately, we were only at the beginning of a process of persuasion which occupied us over the next two months. In January, David Wilson, now Sir David and Governor of Hong Kong, followed me to Peking and took the debate further. Then the Foreign Secretary, Douglas Hurd, took a hand, with a series of messages to Foreign Minister Qian, which have since been published. In the end we obtained agreement to 18 directly elected seats in 1991, 20 in 1997, 24 in 1999 and 30, that is half the legislature, in 2003. The number of seats in 1995 and other arrangements for those elections, the last under British rule, were left unsettled and we reserved the right to approach the Chinese again on the matter. Otherwise we had clear understandings for a larger number of directly elected seats than we had begun with, plus the assurance of a steady increase in such seats through into the next century. These understandings were reflected in the final version of the Basic Law; they would stick.

There has been a tendency in the press to represent these understandings as secret and shameful, directed towards stifling democracy in Hong Kong. Even the Foreign Office, when publishing them, was inclined to adopt a defensive tone, emphasizing the areas of disagreement rather than the common ground. The exchanges were certainly secret. There would have been no possibility of achieving any advance had they been public; and the Chinese government could not afford to admit that their Basic Law had been so influenced by British persuasions. But the Hong Kong government and Exco were involved at all stages. Shameful? In fact, as has been shown, they were the very creditable result of a difficult negotiation, particularly difficult in the post-Tiananmen atmosphere. Far from stifling democracy, they enlarged it: with each round the numbers rose, the future gradient got a little steeper. There was not going to be full and instant Westminster-type democracy in Hong Kong; but there would be steady progress in that direction which, and this was the crucial point, the Chinese had been brought to endorse.

There is perhaps one footnote to be added. It has been argued in Hong Kong that we failed to meet the target set by Exco of 20 seats in 1991; and that we could have met it had we shown more resolution and faith and less fear of China. I do not agree. We went as far as we could in a long struggle; and it was the judgement of ministers and, for what it is worth, my own that to insist on more would have endangered the whole understanding. It is true that at one point senior Exco members urged us to insist on 20 seats in 1991 (as against 18) regardless of the consequences. I warned that that would be more traffic than the bridge could take; the Chinese had repeatedly refused to move on the point; to act unilaterally would destroy the work of the last months. The Prime Minister agreed. Then at the last moment Exco changed their position and decided that 18 seats would suffice. We settled on that basis.

Though democracy was to become the most hotly debated issue in Hong Kong in later years and even the occasion for a radical turn in British policy towards China, it was not, in 1989, the most deeply felt question. That place undoubtedly belonged to nationality. In Hong Kong democracy was sometimes dismissed as a British solution: it cost us nothing. What really mattered in Hong Kong's eyes was the ultimate right of Hong Kong people, or at least those with some form of British passport, 3.25 million of them, to live and work in the United Kingdom.

The subject had a long and sensitive history. In 1962, the Commonwealth Immigration Act removed the right to settle in Britain from Hong Kong citizens, as from those of most other Commonwealth and colonial territories. In 1981, the Nationality

Act compounded the offence, as Hong Kong saw it, by imposing an inferior status, that of British Dependent Territory Citizenship, in place of the old Citizenship of the United Kingdom and Colonies. It was readily assumed in the territory that the 1981 Act was a piece of prudent planning on the part of London, aimed at shrugging off responsibility for Hong Kong people in advance of the main negotiations with China. This was not the case: governments rarely act with this degree of foresight; and the crucial link had in any case been severed eighteen years earlier. But the sense of grievance stemming from the 1962 Commonwealth Act was revived and reinforced.

In the negotiations on the Joint Declaration citizenship links with Hong Kong were further attenuated. The Chinese government were not prepared to allow that anyone born in Hong Kong after 1997 should acquire British nationality by virtue of connection with Hong Kong. The term British Dependent Territory Citizenship would no longer be appropriate after the hand-over; and it was arranged that it would be replaced by a new form of British nationality, which would provide a British passport and, outside China, British consular protection. To Exco's sorrow, we could not obtain agreement on the transmission of this status by descent, as we had hoped. Nationality generally remained disputed ground and had to be left to an exchange of memoranda, in which China and Britain set out their differing, though overlapping, views.

As has been noted, emigration from Hong Kong rose in the years following 1984, with some residents returning after having secured a second base, some staying away. Canada and Australia, rather than Britain, were favoured second homes. And there was a natural reluctance on our part to be seen to encourage the grant of British passports. Our object was to encourage Hong Kong people to stay and flourish in Hong Kong. If we ourselves showed no faith in the agreement, how could they be expected to? It was not in our interest to promote a Hong Kong diaspora. A depopulated and impoverished Hong Kong would have poor prospects of surviving as an autonomous region of China.

Tiananmen naturally aroused deep fears among Hong Kong residents and posed in sharpest form the question: how far did our responsibility for them in an emergency extend?

The Governor put the question directly. He flew to London for a meeting with the Prime Minister on 7 June and asked for rights of abode for the 3.25 million Hong Kong holders of British passports. The request was sharply rejected by the Prime Minister. Her refusal had nothing to do with fears of Chinese reactions, as is sometimes alleged, but everything to do with political realities in Britain. There was no prospect of getting parliamentary agreement, whether on the Conservative or the Labour side, to the admission of immigrants in those numbers. Mrs Thatcher pointed out that in the whole post-war period Britain had taken only half that number.

Nevertheless there was a responsibility and an urgent need for reassurance. How to express it and how far should it extend? On these issues there was lively debate over the next six months.

The Hong Kong case was that our moral responsibility extended to all 5.7 million inhabitants, but that the 3.25 million British passport holders formed an irreducible core. Moreover, if given the right of abode, very few would in fact exercise it. Hong Kong people did not wish to leave their territory and for the great majority it would be merely an effective insurance policy.

On this last point London were unpersuaded. They could not act on the assumption that any rights conferred would never be exercised. There was the domestic political factor. The size of any package had to be far below 3.25 million; but it had to be large enough to restore confidence. Then there was the practical aspect. Should we grant rights of entry, allowing those chosen to stay here for a time and thereby qualify for British citizenship? This was, administratively, the easy route. Or should we grant passports, which would require special legislation?

I argued for a generous package and against entry certificates. The object was to persuade people to stay and work in Hong Kong. Entry certificates would encourage recipients to come at once in order to qualify and out of fear that permission might later be revoked. We could be prompting an exodus. If passports were granted, they would be an insurance and there would be less incentive to move. Experience of business firms in Hong Kong with Chinese employees holding passports suggested that they had been less shaken by events on the mainland than had their non-passport-holding colleagues.

Eventually it was decided to legislate to provide full British passports for 50,000 Hong Kong households (which would mean up to 225,000 people in all), selected under a scheme which laid weight on key groups in the business and economic worlds. The recipients would not need to leave Hong Kong. The aim was to keep essential elements at their posts and to keep Hong Kong flourishing. The scheme was announced in December 1989.

The debate on this issue lay mainly between Hong Kong and Britain. It was a matter of a balance between our ability to accept certain numbers for settlement, if that should ever prove necessary, and our wish to restore confidence, a balance between moral obligation and political practicality. But there was also a Chinese angle. In my visit in early December, which preceded the legislation on passports, we had briefly alerted the Chinese government to the possibility of special measures on passports in order to reassure Hong Kong residents. Robin McLaren spoke to his old sparring partner on nationality questions, Lu Ping. There was little response: Lu Ping merely noted the problem we faced. Later there were objections and claims that such measures would introduce problems of allegiance, even that it was another method of trying to retain British influence in Hong Kong well after 1997. There were threats that holders of foreign passports would be ineligible to serve on the legislature. In practice it was almost impossible to distinguish between one set of British passport holders and another; and we had the defence that our measures were necessary to maintain stability and prosperity in Hong Kong, a task to which both sides were committed under the Joint Declaration. Nevertheless the Chinese did not acquiesce. They inserted a provision in the Basic Law whereby no more than 20 per cent of the membership of the legislature could hold foreign nationality; this provision was in direct retaliation for our nationality measures.

CHAPTER TWENTY-THREE

The Airport Agreement

THE YEAR AFTER Tiananmen was largely occupied by efforts on our side to restore confidence in Hong Kong, usually in the face of resistance from an embattled Chinese government. Two of these measures, more democracy and more British passports, have been described in the previous chapter. A third, the passage of a Hong Kong Bill of Rights, was completed in June 1990. There was another decision, however, in the same category and made about that time, which provoked a more protracted struggle, a milestone in the intensifying effort by the Chinese government to establish a dominant influence in Hong Kong in the final years of the transition. This was the question of the new airport. It developed into the most serious crisis we had faced since 1983; and it was resolved in dramatic fashion by an agreement, which the Chinese at least placed in something like the same order of importance as the Joint Declaration and which seemed at the time to usher in a new era of Sino-British co-operation.

Though the Governor's decision to build a new airport, announced in October 1989, was part of the confidence-building operation, the project had its own compelling rationale. Anyone making the hair-raising descent into the existing airport at Kai Tak, surrounded by high-rise blocks, could appreciate the requirement for a better site. There were also strong economic grounds. The existing airport was near saturation point and would soon constrict Hong Kong's growth. Something of a different order was urgently needed to match the territory's position as a major international financial, commercial and communications centre. There had been the usual history of abortive planning for another location, interrupted by political or financial crises. It was time for a bold move. A site on Lantau Island with associated plans for extensive port facilities was chosen. It was naturally a big project, worth around £8 billion and extending well beyond 1997. But the Hong Kong budget could readily carry its share, and 40 per cent of the money would come from the private sector.

The plan had ample publicity and was spoken of to Zhou Nan. At first the Chinese government expressed no particular interest or objection. They had other preoccupations at the time. By the end of 1989, however, there were ominous mutterings from Peking. They related to cost, fears that the plan might be over-ambitious and, more precisely, that it could leave the Special Administrative Region in a weaker financial position in 1997. We were encountering a more refined version of Deng Xiaoping's worries in 1984 that we would deliberately impoverish the territory before leaving; the airport was seen as a means by which British companies would be enriched and Hong Kong's treasury emptied.

In the Chinese reaction there was no doubt an element of genuine concern about possible burdens that the undertaking would impose on the Hong Kong region after 1997. But there was also an instinctive opposition, enhanced by the post-Tiananmen mood, to any unilateral steps to reassure Hong Kong. And, most important, there was a growing realization on the Chinese side that in this massive project, straddling the hand-over, and critically dependent on private finance (and therefore Chinese endorsement), they had a powerful lever with which to assert their claim to greater control of the territory in the transitional phase.

Between October 1990 and February 1991 the Hong Kong government held expert talks to inform and reassure Peking, three rounds in all. They certainly informed, but they apparently did not reassure; and Hong Kong decisions, relating to preliminary work on the project and coinciding with the first round of talks, gave the Chinese an opening to denounce publicly what they could represent as unilateral moves, 'insincere attitudes' and inadequate consultation. It is true that Peking could have been handled more sensitively; but it is questionable whether this would have affected the outcome. The Chinese used the talks for propaganda purposes and advanced a series of extravagant demands as preconditions for their agreement. These demands were for considerable sums to be set aside from the Hong Kong fiscal reserves and for veto powers, not only on the airport authority, but also more widely in the financial sphere.

Discussion moved to a higher level: the Governor talked to Lu Ping, now Director of the Hong Kong and Macao Office, and to Li Peng, the Chinese Premier. In April and May 1991 a combined Foreign Office and Hong Kong team of officials under Andrew Burns, the Foreign Office Assistant Under-Secretary for the Far East, underwent two long and punishing rounds of talks with the Chinese. The Foreign Secretary visited China in April 1991, tried for an agreement and came very near reaching one.

But the Chinese remained elusive. They shifted their ground. New demands appeared or old demands were resurrected. What they seemed to be seeking were two things. First, they required extreme financial reassurance in the form of guarantees of money to be left in the Hong Kong reserves after the construction of the airport, plus limitations on government borrowing, so that the new site and its buildings would come to them almost as a gift. Second, and most worrying, they sought a generalized right of veto over major Hong Kong decisions in the transitional period. The veto claim was not baldly stated; the Chinese Foreign Minister denied that it was being made; it was concealed in a demand that certain matters should be subject to consultation and consensus; but the meaning was clear enough.

At its most ambitious, the claim was that consensus should be reached on any responsibility or obligation to be taken on by the government of the Special Administrative Region. It was impossible to reconcile this with the British government's responsibility, acknowledged in the Joint Declaration, for administering Hong Kong until 1997. Nor was there, among these large and generalized demands, any sign of the precision and certainty which we needed on finance, on franchises, on consultation, if the Hong Kong authorities were to get on with the project, and which private investors needed if they were to venture their money.

This was the situation in the summer of 1991. A breakdown looked likely. The Chinese were threatening to publish their account of the negotiations in order to demonstrate British 'insincerity'. There was a point fast approaching when the Governor could no longer postpone a public decision: the calls for tenders on two of the main contracts were overdue.

Steps were taken to make plain to the Chinese the essentials of our position. We must have co-operation from them. We must also have clarity and certainty if we were to embark on the work. Failing that, we would reluctantly be obliged to postpone the whole project.

This message almost certainly made an impact and corrected any expectations the Chinese might have had that, since our need for the airport was extreme, their exactions could safely continue.

At this point I became involved as an actor rather than simply an adviser and observer. The Prime Minister, now John Major, asked me to go to Peking as his representative on a make-or-break visit. The main bones of the story follow; but I shall have to draw a veil over the detail of my discussions in Peking: at the time of writing negotiations on the airport continue and I would not want these memoirs to prejudice them in any way.

For reasons which I shall not go into here, the preliminaries to the visit followed a strange and indirect pattern. Final agreement to travel came, as I remember, in a telephone call from Zimbabwe, and my plan to go by Scandinavian Airlines, so as to avoid Hong Kong, was transformed in the telling to a message that I would be flown in by the SAS. But I eventually arrived in Peking, by orthodox means, on 27 June without incident.

Like my excursion in December 1989, it was meant to be a secret visit. It remained relatively discreet until the work was done, though an alert *Daily Telegraph* reporter spotted me in the first twenty-four hours. I travelled alone. This time I had Robin McLaren already at the other end, as our newly installed Ambassador; and I thought the two of us should be able to do whatever was necessary. In the event we drew heavily on the help of his Counsellor, David Coates, and First Secretary, Janet Rogan; and the whole of his Embassy was mobilized in support.

There was no Hong Kong representative present. This was unfortunate but, in the circumstances, unavoidable. The Governor, whom I had seen in London the day before leaving, was very understanding; and he and his Executive Council were kept throughout in the closest touch.

I set out with low expectations, a less than 50 per cent chance of success as I saw it. The ground had been thoroughly worked over and the Chinese demands were extreme. I had about three days: Li Peng, the Chinese Prime Minister, was leaving for the Middle East that weekend. I had to make it clear that this was the last word. The best scenario, it seemed, would be the discovery of enough common ground to support an agreed minute and to justify a further meeting of experts to draw up an agreement. But equally plausible was the scenario in which both sides acknowledged disagreement and, perhaps, tried to limit the damage. It turned out rather differently.

A major factor, which became apparent on the afternoon of 28 June, when I saw him, was Li Peng's interest in an early visit by John Major to sign any agreement we reached. In Peking's planning the airport was therefore to become an instrument in China's full rehabilitation after Tiananmen. This greatly assisted our leverage. Nor was it so extravagant a wish as some of the commentators made it seem: the international 'quarantine consensus' of June 1989 had already crumbled; the Japanese Prime Minister was coming to Peking in August, the Italian Prime Minister probably in September. But there were problems in Li Peng's wish to delay any announcement on the airport until full signature: that could mean months of delay, with leaks and uncertainties in the interval. We wanted work to begin at once, at least on the most urgent of the core projects.

There would undoubtedly be domestic sensitivity about a visit by Mr Major to Peking. But there were powerful arguments in its favour, relating to the airport, Hong Kong's confidence and prosperity, and the recovery of Sino-British co-operation, both over the territory and generally. I put them as cogently as I could in my telegram home, adding that there would be advantage in the Prime Minister raising the issue of human rights on the visit and letting it be known that he had done so.

The Prime Minister had little time to brood on the matter and he was in any case deeply engaged with his European

Community colleagues at a summit in Luxemburg. But he reacted rapidly and favourably and we were grateful to him for doing so. He was prepared to say he would come as soon as his programme allowed. In the continuous process of haggling on which we were now embarked this was whittled down to 'soon'.

The final stages of our negotiations turned on the likely timing of the Prime Minister's visit, the timing of the publication of the agreement and the scope of the construction works that could begin on initialling only. The Chinese fought for a complete embargo until the two leaders had met; and for a time on the last day the whole agreement seemed in jeopardy. But it was eventually initialled on 30 June and published four days later.

It was brief and to the point. In return for certain financial assurances and strictly limited undertakings on consultation, the Chinese expressed their support for the airport, their willingness to take part in its construction and their undertaking to recognize after 1997 obligations entered into by investors. Work could begin on two urgent contracts at once; a long list of core projects could be begun as soon as the agreement was signed.

On the critical question of consultation, which meant the Chinese wish to be involved in the general management of the territory, there was a formula whereby, on important matters bearing on the airport and straddling 1997, the two governments would carry out consultation in a spirit of co-operation and in accordance with the Joint Declaration. This was a safe formula. It restricted consultation to airport issues, as distinct from all issues; and, by reference to the Joint Declaration, incorporated the assurance of continuing British rule until 1997. Though the press made much of the references to consultation, here and elsewhere in the memorandum, treating them as British concessions and Chinese encroachments, they were sensible and harmless. For a project of this size, involving work and expenditure long after 1997, consultation with the successor government was only natural and practical.

On contracts or franchises for the airport straddling 1997, there was language whereby we would provide the details for each application, the Chinese had a month for consideration and then the decision lay with us. The original phrase stating baldly that the ultimate responsibility was ours was excised in the final form of the memorandum out of regard for Chinese sensibilities, but the meaning was clear nevertheless.

Finally, the memorandum contained clauses on the amount of Hong Kong government borrowing to be repaid after 1997 which could be undertaken without reference to the Chinese government and the level of fiscal reserves which would be left for the successor government in Hong Kong after 1997. These clauses addressed the abiding fears on the Chinese side that as a result of the airport project the government of the new Special Administrative Region would find itself with empty coffers on the day after the hand-over.

The agreement was welcomed with relief and enthusiasm in Hong Kong and the Hang Seng Index shot up. A serious crisis had been narrowly averted. The territory now seemed certain of having the airport it needed to ensure its future as a great financial and trading centre. The way was also now open to tackle other practical matters which had long lain becalmed in the Joint Liaison Group.

It remained to secure an early date for the Prime Minister's visit and the signature. I was anxious that the interval should be as short as possible, not only so that the work on the full range of construction could get under way, but also so that it would look less like a tribute-bearing occasion and more like what it was, namely a working visit related to Hong Kong's urgent needs. We had a decisive argument for doubters: if we wanted to help Hong Kong we had to be able to talk to Peking; and we should not be timorous in using it.

The Prime Minister made the trip in September 1991, travelling by way of Moscow, where he saw Yeltsin, triumphant after the failure of the August coup. He handled the talks with the Chinese leaders with great skill, speaking firmly on human rights, but at the same time pushing Hong Kong's interests and extracting an agreement on the Court of Final Appeal there, as well as wider promises of co-operation. He spent two days in Hong Kong on the way home.

It has been widely reported, and become part of popular history in Hong Kong, that the Prime Minister was angry at being compelled to make the visit to Peking and blamed the Governor, whose handling of the airport issue, it was alleged, made this tribute to China necessary in the first place. Travelling with him, I saw no evidence of this. On the contrary, the Prime

Minister was highly satisfied with his travels, as well he might be. Starting with Kennebunkport, where he had conferred with President Bush, he had flown round the world, to Moscow, Peking and Hong Kong, with striking success at each stop. So much so that the polls were highly favourable on his return and the accompanying press corps speculated on a November election.

The decision on the change of Governor had other origins, going back to the time of the Prime Minister's predecessor, and relating to the view that in the final period of British rule a politician's presence was needed. It was a view I suspected, since it seemed to me based on an exaggerated idea of the range of action open to us and to any British Governor in the tightly constricting conditions of the late transitional period. To a marked degree the script had been written and, short of tearing it up altogether, there was little that could be done except to recite the lines with some personal difference of emphasis. But this was not a view that found favour.

The autumn of 1991 saw Sino-British relations, both over Hong Kong and more generally, once again at a high point. And, although neither government entertained illusions, it seemed we should be able to enjoy a smooth passage in our dealings for some time.

It was a false hope. The Hong Kong elections of September 1991, the first direct elections to the Legislative Council, summoned into existence new political parties and returned a strong group of United Democrats, under Martin Lee. Lee, a slight, intense, dogmatic, self-absorbed lawyer, had acquired a great name as an advocate of a defiant policy towards China and a rapid introduction of more directly elected seats on the legislature, in disregard of the Chinese if need be. Indeed he saw a positive virtue in defiance as the only way to win Chinese respect. It was a policy that had a certain appeal for those not burdened with any responsibility. The Chinese, for their part, claimed that Lee sought to overthrow their government and promised his exclusion from the legislature after 1997. There were rich possibilities for trouble here.

Hong Kong political and legal circles also chose this moment to assert themselves by rejecting the agreement on the Court of Final Appeal, so recently and painfully extracted in the context of the Prime Minister's visit to Peking. The issue turned on the number of overseas judges eligible to serve on the court, which would be Hong Kong's substitute for the Judicial Committee of the Privy Council. Some outside element would be valuable in ensuring that the territory remained within the common law tradition. The wording in the Joint Declaration was ambiguous, capable of being read as 'one' or 'several'. The Chinese naturally opted for the narrower interpretation. We had accepted, and the Hong Kong government had agreed, that that was the best we could get; and we were anxious to get the court set up and operating well in advance of 1997. But the Hong Kong Legislative Council and the Hong Kong legal profession insisted on the wider meaning, even though that would mean no agreement with Peking and no court at all. Members of Exco joined in and attacked a deal they had endorsed when consulted earlier. The legislation had to be withdrawn and the court was stillborn. Peking, predictably, found in this performance evidence of a British conspiracy with Hong Kong to undermine the understanding of September and reopen the issue. It seemed to me a self-defeating refusal to come to terms with realities; also a bad augury for the reception of any future Sino-British agreements on the territory; and for future relations between the Special Administrative Region and Peking.

The announcement in April 1992 of Mr Patten's appointment as Governor of Hong Kong also aroused all Peking's latent suspicions, even before he had time to read himself into his new post and decide his policies. He was recorded as speaking at an inaugural press conference, not just about Hong Kong's stability and prosperity, hallowed words from the 1982 communiqué, but also about Hong Kong's freedom. What lay behind the extra word? On a farewell visit to Peking in May I was repeatedly asked to explain. I told the Chinese leaders that the reference was, of course, to the many rights and freedoms enshrined in the Joint Declaration. They should not disturb themselves. They were dealing with a strong, well-disposed British government, enjoying a new mandate from the electorate, and with a Governor in Hong Kong who was particularly well connected in London. This provided the best possible basis for Sino-British co-operation over Hong Kong. But we would like to see more co-operation and less struggle.

Ominously, I found I spent most of my time on that visit, not in polite farewells, but in protracted argument over the airport, which I had thought settled, at least in broad outline, the previous summer. The Chinese were again proving difficult and demanding about the financial arrangements, apparently trying to remove any contingent liability on the SAR government and to assure themselves of inheriting a first-class airport free of charge in 1997. But the larger issue lying behind these mano-euvres now was Chinese uncertainty over the new Governor. Until they could see the colour of his money they were not prepared to give away any tricks over the airport. It was again to be used as a lever for political ends.

At this point my official dealings with Peking drew to an end. Though I did not know it at the time, we were also coming to the end of a chapter in Sino-British relations, of which the governing principle had been the need for steady co-operation over Hong Kong. We were about to move into another phase, where a combination of forces, new personalities and tactics, the strains of accommodation, impatience with Chinese intran-sigence and a greater assertiveness on the part of Hong Kong, were all to erupt in a policy of effective, if not altogether intended, confrontation.

CHAPTER TWENTY-FOUR

The End of Co-operation

THE LAST SECTION of this book has dealt with Hong Kong from the time when it took over as the dominant element in Sino-British relations to the point of my retirement in 1992. That period has a unifying theme in the efforts of the two governments to come to a negotiated settlement on Hong Kong's future and to co-operate in order to ensure a smooth transition in 1997. But it was a course which was never entirely free from controversy; it came under particular strain in the years after Tiananmen; and from October 1992 a new approach and new, more assertive tactics were tried. We moved into rougher waters.

It is worth pausing at this point to look at the origins and force of the criticisms levelled against the policy of co-operation and to ask whether any other route could have been followed.

On the British side, co-operation was virtually imposed by the hard facts of history and geography and by the disparities of power, on this matter at least, between Britain and China. The lease, which we recognized, meant reversion, with or without safeguards. A military response, in the sense of standing fast on the ceded territory and daring China to do its worst, was considered and dismissed at the outset. At any number of points in the course of our exchanges in 1983 and 1984 defiance and withdrawal from the talks would have been possible; it was always the easy option; but it was rightly rejected as destructive and indefensible, given our responsibility for Hong Kong. We were therefore negotiating throughout for the best we could get, pressing very hard, but avoiding a breakdown, for which Hong Kong would have to pay. The same reasoning informed our dealings with Peking after 1984, particularly in the exchanges over directly elected seats in the Hong Kong legislature.

On the Chinese side, the arguments for negotiation were less compelling: they were in a position to dictate. But they sought the benefits which a peaceful and agreed transfer of power offered in terms of economic gain, China's international standing and, above all, the prospects for reunification with Taiwan. Overt use of force or blackmail over Hong Kong would destroy the hopes, which, happily, they still entertained, of recovering the most important piece of lost national territory. For these reasons they were ready to treat, to offer reasonable terms and to honour their new obligations as they interpreted them.

But in Britain the 1984 agreement, however successful and skilfully accomplished, left among many an uneasy feeling, an ill-defined sense of guilt. I recall being asked by Peter Hennessy, in an interview in 1984, whether there was not a parallel with Yalta and the transfer then of large numbers of Russians to Stalin's mercies. I thought it was a bad analogy and said so: there might have been some relevance if we had done nothing; as it was, we had provided the most detailed protection possible. But the fact that such a question could be posed, and by a well-informed analyst and historian, indicated the kind of doubts that arose. The reasoning behind the treaty, it was admitted, was impeccable; but, illogically, the question recurred, could not some other solution have been found?

These misgivings, stemming from the fact of the lease and the nature of the Peking government, were aggravated by the painful history of nationality legislation and the removal, in 1962, of the right of any Hong Kong residents to settle in Britain. The hard political reality, that no British government could contemplate as immigrants the numbers involved, was in practical terms a complete answer. But again there was the nagging doubt. Perhaps we should have done more. Perhaps the territory had to be handed back, but not the people.

There was also a belated sense of guilt over the failure to introduce democracy to Hong Kong well before the negotiations and an exaggerated claim for its efficacy as a defence against

Communist encroachments. What was overlooked was its inefficacy if it merely provoked a backlash, and the certain hostility of the reaction from Peking in the years after the Communist take-over in 1949 to any moves toward more popular government in the colony. The Chinese had made it plain enough both to us and to their contacts in the colony that moves towards self-government would be seen by them as steps along the normal colonial road towards independence and would therefore be out of the question. Talk now of democratic opportunities missed in the 1960s and 1970s is therefore unreal. It is also worth noting how slowly and painfully the Chinese came to tolerate the idea of even an element of direct elections. When, in late 1983, I first raised the possibility of direct elections before 1997 the reaction was one of horrified dismissal. It was a long road from there to the 1990 understanding, which accepted 18 directly elected seats in 1991 and envisaged half the legislature directly elected in 2003.

Much was also made of an alleged failure by London to involve Hong Kong further in the negotiations on its future. The charge rested largely on an inability to appreciate the strength of Peking's objections to any direct Hong Kong participation. This included an angry refusal to deal with Hong Kong as an independent point in the triangle, total resistance to any idea of a referendum in 1984, and non-recognition of the official position of Chinese Exco and Legco members. If it wished to help Hong Kong, Britain had to use the only channels available. As regards consultation between the metropolitan and colonial governments, this was close and constant: Exco were privy to every move. Wider consultation, as with the Legislative Council or the Hong Kong public, during secret negotiations would have been unprecedented and impracticable, even if Peking had acquiesced.

Nevertheless, there were symptoms of malaise and they were given a new edge by the events of June 1989. In that atmosphere of outrage and emotion the rationale of the Joint Declaration and of Sino-British co-operation was forgotten by the commentators and the wish that things had been otherwise became obsessive. We heard much more of the 'hand-over of six million people' and of 'betrayal' and 'appeasement'. The whole process of dealing with Peking in a constructive way became suspect.

The criticism flowed easily, but practical alternative prescriptions were hard to come by. Reviewing the Joint Declaration, or, worse still, denouncing it, as was advocated in the press in 1989, would achieve nothing, apart from terminal damage to Hong Kong. There was never a clear answer to the question: What would you have done differently in 1983 and 1984, or, for that matter, in 1989?

When pinned down, most critics would admit that they perhaps did not want defiance and breakdown in Sino-British dealings over Hong Kong. But they felt that the negotiations had been conducted in too flexible, not to say supine, a fashion, that passes, always unspecified, had been sold, and that there had been a general failure to 'stand up to Peking'. And here appeared the phantom of an alternative line, tougher with China, kinder to Hong Kong, which haunted popular criticism of official policy in the post-Tiananmen years. It was aided by revisionist history in Hong Kong, asserting that the territory would have fared much better had it listened to its own tough instincts and not allowed itself to be beguiled by the Foreign Office experts in London.

These experts, the 'mandarins' or, more exactly, the Foreign Office sinologists, came to occupy a leading role in the demonology of the time. They were alleged to be so besotted with things Chinese, or, alternatively, so overawed by China, that they surrendered automatically to Peking's demands, or even, by anticipation, before the demands were formulated. 'Pre-emptive cringe' was a phrase much employed. It was also claimed that they saw Hong Kong as a tiresome diversion from the main business of Sino-British relations, which was pictured as some twentieth-century equivalent of the 'Great Game' played by Britain and Russia in Central Asia in the nineteenth century.

It was strange stuff. No official I came across had any illusions about the regime we were dealing with in Peking. We had all been through the mill. No one had any doubt of the primacy of Hong Kong in our dealings with China. Nor did we justify British policy on any other grounds. The accommodations with Peking were not prompted by regard for China, but by the calculation that any other course would have been much more damaging to Hong Kong. It was throughout a policy of cool realism, recognizing the immutable facts of the situation and directed to providing the maximum protection for the territory in the difficult circumstances in which it was placed. And it was endorsed and applied by a succession of ministers, none of whom could be described as a sentimentalist on China or a push-over in negotiations. Every position was stubbornly fought, and concessions made only after a scrupulous balance of profit and loss for Hong Kong. If there had been any other practical course we would have been overjoyed to learn of it. Defiance was naturally always tempting. But it was one thing to be defiant when we in Britain would bear the consequences ourselves. To be defiant at the expense of a third party, particularly one to whom we stood in a position of trust, as with Hong Kong, was something very different, an inexcusable self-indulgence.

Nevertheless, it must be recognized that official policy during this period did impose its strains and demand more than usual self-control on the part of London and Hong Kong. However logical and justified, the constant compromises and accommodations with China did not come easily; and even when spectacular settlements were achieved, as over the airport, the period of goodwill and co-operation they engendered proved disappointingly brief. The Chinese were always difficult; after 1989 they grew even more antagonistic and demanding. As they saw it, they were engaged in the final stages of the struggle for Hong Kong, facing all kinds of capitalist wiles. The task of British officials engaged regularly with them, as in the Joint Liaison Group, called for superhuman patience. Moreover, as the period of British rule dwindled, we were being driven, on grounds of pure practicality, into wider consultations with the successor regime and on terms which would grow progressively less favourable. This was inherent in the fact of the transition and the ultimate transfer.

Reduced to its most precise form, the charge of the critics was that we had overestimated Chinese strength and underestimated their tolerance. All our experience, both in the 1983–4 period and later, argued strongly against such a judgement. But there was no conclusive way of proof, except by trial. And in October 1992, probably more by error than by intention, Britain and Hong Kong found themselves engaged in a practical demonstration.

The Patten reforms and the crisis they provoked lie largely

outside the scope of this book. They belong too closely to current events, and also to future developments whose shape we cannot yet clearly see. But they require mention because of the fundamental issues they raise and because they provide an instructive epilogue to the foregoing account of co-operation between Britain and China over Hong Kong.

In essence the proposals were an attempt to establish a further degree of democracy in the final years of British rule, if possible with the consent of the Chinese, but if need be in disregard of their understanding of the political settlement that had been reached over the territory. The object was to give further vitality to Hong Kong and a greater capacity to resist any pressures from Peking after the hand-over. The approach was to be tough and assertive, in an effort to make up for what many commentators saw as the too flexible approach of British negotiators in the preceding decade. Hong Kong was to be the prime mover: the appeal was to be primarily to Hong Kong opinion, though also to that at Westminster. And a leading role was to be assigned to the Hong Kong Legislative Council. The Governor emphasized that he was only making proposals; but he made it clear that, in default of counter and better offers from the Chinese, he would submit his plans to the Legislative Council for them to debate and pronounce in the spring of 1993.

The Chinese reaction was violent, both because of the manner and the substance of the proposals. On the first, although they were told of the substance of the Governor's speech two weeks in advance, their request that they should be consulted (which in their eyes probably meant negotiation) before the speech was delivered was rejected. This was contrary to previous practice and, as they saw it, to provisions in the Joint Declaration, which required closer consultation in the later stages of the transitional period. The substance of the proposals, by greatly widening the electorate, in their view contravened earlier Sino-British understandings expressed in the Joint Declaration, the Basic Law and the exchanges of letters on directly elected seats of 1989–90. (The British naturally contested this reading.) The Chinese rejected the right of Legco, to them a purely advisory body, to pronounce on the future of their territory. To them the reforms and the manner of their promulgation represented a 180-degree turn in British policy on co-operation and convergence. They went further and claimed to detect a conspiracy aiming to enhance Hong Kong's independence and spread the virus of democracy to the mainland. The fact that the United States, Canadian and Australian governments warmly endorsed the Governor's constitutional plans confirmed Peking in the instinctive suspicion that there was international backing for such a plot.

A confrontation rapidly developed. On the Chinese side there was sustained invective and threats to abolish the legislature in 1997 if the new arrangements were implemented and to set up before that date a 'second kitchen', that is an alternative centre of authority for the territory. There could be little doubt of the seriousness of these warnings; which, if implemented, would mean that the reforms could at best bring two years of improved democracy, after the 1995 elections, to be followed by an indefinite period of a more repressive system. To this had to be added the effect of divided authority in the remaining years of British rule and, most worrying of all, the strain on the Chinese commitment to the Joint Declaration itself.

On the British side, there were repeated assurances of readiness for discussion; but at the same time the government expressed their full backing for Mr Patten; and the Foreign Secretary stated that the days of negotiation with Peking over the head of Hong Kong were past. In Hong Kong the Governor was criticized by the business community. Otherwise he enjoyed much personal support, though this was coupled with a strong popular wish that confrontation with China should be avoided, a typical Hong Kong combination. In Britain itself attitudes were less *nuancé*. The press preferred to portray the issue in terms of a simple morality play, in which the Governor fought the good fight against the wicked Chinese in the cause of democracy. The fact that the struggle took place over the body of Hong Kong, and the likely effect on Hong Kong if the reforms were made law and the Chinese threats were put into operation, were aspects that received less attention.

By the end of 1992 Sino-British relations had fallen to their lowest level for a decade. The speed of the deterioration and the strength of the Chinese response suggested that, contrary to popular perception, earlier negotiations had gone near the limits of Chinese tolerance.

Diplomacy was not entirely asleep, however. The British offer of talks without preconditions was maintained; and for some months in early 1993 the British Ambassador, Sir Robin McLaren, conducted delicate talks about talks. After an unfortunate interruption in March, coinciding with the meeting of the National People's Congress in Peking, it was finally announced, on 13 April, that Britain and China would open confidential discussions in Peking on the subject of the electoral arrangements for the 1994–5 elections in Hong Kong.

The talks were to be conducted by two principal representatives, Sir Robin McLaren himself and the Chinese Vice Foreign Minister, Jiang Enzhu. They would be assisted by experts and advisers, on the British side drawn from Hong Kong as well as from London. The arrangements were reminiscent of those in 1982–4 during the negotiations on the Joint Declaration.

The announcement signalled a drawing-back on both sides. On the British side it also implied a somewhat reduced role for Hong Kong. Although the option of breaking off the talks and referring the issue to Legco was never abandoned, and was indeed used by the Governor on occasion as a means of pressure, for the time being at least Hong Kong's legislators seemed content, almost relieved, to await the outcome of the discussions between capitals and ready when they were concluded to pass the appropriate legislation.

In a wider sense also, the agreement to open talks between London and Peking was a watershed in the crisis. For some six months there had been a new approach and style in Sino-British dealings over Hong Kong, an apparent readiness to go it alone and embark on direct trials of strength. In practice it had proved, to put it mildly, counter-productive. Far from establishing an alternative policy, the experience had become a demonstration that, confrontation apart, there was no alternative: Britain and China were condemned to co-operate over Hong Kong. Though there was a natural reluctance to admit it, the two governments were now back on the traditional course of negotiation between capitals, as practised by the mandarins and sinologues of the previous decade.

The negotiations would of course be tough. The subject was highly charged and significant damage had been done. Chinese suspicions had been reinforced and their hostile analysis of

British policy seemingly vindicated. Hong Kong society had been polarized and political intrusion from the mainland accelerated. The terms that might have been secured in quiet discussions in October would be much harder to obtain after six months of trench warfare. But at least there was a return to rational discussion.

The negotiations, however, proved fruitless. They wound on into the summer, the autumn and the winter of 1993, seventeen rounds in all, over a hundred and sixty hours of talks. The British offered some significant concessions, but the Chinese proved unyielding on all major points. This rigidity no doubt reflected the fact that they had been taken to the limit of their tolerance by the earlier negotiations: they had reached a political settlement and, as they had repeatedly warned, they were not prepared to reopen it. But it may also have reflected uncertainty in Peking about the succession to Deng Xiaoping: no one had the confidence to be flexible. For the Hong Kong government there were apparently also technical constraints: dates before which legislation had to be passed if it was to be ready for the district elections of 1994 and the legislative elections of 1995.

At the time of writing (the end of November 1993) it is clear that the talks have collapsed and, though the consequential decisions have not yet been taken, it seems highly likely that the British and Hong Kong governments are now prepared to take unilateral action and to submit the Patten proposals in some form to the Legislative Council.

If this course is followed, I fear we must expect a renewed and probably final confrontation with China. The Legislative Council may of course refuse the cup put to them and cast out the proposals; or they may pass only a watered-down version. But it is unlikely that these manoeuvres, by what they see as a subordinate body, will have much impact on the Chinese, who will concentrate on British government policy and the rupture in the inter-governmental negotiations. As I see it, unless there is a major retreat by London (on the grounds that Hong Kong does not want a confrontation), the Chinese threats, of setting up an alternative centre of authority at once, and of dismantling the legislature in 1997, will undoubtedly be implemented; and there will be an ugly stand-off over the territory in the remaining years of transition. Observers will be driven to the conclusion that the antagonisms of one hundred and fifty years were spectres not after all to be so easily laid; and Britain and China will end their dealings on Hong Kong as they began, in misunderstanding and hostility. With the difference, that this time superior power will not rest with Britain.

In such an event, it will no doubt be argued in justification that honour required us to leave Hong Kong with an improved level of democracy, with credible elections in 1995, and with the attributes of a free and open society. But in fact the effect of the confrontation will almost certainly be to ensure that the legislature is uprooted in 1997 and democracy thereby permanently impaired. It seems only too likely that the 1995 elections will be held in circumstances of unprecedented pressure from the mainland; that their results will be negated two years later; and that, as a result of strains on the Chinese commitment to the political settlement of 1984, the safeguards for the territory as a free society will be weakened. In these circumstances Hong Kong will be left in a worse state than it was in before the new approach was tried in 1992.

It will be a tragedy, the greater for being avoidable. In distributing blame, the future historian will note Chinese intransigence and an apparent wish, contrary to Chinese tradition and interest, to humiliate their opponents. But he will also note, on the British side, a consistent misreading of Chinese attitudes and tolerance. However unreasonable, the Chinese position was well known before the 1992 venture began; and there were plentiful warnings of the effect of disregarding it. Given the balance of power between the two sides, these were facts to be accorded great weight in British calculations; they seem to have been underestimated or discounted. The public nature of the first British approach made dignified retreat hard for both sides. The British objectives remained throughout unrealistically high. And, given the clear prospect of damage to the colony flowing from unilateral action, it will be hard to explain British resort to it except on the basis of a determined refusal to believe that the Chinese meant what they said. How otherwise could a government putting Hong Kong's interests first make the move? It will seem a puzzling as well as a fatal decision.

Bismarck in a reflective mood once used a fine image to illustrate the limits on statesmanship. He pictured the powers travelling on the stream of time, which they can neither create nor direct, but on which they can steer with more or less skill and experience. The key phrase is 'which they can neither create nor direct'. Those in charge of Sino-British relations in the years of co-operation perhaps overestimated their capacity to direct events and to impose a rational framework on irrational forces. They discounted the still unexhausted reserves of prejudice and emotion on each side, the deeper currents in the stream.

It is sad to have to leave the Hong Kong story at this point, with so much to do and so much that has been done brought into question, with the main issue still unresolved and the risk so high that damaging and irrevocable decisions will be taken. We are back on that famous window ledge from which the Unofficials were more than once rescued in the 1982–4 negotiations, and this time saddled with stronger suicidal impulses. But it would be wrong to be totally despondent. Even if, as it seems, we are condemned to follow the dark scenario, the whole achievement of the time of co-operation will not be lost. Those thirteen years, from 1979, when the issue of the lease was first raised, indirectly and with some trepidation, during Sir Murray MacLehose's visit to Peking, have left a foundation work of agreements and habits of consultation which cannot be entirely erased. In particular, even in the worst case, the Joint Declaration, the territory's sheet-anchor, should survive, though under strain. If that happens, it will be ironic, though providential, that the main product of a rejected policy should be the insurance against the full consequences of its successor and should supply the safety net against the casualties of a disastrous high-wire act.

There could be other ameliorating factors. Despite the political rift, practical co-operation over large public works for the benefit of the future Special Administrative Region may still continue. Certainly it should be the object of both sides to ensure that it does; and the Chinese dogma that politics is always in command should not be allowed to stand in the way.

Above all, in a manner quite different from the battles of the 1980s, the Hong Kong economy has so far shrugged off the crisis and led a buoyant life of its own, relying on the territory's close ties with southern China and the mainland's remarkable economic growth. This does not make the political strains irrelevant, as some now assert: challenges and struggles of the order we are

now experiencing will leave their mark, however they are concluded. But it does offer the hope that, in the longer term,
against the immense fact of China's and, in consequence, Hong
Kong's prosperity, the constitutional disputes of these times will
dwindle in importance and be eventually relegated to a secondary place in history.

Whatever the outcome, looking back, I do not believe that
British policy in the years covered by these memoirs, that is from
1979 to 1992, can be seriously faulted. Of course, it would have
been better if, with Peking's agreement, democracy could have
been long rooted in Hong Kong. It might have assuaged some
guilt, though it would have created many new problems, if the
right to settle in Britain had survived. But already we are well
into the world of wish fulfilment. In the situation inherited by
the negotiators, both in China and Hong Kong, I do not think
much more could have been done. The underlying philosophy
has also been vindicated. However the play ends, the events
since 1992 have demonstrated, if further demonstration were
needed, that the policy of co-operation with China for the benefit
of Hong Kong, if not the only conceivable policy, is the only one
that will allow Britain to leave the stage knowing that it has done
its best to fulfil its responsibilities to the six million people in its
charge.

PART FOUR

Envoi

CHAPTER TWENTY-FIVE

A View of China

IT IS TIME to return to the wider canvas of China, the background against which the intricate pattern of Sino-British manoeuvres over Hong Kong has to be set. This book has given a view, necessarily partial and imperfect, of some episodes in China's history over a generation, the years between 1962 and 1992. It has been a dramatic and a violent time. In retrospect, it appears as a battlefield, littered with abandoned ideologies and policies, the bones of dead heroes and the remains of innumerable lesser victims. One can only admire the endurance, the adaptability, the resilience of the Chinese people which has enabled them to survive such extreme experience and retain their human nature, even if sometimes sadly scarred.

The first years of the story, inevitably, are dominated by Mao Zedong. It is possible to take a variety of views of Mao, as of any other great historical figure; and it can be argued that his demonic qualities were needed to break the mould of failure, invasion and civil war, and to bring China to unity and a measure of peace in 1949.

But beyond that point justification is harder. As Chen Yun said,

Had Chairman Mao died in 1956, there would have been no doubt that he was a great leader of the Chinese people . . . Had he died in 1966, his meritorious achievements would have been somewhat tarnished, but his overall record still very good. Since he actually died in 1976, there is nothing we can do about it.

If only. But this story has been concerned with his later years and here even his colleagues could not avoid the most severe censure. To me he seems an affliction, a scourge. His country would have been infinitely happier and more prosperous in duller hands. It need not have been the terms of Walter Scott's spell:

> Vacant heart and hand and eye,
> Easy live and quiet die.

But it could have been life at a much lower level of dogma, egotism, illusion and destruction. China itself, its size, population and poverty, would have provided drama enough, without the excesses imposed by a disastrous old man.

Nor did he pass entirely into history. His mausoleum, and his ghost, are still there, his name still invoked. In 1981, the Party found it could not cut itself free. Like his hero, the first Emperor, he is now part of that weight of history and tyranny which China has to bear and which makes political change there so convulsive and painful.

Deng Xiaoping, vastly more human, reasonable and successful, inherited the same role of absolute ruler, which Chinese conditions and traditions apparently demand. But with him it was possible for the first time to apply normal standards to China's behaviour. And the first years of Deng were undoubtedly years of relief and hope, as well as positive achievement. The pragmatic approach, the opening to the West and the reforms in agriculture and industry laid the foundation for the remarkable economic growth, which is now China's most striking attribute. The famished and disaster-stricken country I first encountered in 1962 has become the world's fastest-growing economy and, if the projections are sound, one which in the early decades of the next century could be the world's largest.

I am not so sure about the projections: a country with 1.2 billion people and its population growth out of control has an inbuilt constraint of the most extreme kind; and this is not to speak of the inherent tendency of the economy towards overheating, let alone the overriding political uncertainties. But the economic achievement is undeniable; it must be Deng's chief claim to greatness; many of the reforms are now irreversible; and the Party Congress of October 1992 provided the political blessing for the continuance of the reform process. So that there are grounds for saying that the performance could be sustained.

Growth of this order for a country of this size would have large strategic implications. It would mean a shift of economic and political weight to the Pacific region and justify visions of China as a world power, no longer just a regional power, early in the next century. In such a situation, areas of China's foreign policy which have interested, but never wholly absorbed, Britain, and have taken second place to pressing bilateral issues like Hong Kong, subjects such as China's behaviour on the Security Council, attitudes on arms control, relations with the Pacific states, would all assume a new significance. Sino-Japanese relations would become even more important, and probably even more delicate. China's military policies would demand closer study. The West would have to adjust its thinking and its dispositions.

Economic success, however, has been attended by political stagnation and crisis. The improved living standards, the flow of consumer goods, the openings for business enterprise are all there, but so are political institutions and inhibitions that have changed little since Mao's day. The Party is still the ultimate authority. As one Chinese writer puts it, 'the Communist Party controls everything except the Communist Party itself'. The old machinery of dictatorship – Party, security police, labour camps, propaganda organs – functions as before. The intellectuals despair; the student idealists learn to stifle their discontent. It is a richer, more comfortable society; but it is harsh, repressive, corrupt, materialist and cynical.

Deng's formula, economic reform within a framework of tight political control, has been from the outset a cautious one, reflecting a deep scepticism about the stability of the Chinese political order and a fear of the chaos into which it could only too easily descend. It has also been a brittle formula: Tiananmen was the most dramatic illustration of the strains it provoked; but, as even the superficial survey in these pages has shown, there have been a series of lesser tremors on the same fault-line, revealing the contending forces at work below the surface; and the battle goes on. From time to time Deng has tried to soften these tensions by venturing into the field of political reform; but it has proved too risky and he has always had to draw back. His attempts to stabilize the future by establishing his lieutenants as Party leader have turned out badly: Hu Yaobang and Zhao Ziyang have come and gone; and now, as he prepares to be reunited with Mao, or Marx, there is an alarming uncertainty about the succession. Ten years ago I wrote in my farewell despatch from Peking that far too much hung on the health of one old man. It is still true and that is a measure of China's danger.

The theme of the last fifteen years has therefore been the efforts of a Communist regime to carry out partial reform. It is an unfinished story and, as often with China, it could have a tragic ending. Can a totalitarian state transform itself? And are the forces it has released capable of control?

It is hard to avoid the conclusion that two forces at least will in the end prove irresistible: the political fall-out from the growing economy, particularly the non-state sector; and the relentless pressure of the outside world on the one great surviving Communist system.

But, if eventual political change is inevitable, it need not be imminent; and a great deal will turn on the timing and the manner. On timing, it would be unwise to expect a rapid alteration. China has a number of special characteristics differentiating it from Eastern Europe. The first is the government's economic success and the popular perception that living standards are rising. This is hardly the seed-bed of revolution; and the contrast with the turmoil and deprivation in the former Soviet Union drives the point home. The second is the fact that the great mass of the population still live in the country and in general since 1978 the peasants have done well. They were indifferent to the student agitation in May and June 1989. Of late there has been discontent as peasant incomes have failed to keep pace with inflation, and levies by local officials have increased. There is danger here; but the central government seem alive to it and have taken emergency measures. So that the all-important rural base still seems reasonably solid. Third, there is throughout the country a fear of disorder, sharpened by memories of the Cultural Revolution. And the Party, though corrupt, is still pervasive and effective, at least as a means of perpetuating its own power. These are not necessarily insuperable obstacles to major change; but they suggest that it may come slowly and could be deferred until long after Deng Xiaoping's death.

As regards the manner of change, there is a benign scenario, for which the Chinese concept, the New Authoritarianism, could provide the title. According to this, the centre would remain true to the letter of Mao Zedong Thought and socialist theory; but practice, particularly in the provinces, would steadily diverge. China would increasingly come to resemble other Pacific-rim states, like Singapore, South Korea and Taiwan, where an authoritarian political system exists side by side with a thriving economy. Nothing need be explicit: Communist dogma would wither; central state power would remain. Already Chinese life has been much depoliticized; this would take the development a stage further.

It is an attractive theory and it could even be the way events move. But it neglects the violent strains which have built up below the orderly surface of Chinese life, the contradictions between the power-holders and the idealists, between reformers and reactionaries; and the need, on the part of the most active and articulate part of the population, for slogans and sharply enunciated principles. The pretensions of the Party and its record of successful repression, without outside help, also argue against the benign scenario. Can such a tyranny bow quietly off the stage? It will not be easy. This suggests, not an imperceptible move away from dogma, but a sharp break, a revolutionary incident and a visible, probably physical, clash between two ideologies. This form of change, a revolution with banners and principles, is likely to be bloody. But China may find it hard to avoid.

These are large uncertainties, which warn against confident prediction. But, whatever form change takes, China's strength seems fated to grow; and the remarkable qualities of its people, which have enabled the country to survive and revive after the turmoil and ruin of the last generation, seem certain to drive it on. In consequence, Britain's relations with China will grow in importance. Even more than now, we shall need to study the country. We shall need an expanding corps of experts, who have some facility with the language and have devoted some time to the study of Chinese history and habits of mind.

Looking back, not only over the thirty years of this personal history, but also over the longer vistas of Sino-British dealings, it is clear that the inevitable contradictions of cultures and political systems have been exacerbated by the fact that both sides have enjoyed at best partial vision. To us they were the inscrutable Chinese; to them we were the unfathomable barbarians. Aubrey's story of the axes in the dark cellar may not be an entirely extravagant image. On the British side certainly, much of the trouble has stemmed from a failure on our part to forecast Chinese reactions accurately and with sensitivity, to allow for the idiosyncracies of their approach, to give sufficient weight to Chinese pride and nationalist sentiment, even at times to admit that there was a distinct Chinese position deserving attention and a measure of respect. We are not by nature an emotional or imaginative people and are prone to attribute to others our comfortable ways of thought. Whereas the essential gift is the ability to put oneself in the other's shoes. As the great Chinese military philosopher said, 'Know yourself; know your enemy.' It has been a failure of imagination rather than goodwill.

In the country of the blind the one-eyed man is king. What the diplomats and sinologists can do, by accurately reporting conditions in China and its government's ways of thinking, is to make the official, and perhaps even in time the popular, vision less distorted and give political leaders a chance to see issues from the point of view of the other side. By so doing the interpreters will risk incurring the charge of having gone native; but such insights can be critical and can preserve governments from serious policy misjudgements, misjudgements which can be less easily afforded when the balance of power is no longer in our favour, as will increasingly be the case.

So future sinologists will be needed; and they will occupy the same ambiguous and exposed position as their precursors today. They too will serve as interpreters between very different worlds. They too will find China an acquired taste, much of it bitter. They will have to study a society which will probably remain alien to Western concepts and handle the harsh and assertive policies of a regime of growing power, which, even if no longer Communist, will certainly remain strongly nationalist. As those before them, they will no doubt find intellectual satisfaction in following the obscure course of Chinese internal politics and the struggles between Chinese leaders, and in reporting these events to uncomprehending departments at home. But they will also surely find that China in its wider sense, that of the land and its civilization, is large and rich enough to allow them to construct from its history, its literature and its art, from experience of its people and scenery, something to allow them to justify their addiction. For, like all who have lived there any time, they will be addicts, fascinated, if at the same time repelled.

In classical China, the scholar-official, freed from his duties, perhaps out of favour with the court, traditionally withdrew to his country retreat, to enjoy his books and his wine, to reflect on events, put his career in perspective and come to terms with the natural order. In the seventh century the poet Wang Wei, musing, after a not very successful official life, on the vanity of the worldly bustle, the 'ten thousand things', wrote some lines in this vein:

> In the evening of life I seek only tranquillity,
> The affairs of the world no longer concern me.
> Having measured my own limits,
> I only want to return to my old woods.
> The wind in the pines plays with my sash,
> The mountain moon shines on me at my lute.
> You ask what is the ultimate answer?
> It is the song of the fisherman sailing back to shore.

These are the higher serenities, not to be matched. But, at a much humbler level, the model is worth emulating; and this book begins the necessary process of reordering and detachment. In the course of writing, the events and actors it describes, though still vivid, become in some way smaller and more manageable, like pictures in an album, to be fitted in their setting: the flames of the Cultural Revolution, the crises in the negotiations, the scenes in the Cabinet room and the Great Hall of the People, the procession of leaders, ministers and governors, all taking their place along with the subjects of the group photographs and the figures on the Residence lawn at Queen's Birthday Parties, as images of a past experience, the shapes and ferments of another age.

I am glad to have known them. It has been, I am afraid, more a matter of struggle than of contemplation, more a clash of philosophies and interests than a scholarly enquiry. But it has been instructive; and the struggle too has had its compensations and its pleasures. It has been a privilege to have been so involved when large issues were at stake and to have been able to advise, argue and negotiate for this country and for Hong Kong. I am grateful for the kindness and tolerance of two Prime Ministers. I record my debt to all those who worked with me. I should also like to make a small bow to those who sat at the other side of the table, with a different brief, in a different interest, and proved themselves formidable adversaries and sometimes, though too rarely, helpful collaborators. I hope the agreements we reached will prove of lasting value to both our countries and that even where co-operation was not possible, our disagreements will have proved enlightening. For though Britain and China may not always find it easy to agree, they must, at all costs, understand one another.

Index